THE DISCOURSE OF SELF IN VICTORIAN POETRY

Victorian Literature and Culture Series
Karen Chase, Jerome J. McGann, and Herbert Tucker
General Editors

ANTHONY WINNER
    Culture and Irony: *Studies in Joseph Conrad's Major Novels*

DAVID G. RIEDE
    Matthew Arnold and the Betrayal of Language

DANIEL ALBRIGHT
    Tennyson: *The Muses' Tug-of-War*

JAMES RICHARDSON
    Vanishing Lives: *Style and Self in Tennyson, D. G. Rossetti, Swinburne, and Yeats*

ANTONY H. HARRISON
    Victorian Poets and Romantic Poems: *Intertextuality and Ideology*

JEROME J. McGANN, EDITOR
    Victorian Connections

E. WARWICK SLINN
    The Discourse of Self in Victorian Poetry

The Discourse of Self in Victorian Poetry

E. WARWICK SLINN

*Senior Lecturer in English
Massey University, New Zealand*

University Press of Virginia
Charlottesville

© E. Warwick Slinn 1991

All rights reserved. No reproduction, copy or transmission
of this publication may be made without written permission.

First published **1991**

Published by
MACMILLAN ACADEMIC AND PROFESSIONAL LTD
Houndmills, Basingstoke, Hampshire RG21 2XS
and London

Companies and representatives
throughout the world

Printed in Great Britain

First published 1991 in the United States of America by
the University Press of Virginia
Box 3608, University Station
Charlottesville, Virginia 22903

Library of Congress Cataloging-in-Publication Data
Slinn, E. Warwick, 1943–
The discourse of self in Victorian poetry / E. Warwick Slinn.
p.   cm. — (Victorian literature and culture series)
Includes bibliographical references and index.
ISBN 0-8139-1309-8
1. English poetry—19th century—History and criticism.   2. Self in literature.   I. Title.   II. Series.
PR595.S44S55   1991
821'.809—dc20   90-41724
                                                                              CIP

For Suzann and Sordello

Contents

Preface vii

Introduction 1

1 Consciousness as Self 9

2 Consciousness as Writing 38

3 Absence and Desire in *Maud* 64

4 Fact and the Factitious in *Amours de Voyage* 90

5 Language and Truth in *The Ring and the Book* 119

6 The Politics of Self in *The Ring and the Book* 149

Afterword: On Poetry as a Significant Discourse 185

Notes 188
Index 210

Preface

> Human thought is not constituted like an originative, infinite, on looking mind. Rather, it can only grasp what is, in discursive development of its thoughts.
>
> Hans-Georg Gadamer

This book is a study of Victorian poetry in terms of dialectical process – not dialectic as definition by opposition, but a non-dualist, Hegelian dialectic which anticipates the open-ended discursiveness of deconstruction. Within such a context, the poetry becomes more philosophically radical. Criticism has often insisted upon the purely subjectivist nature of Victorian poetry, but such readings have tended not to demonstrate the full range of its dramatic subtlety or 'discursive development'.

Robert Browning's monumental poem, *The Ring and the Book*, provides the climax for this approach on the polemical grounds that it is the triumphant work of the century, a work which has too often been misrepresented as a sort of *Paradise Lost*, representing the ways of God to men – two centuries too late. Rather, it is as much concerned with *ways* of representing as with representing, developing through that concern a critique of both the powerful Romantic aesthetic of transcendence and the equally powerful Cartesian *cogito* that has dominated so much Western thought and literature since the seventeenth century. Such a critique makes it one of the most challenging poetic experiments of post-Romantic writing.

For the last three years I have taught a graduate course at Massey University (New Zealand) that has been modelled on the structure and content of this book. The students who have taken this course, writing essays and theses on its content, have frequently stimulated my own thinking about the issues involved. Often they have drawn on my suggestions and I have in turn drawn on their responses in an act of dialectical learning. In particular, I should like to acknowledge the work of Douglas Standring, Tina Sutton, Kim Worthington, Pauline Simonsen and Lisa O'Connor.

I am especially grateful to Herbert Tucker (University of Virginia) and Simon Petch (University of Sydney), who have given generously of their time and knowledge in reading drafts of several chapters and in making many valuable suggestions for improvement. Isobel Armstrong (Birkbeck College, London), Clyde Ryals (Duke University), Linda Hughes (Texas Christian University) and Graham Oddie (Massey University, NZ) have also read sections of the manuscript and I am indebted to them for their encouragement and comments. Like so many before me, I am also indebted to the writers of the books and essays which have influenced and inhabited my own unceasing 'discoursive development'.

Parts of Chapter 2 and Chapter 5 have appeared as articles in *Victorian Poetry* and I am grateful to the Editor for permission to reprint those sections here.

Finally, this book is dedicated to Sordello (my 20 megabyte hard disk) for carrying the charge of textuality, and to Suzann Olsson (my 20 megavolt partner) for carrying the charge of provocation and resuscitation.

EWS
August 1989

Introduction

I

This book reads Victorian poetry within the context of a radical shift over the last 150 years in the key European model for human definition and experience: from the metaphor of self to the metaphor of text. The movement in thought from Hegel to Derrida produces a shift in the dominating metaphor for human experience from consciousness as self (there is nothing outside self) to consciousness as writing (there is nothing outside text). When placed within this changing process of mediation, Victorian poetry develops the problematics of selfhood, pursuing a post-Romantic displacement of the self as an originary guarantor of meaning and truth.

Within the context of a generally idealist emphasis, Romantic poets tend to privilege imagination as the mode of consciousness which most closely represents the truth of self and which is the most fruitful path to unity and self-realisation. This strain of Romantic thinking seeks to transcend language and temporality through appealing to the powers of imaginative synthesis. Such a desire for unmediated knowledge of the self appears to have been a controlling impulse in reaching for the realms of prophetic vision, the Romantic sublime of a transcendent, whole self. This desire coexists, however, with the role of imagination as a transforming power – consciousness, mind, as itself the agency of transformation. Hence consciousness becomes both the instrument for transcendence and the guarantor of an authentic self. It is both origin, the authorising source of knowledge and integrity, and mediation, the means of representing the self to itself. Consciousness is the means therefore of producing that process of self-recuperation – that seizing of the self as object in order to validate the self as subject – which is the classic sign of Romantic idealism.

In Victorian poetry the desire for a reality beyond representation persists, but a greater emphasis on the ironic ambiguities in the double role of consciousness intrudes and persists equally forcefully. A key effect of the move towards ironic disruption is that it foregrounds the textuality of all representations of voice: consciousness not as the authentic self but as a mode of writing becomes an increasingly possible metaphor. Closure, teleological purpose, become less certain as the means of controlling meaning, and speakers increasingly reveal their attachment to acts of representation, to a fractured lyricism which proposes the self as a factitious construct. A growing sense of flux in all things, the intrusions of an irony not based on fixity, the realisation of the role of language as a dominating epistemological force, all lead to a discourse of self which is characterised by division and displacement. Temporality and process become more problematic in poetic structures while unity becomes increasingly dialectical – unity as difference.

Victorian poetry, more perhaps than the Victorian novel, probes the subtleties and contradictions within the drama of the human subject. The result is a literary discourse whereby the self and its primary human concerns (truth, perception, morality, feeling) become produced through the conditions of textual process (the dependency on figural representation, for instance). Poets, speakers, subjects face a terrifying prospect in Victorian poetry: they speak in order to establish the presence of their authority; they argue for their place in the scheme of things in order to establish the self, if nothing else, as a viable centre in which to locate value and meaning. Yet the moment they speak, they commit the self to inevitable division, to a textual disjunction which ironically challenges their authority in the very act of attempting to establish it. The converse, however, is also true. As lyrical modes of utterance are placed within extended contexts which disrupt the autonomous lyric voice (in the dramatic monologue or long poem), the speaking subject is divided. Nevertheless, through that very process of division, the self is brought into existence as subject, constituted through difference.

My aims in this discussion are several: to indicate the philosophical and psychological challenge of a poetry which disrupts the assumptions of lyrical idealism; to demonstrate the dramatic subtlety of Victorian poetry in its exploration of the dynamics of the self in language; to place Victorian long poems, particularly *The Ring and the Book*, firmly in the forefront of critical attention; and to (re)construct a historical process whereby the metaphysics of Romantic idealism give way to the more problematised perceptions of a consciousness tied to textuality. The history of modern or post-Saussurean thought, in its movement from formalism to textualism, was anticipated, then, within the productions of Victorian poetry. At the same time, this claim is itself tied to a historical production (this text) which allegorises and celebrates the appearance of its own action within earlier textual activity (Victorian poems).

II

My approach incorporates overlapping features of literature and philosophy. The philosophy, however, is not used to justify the literature, nor is it to be put in opposition to literature. It provides a context for establishing significance and providing conceptual explanation. The themes of the literature are to be seen as continuous with the philosophy not in opposition to it, although the implications of the literary text may well be given different shape, reformed in terms of a redefined context.

The link between Hegel's version of philosophical knowing and the narrative ironies of Victorian poetry provides a way of understanding the cognitive seriousness of the literature. The philosophy neither guarantees poetic meaning nor provides a proof of poetic truth; indeed, Hegel seeks to outreach 'proof' in either its empirical or idealist sense (that is, scientific experimental proof or the proof of one's subjective experience). Nor is the question of influence relevant. What is to the point is the explanatory power provided by the implications and claims of Hegel's discourse and by its links with recent post-structuralism and deconstruction. The text of his *Phenomenology* and the text of Derrida's writing on textuality provide contexts which produce a revised reading of Victorian poetry. In this way the philosophy facilitates an understanding of the changing forms of human experience.

The shift in conceptualising from Hegel to Derrida is explained in the first two chapters. In one sense these chapters provide a 'Hegelian' narrative – a development that is governed by a post-hoc teleology where significance is determined from the point of view of an established present. Development is thus a shifting proposition according to the way the present (or end) alters with transient arguments and temporary conclusions. For my purposes, the concept of writing as a metaphor for consciousness is the end which determines the starting point (*The Phenomenology of Mind*) and the significance of selected moments along the way (*Maud, Amours de Voyage, The Ring and the Book*).

Specifically my approach means that texts are read in a context where metaphysical transcendence is rejected as a delusion of epistemological making: subject and object are separate and yet cohere in textual interdependence; reality is constituted through an interplay of physical existence (textually conceived) and individual perception (textually produced) to the point where outside and inside become indeterminate, undecidable even. Consciousness is the model for understanding and for discerning value and meaning, although consciousness is itself conceived through textual metaphors, whether in terms of the idealist metaphor of self or the deconstructionist metaphor of textuality. The titles for Chapters 1 and 2 should not be taken, therefore, as signs that consciousness is a reified, separate phenomenon which is somehow indicated through changing representations. My concern is with the varying conceptions which have formulated and thereby produced its existence.

I found it necessary to elaborate my teleological narrative, because the continuities from Hegel to Derrida have tended so far to remain a vague and unspecific gesture within literary theory. Also, most references to Hegel in literary contexts stress the metaphysical Hegel, the Hegel of spiritual absolutism. My concern, on the other hand, is rather with the non-dualist Hegel, the Hegel of dialectical process. It is my contention, for instance, that the strong affinities between this Hegel and Victorian poetry provide a means for theorising the dominant use of the monologue form in post-Romantic writing.

III

Two conceptual networks which act as meeting points for philosophy and literature are representation and relationship. Representation raises questions about mediation (and relationship) which involve realism, mimesis, imagination, and language.[1] Relationship invokes epistemological questions – about the dualism of self and world, about being as being-known, about the truth of experience. Within literary criticism relationship involves meaning, value, point of view, metaphor (the main means of producing 'relationships' in literary modes) and imagery generally.

These networks are located within the subjective self by idealist phenomenology, but they are located within discourse by structuralism and post-structuralism. The advent of semiology shifts attention from author to text, from subject to signifier, relocating the origin of meaning within language itself rather than in the author of discourse.² At the same time, within most post-structuralism, signification still cannot be considered apart from the subject.

By calling this discussion the discourse of self, then, I am deliberately combining terms from idealism and from post-structuralism in order to make the point that Victorian poetry already demonstrates the problematics entailed in the shift in emphasis from self to discourse: specifically the poetry displays the psychological drama which follows from the sense that the self is inseparable from language (that is, from representation). My concern is with both subject and language, with the interplay through which they constitute each other and without which, conceptually speaking, neither would exist. For those who think the title ought to be plural, it is not a matter of separate discourses (although they will be the object of discussion), but rather the conceptualising of a thematic strand in Victorian poetry, a strand that is endemic within the period.

My concern with discourse also rests upon the implications of dialectical thinking, implications which can be traced as far back as Plato. These implications will be explained further in Chapter 1, but what is crucial is the notion that no idea exists in isolation – that there are no single ideas, no sign that has a meaning which is separate from other signs. In Derridean terms the point is simply that there is no 'transcendental signified', that meaning emerges from chains of supplements and mediations, although the issue is as old as dialectical thought. Hans-Georg Gadamer, for instance, observes that for Hegel what is paradigmatic in Plato is 'the concatenation of ideas':

> Plato's underlying conviction, which we find developed above all in the *Parmenides*, is that there is no truth of a single idea and, accordingly, that isolating an idea always means missing the truth. Ideas exist only linked, mixed, or interwoven as they are encountered in discussion or are 'there' each time in the discourse of the soul itself. Human thought is not constituted like an originative, infinite, on looking mind. Rather, it can only grasp what is, in discoursive development of its thoughts . . . . There are no single ideas, and it is the purpose of dialectic to dispel the untruth of their separateness.³

The problematic of ideas or signs as separate (in order to be known) and yet not separate (in order to have meaning), as differentiated and yet linked with others in a chain of signification, helps to explain the contradictory movements which often appear to be operating simultaneously in dialectical thought.

IV

In her important and highly articulate account of idealist language in the nineteenth century, Isobel Armstrong stresses Hegel's model for knowing – the possession by consciousness of the self as object, or the self-generating process of knowing through self-objectification – in order to explain the implications and forms of Romantic idealist poetry.[4] Her main argument is that 'it is possible to regard the language and form of nineteenth-century poetry as a model of the structure of consciousness or being itself' (p. xiii). Hence a careful reading of this literature 'depends on an understanding of the constitutive nature of mind with which the poets were concerned' (p. 20). Romantic poetry in Armstrong's reading is seen to imitate not time or external phenomena, but 'the self-comprehension of the mind which goes on simultaneously with conscious life' (p. 34). Since this process of a mind-created world is necessarily extended in time, the poems will be long: 'A poem of this kind has to be long enough to have a past on which it can reflect, long enough to contemplate itself, to interpret itself to itself, to transform and create new experience out of its own elements' (p. 34).

The recognition that the supposed prolixity of nineteenth-century poetry is related to sophisticated conceptions of mind, and to their associated mimetic constructions in literature, is responsible in part for my focus on long poems. But my emphasis also develops from a polemical claim that the poetry of the time is fundamentally subversive.

The simple-minded among Victorian poets followed the more sentimental strains of Romanticism into effusions of mere personal sensibility, touting a somewhat crude form of subjectivism where the world is coloured by poetic feeling. Such work hardly shattered the illusions of a utilitarian value-system which marginalised all art as trivial in the first place. But the more serious poets incorporated issues raised by idealist epistemologies, provoking fundamental questions about consciousness and language. Hence their poetry provokes questions about prevailing beliefs in individualism and, implicitly, about bourgeois liberalism itself.[5]

Dorothy Mermin has explained how Victorian readers tended to look in the poetry for qualities which they found in the novel, and how the reviewers of poetry in the 1830s and 1840s 'paid an extraordinary amount of attention to the slightest hints of narrative and characterization'.[6] Yet as the poets develop their larger poetic forms in the 1850s and 1860s, their structures usually disrupt rather than confirm expectations about narrative and character – about the structuring principles of narrative order or teleological purpose, and about the self as autonomous and discrete. In addition, by extending the context of lyrical self-expression in longer poems, particularly forms such as *In Memoriam* or *Maud* where narrative movement is disjunctive and uncertain, Victorian poets fostered what Tilottama Rajan has called 'the intertextualization of lyric' – a process which makes the lyric interdiscursive, challenging its assumptions of a self-enclosed subjectivity. Such a process began, Rajan claims, within Romanticism itself.[7] Hence the Victorian long poem challenges assumptions underlying both narrative and lyrical traditions.

Mermin argues that the development of the monologue form, particularly its use of auditors, was a means of establishing poetry within the social world of the fiction of the time, and a means of considering 'how and to what effect one can speak publicly of imaginative visions and private feelings in that world' (p. 11). Indeed, discourse is a public enterprise and monologues are inevitably dialogic. My focus on the drama of the subject within poetic language and my attention to Hegelian dialectics is precisely to urge the point that intrasubjective perception is also an intersubjective structure. But Mermin's formulation tends to privilege an epistemological subjectivism, maintaining private feelings and social world as separate realms, whereas it is through tying both private and public to the mediations of discourse that Victorian poetry, at one level, develops its social and intellectual critique.

An important part of the poetry's radicalism emerges from the tendency of dialectical process to diffuse the boundaries between inside and outside, or between reason and unreason. Madness, for example, is often defined in nineteenth-century English literature, as Robert Lougy has observed, by an outside world whose moral and rational categories keep separate the worlds of insanity and reason.[8] In *Maud*, Tennyson deliberately breaches these divisions; in *Amours de Voyage*, Clough's letter-writing protagonist intricately and endlessly tries to sort out fact from the factitious in order to maintain the poise of rational and cultural equilibrium; in *The Ring and the Book*, Browning mounts a formidable and searching critique of popular, post-Cartesian assumptions about the separations of truth and falsehood, self and world, meaning and discourse. By blurring the distinctions that sustain an ethos of individualism and rationality, these works threaten the cultivated urbanity of a middle-class hegemony. At the same time they expose the acts of differentiation which bring the self into being, the textual divisions without which the self as subject would not exist.

The movement from Hegel to Derrida is the movement from a totalising process to a process without totality. This is precisely the movement that occurs within Victorian monologues and Victorian long poems. The urge to proffer a total vision, to flaunt a language of transcendence, is increasingly thwarted, subjected to textual disruption. It is a movement from Hegelian difference – the prospect of a unity of consciousness that is constituted through division – to Derridean *différance* – the unity or closure that is continually deferred.

1
Consciousness as Self

Modern consciousness began, according to Richard Rorty, in the seventeenth century when Descartes invented the mind.[1] The notorious Cartesian *cogito*, 'I think, therefore I am', led to a theory of knowledge based purely on mental processes and to an epistemology based on the separation of mind and world that have been the focus of philosophical debate for the last three centuries. This founding of all knowledge on the principle of 'my own thinking existence' has tended to dominate European and Anglo-Saxon thought, providing most of the images which govern our thinking about ourselves and our place in the scheme of things: self and object become separated into realms of 'inner' and 'outer'; knowledge becomes a transaction between a 'knowing subject' and an external 'reality'; mind becomes a mirror which reflects the world of nature (hence the importance of ocular metaphors in our claims to truth); the self becomes the centre of experience and potentially the governing principle in everything we perceive.

Consciousness is thus assigned a crucial and powerful role in human affairs. All events and objects are perceived as images or impressions cast upon its screen, and consciousness then acts as a command centre, overlooking, mediating and judging the data it receives. With consciousness in command in this way, we can truly feel that we are in control of our world, masters of our destiny.

Or so it seems. For the model is far from straightforward and three centuries of debate have produced many disputes and many doubts. Where is this screen of consciousness to be found? (At the back of the mind? Behind the eyes? What happens when a retina is detached?) To what extent do dreams or hypnotic recall challenge the omniscience or unified presence of consciousness? Is there any difference between having an impression or idea in the mind and constructing a proposition about that idea? Most importantly, how do we relate the images of consciousness to the external world when consciousness is all we have? How do we establish the truth or otherwise of the reflections in our mental mirror? Despite the many and sophisticated responses to these and other questions, such difficulties remain for those who would equate selfhood with consciousness, and locate both at the centre of experience.

Eventually thinkers usually regarded as outside the mainstream – Nietzsche, Heidegger, Derrida – were to develop more radical solutions, pointing to the problematic nature of the assumptions which underwrote this whole model of consciousness, and rendering as hopelessly spurious the mastery of the human subject over its meanings and its consciousness. At the beginning of the nineteenth century, however, the Cartesian tradition still remained powerful, dominated by two contending views: empiricism, which argued that the mind is a passive receiver of impressions imposed upon it by a given, objective reality, and idealism, which argued that the mind plays an active part in constructing that reality. In simple and somewhat crude terms, the former locates reality within an external, material world, and the latter maintains that the world depends on ideas, that objects exist only insofar as they are objects of consciousness.

It is worth noting, following the teaching of Rorty, that despite their apparently opposite views, empiricism and idealism are both founded on Cartesian assumptions about mind as the foundation of knowledge and mind as a metaphorical mirror. It is the metaphor of the mirror which is the key link, being assumed and yet interpreted variously by each school. For the empiricists the mirror is reflective and representational, while for the idealists it is transformational and potentially constitutive. For both, the mind as mirror is a limiting factor, never capable of pure transparency and always in some sense a representation. After all, an unclouded mirror or mirror which gave direct access to what it imaged (a non-inverting mirror perhaps) would propose the concept of a mirror which was indistinguishable from what it mirrored, and therefore would not be a mirror at all (Rorty, p. 376). It is the way this model of mind places empiricists and idealists on either side of the one metaphor that leads to the suggestion that they are contending dualists bound by the limits of the same binary system. This binarism is the radical separation of mind and world, internal experience and external reality, knowing and being.

Poets and other writers in nineteenth-century England inherited, then, an intellectual and cultural situation which was characterised by dualisms of various forms and by divided and apparently opposed views about the role of the intellect in human understanding. The empirical stance promoted the value of scientific enquiry into a physical universe which functioned independently of human perception. It supported the view that language is referential, with meaning being established, and therefore verifiable, through a strict relationship between words and their corresponding objects. Idealism, on the other hand, advanced a more active role for mind. It allowed for the realities of spirituality and abstraction, and argued that through representation the mind may constitute the world as humanly perceived and understood: language is thus creative and transformational. During the first part of the century empirical and scientific views which stressed the representational aspects of the mirror of nature tended to prevail, bringing poetry under attack as the organ of mere illusion.

The story of how certain empiricists dismissed poets of the time as tellers of mere fictions is now relatively well known, through Shelley's response to Peacock's claim, in 'The Four Ages of Poetry' (1820), that literature is neither useful nor true, and through accounts of Bentham's utilitarian charge that poetry is of no more value than push-pin.[2] Quite understandably in this environment, writers and poets responded more sympathetically to the creative possibilities allowed by idealist explanations, although it would be a gross simplification to imply that their aesthetic views were merely a matter of emotional preference. Arguments about epistemology were central to battles over ideology and value, and what was at stake was the status of literature amidst the growing prestige of inductive science and the claimed superiority of philosophy.[3]

Within the established epistemological context of the end of the eighteenth century, English Romantic poetry is characterised by self-consciousness and by the ability of poets to become artificers of worlds. What the Romantics thereby bequeathed to the Victorians was a poetry of idealist language, the nature and consequences of which have been brilliantly discussed by Isobel Armstrong in *Language as Living Form in Nineteenth-Century Poetry*.[4] In this important study, Armstrong is careful to point out that idealist epistemology is not to be equated with superficial subjectivism – with the simple devices of pathetic fallacy, for instance, whereby the poet's feelings are merely projected onto some chosen phenomenon. Serious idealism deals instead with the more complex matter of 'the cognitive structure of mind'.

Armstrong also rejects the presupposition of so many readings of nineteenth-century poetry that the subject is transcendent, that a unity of consciousness and world is achieved through 'the free autonomous self and its agency' (p. xiii). The consequence is crucial I think: 'A study of the language of nineteenth-century poetry suggests rather that it works to de-mystify the relation between subject and object, and does not assume a primal unity on the part of the perceiving mind' (p. xiii). She acknowledges, as we all must, that the affective quality of much of the poetry in the period tends to promote readings which equate the poem with the subjective life or selfhood of the poet, but the achievement of her study is to show how this affective language is used with precision by the poets and how it becomes available for quite different kinds of reading once its epistemological base is granted. In my reading, Victorian poetry may even question the assumptions of epistemology itself.

I start then from Armstrong's premise that nineteenth-century poetry is characterised by idealist language and by its concern to dramatise the conflicts of a mind-based, epistemological tradition. There were various forms of idealism current during the nineteenth century, but it is Hegel's particular brand of dialectical thought that I wish to take as my model. Furthermore, whereas Armstrong approaches Hegel through comparisons with Hopkins' reaction against the 'chromatic' thinking that he associated with Hegel, and with Marx's critique of Hegel, I wish to stress those aspects which provide the antecedents for recent post-structuralist thought – dialectical transformation, non-dualist thinking and the refusal to privilege either subject or object.

As Armstrong acknowledges, Hopkins was reacting to Hegelianism, Victorian impressions of Hegel, rather than to what Hegel actually wrote. Hopkins resisted what he saw as the destabilising aspects of Romantic writing, where words were unfixed from things and became 'autonomous, the agents of change and transformation' (Armstrong, p. 4). What troubled him was the prospect of a radically unstable language and an impoverished perceptual experience; he associated Hegel, as the philosopher of process, with this sense of a dynamic world continually in flux. In particular, he was opposed to the notion of knowledge as a process of becoming and to the notion of the self as 'the determinant and creator of experience' (Armstrong, p. 19). The latter, however, is more to do with Kant or Fichte than with Hegel. Marx's critique is similarly unfair to Hegel, as Armstrong also acknowledges. Marx complains that Hegel privileges the subject over objects, that he dissolves the real, sensuous world and that he conceives of the self as its opposite, as the physical world. But Hegel did not privilege subject over object, he does not deny the existence of substance, and Marx appears to misconstrue the abstractions of a dialectic where self is not conceived *as* its opposite but rather in terms of the *possibility* of its opposite, in terms of the process by which the opposite is differentiated. My concern here is precisely with Hegel's stress on movement and process and with the dialectical proposition that there is no unity except through differences.

Victorian Hegelianism tended to respond to the potentially transcendent aspects of Hegel, the movement towards a spiritual Absolute, or an apparent shift from material forms to categories of thought – even though Hegel actually says in his Preface to the *Phenomenology* that the need is rather to reverse this trend, to 'actualise' the universal rather than to make the individual 'a substance that thinks and is grasped in terms of thought'.[5]

This focus on metaphysical transcendence leads to the notion that objects disappear as phenomenal entities and exist only as they are known in the mind: 'We can never get directly at the world or at the unique particular sensory otherness of objects because what is knowable is our constitution of them' (Armstrong, p. 24). A formulation such as this is produced, however, within the discourse of conventional epistemology (a discourse we can only with acute difficulty step outside or supersede), where the underlying dualistic separation of subject and world is sustained by the phrase, 'unique particular sensory otherness of objects'. In this instance the role of consciousness is shifted towards its idealist function as a constituting power. There is nothing necessarily wrong with that, except for ambiguity about the phrase 'our constitution'. If 'our' refers to our personal and individual acts of constitution, as it would tend to do within the discourse of epistemology (objects are known in terms of *my* constitution of them), then the formulation is to be read as a version of what Richard Harland has recently called subjective idealism, as opposed to objective idealism, and it is neo-Kantian rather than Hegelian. If, on the other hand, 'our' refers to a more collective or systemic act of constitution, the constitution of some social, mythological or other semiotic system of which individual experience forms but a part, then the formulation is closer to Hegel's version of objective idealism.

While his focus on the question of how consciousness becomes self-consciousness places him within the tradition of Cartesian subjectivity, Hegel is also to be placed within a metaphysical tradition going back at least to Plato that posits systems of ideas which exist outside or independently from *individual* minds (although not from mind): 'Such systems of ideas are not thought *by* or *from* our minds; rather, they "think themselves", only passing *through* or *into* our minds.'[6] Descartes and Kant also posit systems, of innate ideas or *a priori* categories, but their systems are located within the experience of individual subjects. It is subjective idealism of their sort and particularly of the Fichtean sort ('I am wholly my own creation') which is potentially solipsistic, running the risk of getting trapped inside the individual skull, like Browning's lover in 'Porphyria's Lover' or Tennyson's manqué saint in 'St Simeon Stylites'.

In Hegel's objective idealism on the other hand, 'mind ... becomes object' and the notion of the individual self does not arise directly from personal experience; it emerges rather through a dynamic, dialectical process of production which embraces both inside and outside (to employ the distinctions of conventional epistemology). This does not mean that Hegel denies or repudiates human experience, as some recent forms of structuralism have done, for instance. Indeed, Hegel says that 'consciousness knows and comprehends nothing but what falls within its experience' (Pref. 96), but he attempts to outleap experience as conceived in epistemological terms – conceived, that is, as a condition or event where outwardly objective things make contact with inwardly subjective ideas, where origin or causation is located in *either* external reality *or* the centre of the individual self. Instead, for Hegel, 'substance shows that it is in reality subject', and, when attaining 'true knowledge', the processes of mind 'no longer involve the opposition between being and knowing' (Pref. 97).

The popular view that Hegel was an unabashed metaphysician, ignoring the lessons of Kant, is therefore unfounded. Kant is supposed to have concluded that no objects of knowledge exist prior to their constitution through the action of the mind, beginning the shift of knowledge from a relationship between person and object to a relationship between person and proposition. He also replaces the distinction between ideas and the real with a distinction between *phenomena* (objects as they appear to us) and *noumena* (things as they are in-themselves). We can have no knowledge of *noumena*, since objects 'in-themselves' are outside human perception. For Kant, then, Cartesian dualism is not exactly denied but is at least rendered irrelevant in the sense that the world as we perceive it *is* the real world: what it is like independent of our experience of it makes no sense. Human consciousness involves both experience and the understanding of experience; knowledge, consequently, is concerned with both the object and the method of knowing that object. Since the world *is* the world as we know it, it is actively regulated by our understanding of it.

At the same time, it is important to notice the sense in which Kant retains the implication of a world that is outside or behind our perception. Since we cannot know anything as it is 'in-itself', we can only know the world of *phenomena*, the world as it appears to us, the world that is constituted in consciousness through the combination of experience and proposition. It is this Kantian retention of a dualism between what we know and what we cannot know that leads Robert Solomon to claim that it is rather Hegel than Kant who is the great anti-metaphysician, 'purging philosophy of every vestige of "the thing-in-itself," the world behind, or beyond, the scenes'.[7] Solomon continues:

> It is Hegel who reduced all questions of *being* (or ontology) to questions about the structures and forms of human experience . . . . To say that Hegel is an *idealist* is to say that, at every turn, he argues that the world is thoroughly *knowable*, and it is nothing 'beyond' the realm of conscious experience . . . .There is no 'reality' beyond human experience, and no set reality within human experience . . . which our concepts and judgments must conform to. There is just this – *experience*, and the business of philosophy is to describe this, in an all-encompassing way. (pp. 8–9)

While this approach might suggest that Hegel is still an epistemologist, following the Cartesian tradition that is concerned with the nature of knowledge and the relationship between experience and reality, Hegel also opposes that tradition, rejecting the duality of self and world, the separation of experience 'inside' from reality 'out there'. To the extent, therefore, that this dualism and its problems have defined epistemology, Hegel is no epistemologist.

He also rejects the metaphor of consciousness as a mirror of nature, so that his brand of objective idealism radically questions the conventions of epistemology that have done so much to govern mainstream philosophy. In many respects, then, the real beginning of the nineteenth century, and even the beginning of modern, post-Romantic thought can be located in the writing of Hegel's *Phenomenology of Spirit* in 1806. I shall use this text, consequently, as a focal point for my discussion of the Hegelian discourse of consciousness. In rejecting the excesses of subjective idealism, this book took a leap beyond Romanticism, and it can be placed at the beginning of what Christopher Norris has referred to as a counter-tradition of speculative thought: a development from Hegel via Nietzsche and Heidegger to Derrida, in opposition to conventional analytic philosophy. The figures in this counter-tradition challenge the assumptions of conventional epistemology, redefining the concept of reason, problematising the relation 'between word and concept', transforming 'the relations between knowledge and truth', and generally undercutting those who still believe in 'truth, logic and sufficient reason' (Norris, p. 140).

It is clear that recent developments in deconstruction, Marxism and feminism have collectively shifted attention from product to production, and from fixed meaning to textual mobility. However, the beginnings of this move were already occurring with Kant, where the theoretical focus alters from experience itself to the conditions for experience to occur, away from the real thing to the circumstances of its production, to the 'necessary conditions' for any experience to occur. Hegel's *Phenomenology* then takes the further step of attending to the forms of experience rather than its pre-conditions. For Hegel, pre-conditions, *a priori* principles, are beyond conscious experience and to all intents and purposes do not exist, except perhaps as hypothetical fictions produced within the terms and assumptions of epistemological discourse. What can be known are the ways in which experience is understood – its forms or conceptual processes. 'Hegel's *Phenomenology* is not so much about experience as it is about *changes* in experience, changes in the *forms* of experience, transformations of the *concepts* through which we give form to our experience' (Solomon, p. 13).

This focus on change and transformation produces a discourse which is dominated by the notion of living substance as restless and active, as a continual process of differentiation, where truth, in Hegel's disruptive metaphor, is a 'bacchanalian revel' (Pref. 105). It is therefore a discourse dominated by the flavour and mode of dialectical thinking with its transformations and fluctuating abstractions. Such a focus also means that fixity and finality belong to some other mode of knowing. For Hegel, the quest for meaning and understanding has little to do with the sort of knowledge which produces 'a fixed and final result' – that which he dismisses as 'dogmatism' (Pref. 99).

Finality of argument in any empirical or analytical context would require proof, but in Hegel's discourse grounds or proof belong to external knowledge only (Pref. 123). The claim of his philosophy instead is that it is a 'conceptual' way of knowing which is continually in a state of transition and which embraces the inner nature of both object (Pref. 103) and subject.[8] His philosophical knowing 'affects' the object of its knowledge, so that the object is not external to the knowledge as is the case, for example, in mathematics. Only fixed, lifeless propositions emerge from studies of what Hegel terms mathematical 'unrealities' – space, numerical units, or, in a word, quantity. To quantitative questions of a mathematical or historical kind there can be direct answers, but that sort of truth is different from 'philosophical truth' (Pref. 100), because it does not arise from the nature of the subject matter itself (Pref. 103). 'Conceptual' truth, on the other hand, is based on the model of self-consciousness and is characterised by what he calls 'the twofold process in which the whole comes to be' (Pref. 101).

The two movements which constitute the whole are the movement of substance into outwardness or externality – itself for another – and, what is more problematic, its simultaneous withdrawal into inner essence – itself for itself (Pref. 101). Philosophical knowledge unites these two movements. Perhaps a clearer expression of this proposition is provided when Hegel says that speculative philosophy is the expression of a 'method, which consists partly in being inseparable from the content, and partly in determining the rhythm of its movement by its own agency' (Pref. 115). The notion of 'method' has to be carefully handled here, for it is a method that is at once more than method in the usual sense of a technique or procedure which has features that can be defined and objectified – features, that is, which are external to or can be separated from their user.

Hegel's philosophical method amounts to a form of knowing whereby the means of knowing is inseparable from the knowledge gained, as I have already hinted. Such an intertwining of method and content helps to explain the monistic nature of objective idealism. Too often idealism appears to literary critics as a version of total formalism, where content is reduced, it is sometimes suggested, to mere self-referential patterning. But Hegel separates his idealism from what he calls 'formalism of an external kind' (Pref. 115). Content is form for Hegel, but not form in the sense of form as structure, as a fixed, detached shape which is known in a manner external to its material. Rather, content is form in a dynamic sense, whereby form is a state of 'transition *into* a formal shape' (my italics). Form, then, is 'the indwelling process of the concrete content itself' (Pref. 115).

As always in Hegel, everything is characterised as becoming, as flux and process; therefore, form itself, the shape of all living reality, is paradoxically unfixed, not a static product of existence, but the movement of existence itself into shape. In this definition, form is intrinsic to the object or content of knowledge, so that Hegel's formalism is the formalism of concrete content, not mere abstracted or produced patterning. Nor is it 'produced' as an end result of observing or knowing, because knowledge is itself inseparable from its own process of production.

There may appear to be a certain circularity here, but it is the circularity that relates to Hegel's recognition that consciousness cannot step outside the examination of its own functioning. Method and content are combined, as stated above, and since method is both inseparable from the content and an active participant in producing that content through its own role as agent, knowledge as known within the conscious mind at once embraces the object as content and itself as participating subject. There is, therefore, no outside consciousness, or in more strictly Hegelian terms, no outside self-consciousness. It is necessary of course always to remember that Hegel is not talking about the knowledge of everyday life, where 'the mind finds its content in . . . experiences of various sorts, concrete facts of sense, thoughts, too, and principles, and, in general, in whatever lies ready to hand, or passes for a solid stable entity, or real being' (Pref. 107). That realm is where the mind 'runs its content back to some touchstone of certainty', to the security of some familiar referential 'resting-place' (Pref. 107), which in a literary context would be rendered as the sort of subjective realism found in the standard Victorian novel, from Elizabeth Gaskell to George Eliot. For Hegel, that is where knowledge is external to its material and, therefore, 'the expression of inert lifeless understanding' (Pref. 110). He is concerned instead with the knowledge, or rather the knowing, of speculative philosophy, which is the attempt to understand the nature of living being, living reality, not dead representations after the fact. The attempt to produce this sort of dynamic, dialectical discourse, where the subject is demonstrably an active agent within the process of a textual production that is continually shifting and mutable, is to be found widely in Victorian poetry.

There is a sense, however, in which Hegelian thought is always itself after the fact, since reflection and thought inevitably follow the phenomena and events they apprehend, and his historical awareness makes his approach analogous to narrative writing. In effect, Hegel's manner is a method of narrative reconstruction which is dominated by the concern with meaning, with interpreting past phenomena as part of a philosophical quest for knowledge and value. Hegel's philosophy is neither an attempt to posit causation nor a taxonomical task of assigning phenomena to a class of event, but it is something of a process of active reinterpretation that seeks to demonstrate how a certain end was attained, or how the present is an end to the past. As Solomon explains, 'the business of philosophy is *post hoc* teleological explanation'.[9]

Such a formulation could equally be a definition of any first-person narrative where the end is known by the narrator before the act of narration, or, indeed, of any narrative form which employs a plot structure as opposed to a mere series of picaresque episodes (in the sense that the picaresque generally eschews 'explanation'). *Post hoc* teleological explanation is a form which reaches its zenith in Victorian literature with Browning's *The Ring and the Book*, where each of the speakers is concerned to produce an explanatory and retrospective narrative which places the events of the Pompilia/Guido story into a structure of moral and social inevitability. Speakers in many other Victorian poems could be said to fall into a similar category, although those who speak in a manner closer to conventional lyricism might not be so concerned with the teleological nature of their structure. The more fragmented forms of *In Memoriam* or *Maud* do not allow their speakers to know their end in the way such a method would require; at the same time, the poems themselves involve structures which explore and exploit the nature of teleological purpose. *In Memoriam* through its preface and conclusion certainly presents experience as moving towards a universal and inexorable end, and *Maud* presents an end which is implicitly the product of the earlier means.

Hegel's point that the whole is a simultaneous double movement of externalising and internalising is characteristic of the fusion of lyric and narrative structures that these poems employ. They dramatise the outward representations which involve social actions that externalise the self for others, and yet at the same time these representations involve complex internal movements of thought and feeling, of self-consciousness (in the Hegelian sense) and differentiation. The effort to explain the past is an attempt to produce a sense of ordered movement and progress. For Hegel this advance is towards Absolute Spirit, the working out of universal truth through its transitions and transformations – as knowledge changes, so what is known changes also. For monologuists of various kinds this advance may not be quite so abstruse: it may be evidence for their secular rightness or spiritual righteousness (St Simeon Stylites, Fra Lippo Lippi, Saul's David, St John in the desert), proof of their belief (Johannes Agricola, Cristina's lover), demonstration of their power over the world and its inhabitants (Porphyria's lover, the Duke of Ferrara), or a rationalisation of their need to pursue what they desire despite conditions that are inhibiting (Ulysses).

Also, Hegel's point that knowledge cannot be investigated outside the bounds of its own processes is a recognition of the problem that the mind cannot examine itself from outside itself. The mind becomes object for Hegel, but the process of that objectification or externalising is a process which simultaneously enacts the internalising of the subject. The manner of analysis is therefore inseparable from the object of analysis.

This point too is characteristic of narrative form, where the manner of the telling is constitutive and affective of the content of what is told. As the narrator takes the story to its inevitable conclusion where the events of the narrative and their explanatory connections show the way the end was a necessary product of what went before, so the narrative method is inseparable from the narrative conclusion and meaning.[10] This is not a point always appreciated or required by a novel, but the use of irony in monologues, by Tennyson and in particular by Browning, makes it necessary for the reader to appreciate that the belief and truth of the speaker is inseparable from the manner and mode of presentation of that speaker. Claude's dilemma in Clough's *Amours de Voyage* is precisely his sense of the simultaneity of outward, socialised production and inward enclosure within the productions of self-consciousness, with the consequent difficulty for separating the real from the factitious.

So far this discussion of Hegelian form and its consequences has already illustrated the dialectical process whereby one concept, form, is the transformation of its opposite, content. It is necessary, however, to discuss the dialectical model more directly. Perhaps the first point to make is that the triadic dialectical structure (thesis-antithesis-synthesis) was not invented, as popularly thought, by Hegel. It comes from Kant and, notably, Fichte. Hegel refers to the formula in the Preface to the *Phenomenology*, but he does not use it himself either in the Preface or the main text (see Solomon, pp. 23, 268).

The related point to make is that while the concepts of dialectic and *bildung* (individual growth and development) go together in the *Phenomenology*, this does not mean that Hegel's text itself embraces the end of Absolute knowing. There can be no end to the process while we are still living it. David Shaw's representation, therefore, of the Hegelian model as 'an escalator, a moving altar-stair that slopes through darkness up to God' (Shaw, p. 5), emerges from a quite different reading of Hegel.[11] There is no achieved Absolute and no staircase. As Solomon points out: 'the dialectic is more of a panorama of human experience than a form of cognitive ascension . . . . it is the journey, not the final destination, that gives us our appreciation of humanity, its unity and differences' (p. 26).

What *is* central to the Hegelian model is the disruption of conceptual oppositions – substance and spirit, being and knowing, essence and form, form and content, false and true, ego and object, substance and subject. The intricacies of formulations which present a diffuse accumulation of such terms are characteristic of much of Hegel's writing.

At the same time, disruption of this sort does not entail loss of distinction. A key concept, for instance, is the play with substance and subject as at once unified and differentiated. One typical example is where he attempts to present a conception of the unified and yet disparate elements of what he calls 'ultimate truth':

> In my view . . . everything depends on grasping and expressing the ultimate truth not as Substance but as Subject as well. At the same time we must note that concrete substantiality implicates and involves the universal or the immediacy of knowledge itself, as well as that immediacy which is being, or immediacy *qua* object *for* knowledge. (Pref. 80, his italics)

The existence of the object *for* consciousness or for a subject (here for knowledge) is a frequent formulation for Hegel, and I take him to mean here that 'ultimate truth' involves the fusion of substance and subject in a conceptual act which is conscious of its own action and its own content. 'Truth' does not just involve a truth about existence or about the object as pure being (it includes that truth – the 'immediacy which is being'), but also includes the act, the immediacy, of knowledge itself. In other words, 'truth' includes the consciousness which understands and which is partly produced by the dialectical link between substance and subject.

Any sense of the separation of substance and subject at this point breaks down, and yet that separation must at the same time be maintained since it is part of the act of knowing, of understanding, of 'grasping and expressing' the 'truth', activating it within consciousness. Even then, however, the phrasing 'within consciousness' is misleading, since consciousness is to be conceived as simultaneous with the grasping and the expressing, and 'truth' is not therefore separate from consciousness – neither within nor without. Note, for instance, that Hegel's formulation does not privilege subject over substance, but places each equally – subject *as well* as substance.

Part of the challenge in reading Hegel is that, like Derrida, his concepts are embedded in a textual process that weaves its meaning within its own ongoing, continually redefining and enveloping web. As for Derrida and post-structuralist thought generally, meaning is established through context, and consequently it can be misleading to withdraw statements from their context and expect them to carry their meaning within the bounds only of that statement. In terms of the extract just considered, for instance, Hegel aids our understanding by developing on the next page a link between form and essence – another dialectical transformation. It is incorrect, he says, to suppose that knowledge can grasp essence without form, and therefore 'absolute reality must not be conceived of and expressed as essence alone, i.e. as immediate substance, . . . but as form also, and with the entire wealth of the developed form' (Pref. 81).

Substance and subject, essence and form, object and consciousness, being and knowing, become concepts that incorporate each other, subsume each other, turn into each other in acts of mind which at the same time distinguish them from each other. Such paradoxical propositions are perhaps at the heart of what is so difficult to grasp in Hegel's dialectical thinking, since they disobey the formal conventions of non-contradiction which require that A cannot be both *a* and *not-a*.

What is required is an acceptance of the shifting qualifications of a process that dissolves divisions in the very act of making them. This process rests on the inseparability of knowledge from making distinctions, from differentiation – 'Difference itself continues to be an immediate element within truth as such' (Pref. 99). But the distinctions are not static, fixed affairs; they are continually transforming themselves. All living substance (basically all reality, which Hegel equates with Spirit) is thus known – given consciousness and definition – by its development of 'distinction within its essential nature', by the attainment of 'essential opposition or unlikeness', but also by the 'transition of one opposite element into its other' (Pref. 103).

Life is characterised by its 'sheer restlessness' and by 'its absolute and inherent *process* of differentiation' (Pref. 104; my italics). All is governed by movement, and the dialectical force of this movement is perhaps most clearly represented as the 'transition of one opposite element into its other'. Within such a context, self and other do not exist as opposites, but as the indispensable element of each other. The essence of self is its otherness: it has no essence separate from its other.

What is also required is a level of awareness that perceives how the difference between two concepts, say between self and other, also incorporates the conception of difference itself. That which is distinguished then exists for or in relation to the distinction: neither the self nor the other exists for its opposite so much as for the 'very distinction' between them (IV.223). And the distinction between them is constituted through another distinction which incorporates the act of making distinctions, and so on. We enter a maze of unending dissolution and conflation, which is effectively the process of life: 'The simple substance of life . . . is the diremption [separation, differentiation] of itself into shapes and forms, and at the same time the dissolution of these substantial differences; and the resolution of this diremption is just as much a process of diremption, of articulating' (IV.223). Ultimately this process is linked to consciousness, since it is known, itself articulated and given distinction, through its existence for consciousness. Or perhaps it would be better to say through the coming into existence of self-consciousness.

Consciousness is also given definition through internal disruption and division and is also to be linked with change and process – it is neither complete nor a product – so that the level of understanding which incorporates this conception of a totality which is difference is expressed rather at the level of self-consciousness, with its implied self-reflexive and self-divisive awareness (the very divisiveness which bestows its sense of unity). It is thus consciousness which becomes the dominating universal concept which subsumes all else.

It could appear at this point that we are back at square one, with epistemological or subjective idealism, with Hegel positing a Fichtean subjectivism where consciousness or the self constitutes all reality. But consciousness in the *Phenomenology* is not to be understood as a particular person's awareness; it refers rather to knowing in general.[12] It is a peculiarity of Hegel's discourse that he uses phrases such as 'externalises itself' and 'comes back to itself' for the object, whatever it may be, whether a sense impression or bare thought (Pref. 96, and *passim*). He does this in order to convey the sense of action and process which is not tied to an individual mind or consciousness.

This concept of consciousness as the dominating image for all reality and experience in an abstract, general sense must include the recognition that it subsumes any epistemological distinction between reality and experience. What is experienced as 'a dissimilarity . . . between ego and object' is equally the internal division of substance within itself: 'What seems to take place outside [substance], to be an activity directed against it, is its own doing, its own activity'. Within such a circumstance, 'substance shows that it is in reality subject' (Pref. 97). Again distinctions between substance and subject dissolve, but the sense of what is outside substance/subject also disappears: there is no outside substance/subject, or no outside consciousness, no outside-self. I phrase this proposition as no 'outside-self' in order to prevent any implication that there is no outside 'the' self, with its suggestion of the individual, singular self. That would indeed restore the extremes of subjective idealism. Self, like consciousness in this context, is generally to be read as the concept of selfhood or of self-consciousness as general process.[13]

Towards the end of the Preface, Hegel stresses the role of dialectical form in speculative philosophy for realising truth; he suggests that philosophical exposition must 'retain the dialectical form, and exclude everything which is not grasped conceptually and is conception' (Pref. 124). In these terms, then, there is no outside conception, no outside the dialectical form. What these various formulations amount to is the proposition that there is no meaning, no value outside consciousness, where consciousness is conceived on the model of self – in terms of the fusion of consciousness with substance. For all practical purposes, there is no existence outside-self.

This is a proposition very similar to Derrida's 'no outside the text' or 'no outside-text', where 'text' is to be conceived generally as textuality. The text may be a specific text, just as consciousness for Hegel may be a specific, individual consciousness (indeed, insofar as what is known is bound to consciousness, it must at some point be found within individual mind), but the concept is more generally inclusive, embracing both the individual text and its general concept, textuality.[14] Such a combination of the particular and the general is common to both Hegel and Derrida. Both point to the way all conceptual/textual action is at once particular and general. For both, then, the individual self is at once itself and its other: for itself and for an other (in Hegelian phrase), or written in the very act of writing (in Derridean phrase). Such a double action is basic to dialectical thinking where self and other are opposites that are no longer in opposition and where writer and reader or reader and text similarly are opposites that become conflated, that define the indispensable elements of each other (again these are transformations which do not deny the distinctions which they disrupt).

Within Hegelian discourse, then, the epistemological model of the mirror for mind-world or experience-reality relationships is replaced with a dialectical model of self-consciousness. It is a model characterised by process, continual change, transformation and temporality. It is a dynamic model (as opposed to the static structure of the mirror), where relationships are unstable, and it implicitly contains the proposition of nothing outside-self.

The discourse of self within this context is therefore of course dialectical. It is tied to the concept of the subject as 'a process of splitting up what is simple and undifferentiated' (Pref. 80), and thus it is brought into being through active dislocation, through that 'disruption of fluent undifferentiated continuity' which constitutes the 'setting up, the affirmation, of individuality' (IV.223).

It is a dialectic which is self-affirming while it is self-dissolving, and it is bound to the active development of self-consciousness: 'The living substance . . . is that being which is truly subject, or, what is the same thing, is truly realized and actual (*wirklich*) solely in the process of positing itself, or in mediating with its own self its transitions from one state or position to the opposite' (Pref. 80). There are several factors involved here: (1) the process of shifting from one conception to another, of being part of a continual stream of transformations; (2) the act of self-representation, the subject positing itself; (3) mediation, the mode of presentation, knowing the self and its processes through representing them, rendering them as an object for the mind which reciprocates by seizing them as its own possession, making them its own;[15] and (4) the continual act of differentiation, whereby the subject does not merely perceive static forms, objects that are external to itself, but, of necessity, as part of the definition of being a subject, actively participates in those forms, through acts of separation, making distinctions, differentiating.

The subject is clearly not inert or passive within this discourse: it is 'a self-determining active concept' (Pref. 118; we are always talking of the subject as concept – no outside conception/consciousness). There is, consequently, a formidable challenge to the fixity or solidity of the subject, which Hegel openly acknowledges. The subject 'enters into the different constituents and pervades the content' and instead of remaining in opposition to a determinate content, it in fact 'constitutes . . . that very specificity' (Pref. 119). In other words, the subject actively produces the differentiation which allows the content to be perceived as such, as content.

Such a conclusion is threatening to any empirical notions of the passive self: 'Thus the solid basis, which ratiocination found in an inert subject, is shaken to its foundations, and the only object is this very movement of the subject' (Pref. 119). All substance is subject and the subject is characterised by movement, by the continuing action of differentiation and constitution. Again, there is no outside-self. Here this concept appears in the sense of there being no object, no substance which is not at once the movement of the subject – that is, the object as a determinate entity of knowledge is the combination of its differentiation *and* 'the process of bringing this about' (Pref. 119).

But this account of the active subject is not to restore the all-powerful ego of subjective idealism and widespread common belief – the consciousness which acts as its own command centre. Typically, the dialectical account observes the conflation of subject and predicate and concludes, therefore, that the subject as knowing ego does not achieve total control over its predicates, 'knitting or combining' them in the role of some grand, omniscient narrator.

Rather, the knowing ego discovers the presence of the objective self which it seeks to transcend (the self of sensory perception and physical experience) in the very predicates which it seeks to control, with the consequence that 'instead of being able to be the determining agency in the process of resolving the predicate', it has 'really to deal with the self of the content'. Crucially, it has 'to exist along with this content' and is 'not allowed to be something on its own account' (Pref. 120). The observation which denies the governing control of the knowing ego has enormous consequences for modern thought in all fields, from psychology and psychoanalysis to sociology and recent Marxism, and it certainly anticipates the arguments from structuralism and post-structuralism generally that the human subject is not master over its meanings and its consciousness.

For Hegel, the subject is already conceived, both in being known and in being brought into existence, in terms of a breach or division. It is through putting the other within itself that simple substance 'sunders that simplicity' and thereby produces the division which is basic to a sense of self, to the concept of individuality. It is the 'disruption of fluent undifferentiated continuity' which constitutes the 'setting up, the affirmation, of individuality' (IV.223).

Engaged in such aggressive processes, the subject is associated with acts of consumption and negation. Individuality, Hegel says, 'preserves itself', gives itself the feeling of unity, at the expense of the universal: 'what is consumed is the essential reality'. And yet it is the contrast with the universal which establishes individuality in the first place. Individuality thus 'cancels its contrast with the other, by means of which it exists for itself' and thereby consumes, takes possession, of 'essential reality' – differentiation, or universal consciousness (whose defining principle is differentiation). 'The unity with self, which [individuality] gives itself, is just the fluent continuity of differences, or universal dissolution' (IV.223). The unity of self, in other words, is not merely defined by its opposite – dissolution – it *is* that opposite, although in the act of affirming its unity as an individual the self suppresses this knowledge. This also means that the unity of individualism, the subject's unity for itself, is a conceptual illusion based upon the negation of the other, and the principle of negation figures strongly in the means by which the subject seeks to confirm its own existence.

'Self-consciousness', Hegel says, 'is *Desire*': the urge to negate 'the independent object', and thereby acquire 'the certainty of its own self' (IV.225). The act of negation is effectively an act of absorption. We affirm our own existence through possessing the world, whether through eating it, owning it, naming it, or otherwise persuading it to respond to our power – in the manner of so many monologuists, from the Duke of Ferrara to Caliban, who attempt to fix their own identity through possessing their surroundings. At the same time, in the satisfaction gained from this act of cancelling, consciousness 'has experience of the independence of its object', since that object has to exist 'in order that this cancelling may be effected' (IV.225). The need for a separate and independent other in order to establish identity then leads Hegel to the proposition that only when 'a self-consciousness has before it a self-consciousness' is *self*-consciousness in fact produced. The implication is that the self does not exist as a self-aware subject by itself, in the manner of some self-defined monad or self-created subject, but is only brought into fully self-conscious existence through the interpersonal relationship with another subject.

In this proposition Hegel clearly rejects the Cartesian *cogito* and all that followed which posited the fundamental existence of the individual self as a discrete, self-experiencing entity. Perhaps it is this implication more than any which is the most provocative for both the epistemological tradition and for literary study, since it challenges one of the most pervasive assumptions of all – the singularity and authority of my own experience as a source of knowledge and truth, what deconstruction would call the metaphysics of presence, or self-presence as the guarantor of meaning. The whole Hegelian dialectic offers such a challenge, since it produces the self as part of a continuing, universal action of differentiation where self and other, subject and object, play reversible roles.

On a personal and social plane, reality becomes an interpersonal affair (an image whose illicit prospects are explored by Browning in *Fifine at the Fair*, where the speaker argues that his personal reality requires an interpersonal affair with a lady other than his wife). Nature, as Solomon suggests, becomes 'the stage of our interpersonal world' (p. 441). But it is important to recognise that this metaphor still does not privilege external object or internal subject. Desire and identity within the individual subject are 'conditioned by the object' (IV.225) – they are determined by the existence and impact of the opposing consciousness – but they also act on their own behalf – they exist in and for themselves.

The negation of the other amounts in this process to the production of self-consciousness through mutual definition, and this is a proposition that is developed by Hegel through the Master–Slave parable that was later made famous by Marx and Sartre. It is quite specifically a reciprocal formulation, where 'there can be no master without a slave, no slave without a master (though the two can co-exist in a single person)'.[16] It is a complex process whereby each member of the interaction is at once dependent and independent, dependent on the other in order to mediate itself and independent of the other in acting for itself:

> Each is the mediating term to the other, through which each mediates and unites itself with itself; and each is to itself and to the other an immediate self-existing reality, which, at the same time, exists thus for itself only through this mediation. They recognize themselves as mutually recognizing one another. (IVA.231)

Each is a separate reality, but a reality that exists through a dependent conception. They gain the satisfaction and security of recognising themselves through negating the other, and yet that recognition is dependent on further recognising the mutual and reciprocal act of recognising each other.[17] In this process, the model involves the duplication of a double action. Each subject both acts and is acted upon, and this separate double action is required of both participants in order for the process to occur. There are, consequently, psychological and moral implications which are equally paradoxical. Each person insists that he or she be recognised as a free and independent being, but at the same time that very recognition is dependent on the other person. The self, therefore, is not a free or self-sufficient being, since it is 'conditioned by the object', dependent on the other for recognition and self-consciousness; and yet at the same time it is produced as a free and separate person.

It is perhaps through this conception of selfhood as both determined by the structures of an interpersonal exchange and free to pursue and satiate personal desires that we may understand Hegel's contradiction about consciousness: 'Consciousness finds that it immediately is and is not another consciousness' (IVA.231). It is also through this conception that we can observe one of the reasons why Hegel departs from purely subjective idealism.

Without such a model of mutual definition, idealism remains subject to the charge of solipsism, since the conscious self has no means of determining the reality or otherwise of any object within its cognition, including the object of its own self. Not only the world but the self too may be a mere dream. Only when the object of consciousness is an independent consciousness does it thereby validate the existence of the perceiving self and show that its cognitive experience is not a delusion of its own making. The negation of the other is a fight to the death, as Hegel suggests, since the very existence of selfhood as such depends on it, although the contest would be literal only in the most primitive of circumstances. Negation is also a force for the positiveness of interdependent structures.

I should reiterate at this point that Hegel's objective idealism is a recognition of what Kant before him and structuralist thinking after him have made plain – that the very possibility of human awareness and understanding is bound to the structures and patterns which give them definition. The consequence for the self is that its freedom is a freedom defined by limits, for without limits, without structures, we do not exist. As J. N. Findlay explains when introducing Hegel's work: 'To be a conscious, thinking subject is to recognize limiting, organizing universals in things or to impose them on things: remove the limitation and the organization and one liquidates conscious subjectivity.'[18]

But for the experiencing self this grand conception of objective and reciprocating dependency is not always so straightforward or so obvious. After all, while interpersonal action is produced within Hegel's process of general consciousness and is not subject merely to individual definition, it is experienced first of all as an intrapersonal mode of consciousness. Further, given that mediation allows the individual mind to make false representations to itself, it is quite capable of fictionalising the very process of reciprocal recognition – or any other form of recognition for that matter. The divisions that are a necessary accompaniment to the development of the conscious subject are thus fraught with potential danger.

Through 'attention', as Hegel later says in *The Philosophy of Mind* (pp. 196), the mind is able to abstract itself from its surroundings, and the consequent ability to formulate an abstraction not only of those surrounding objects but also of the self is a privileged feature of human experience: 'Man alone has the capacity of grasping himself in this complete *abstraction of the "I"*' (*Mind*, p. 128; his italics). The danger arises from the fact that the abstract 'I' is initially devoid of content, and able, consequently, to be filled with 'nonsensical ideas'; danger also arises from the possibility that the abstract concept of the self may be developed out of harmony with the concept of the world. Such, for Hegel, are the conditions of insanity. The privileged ability of human consciousness to formulate abstract concepts is therefore equally 'the privilege of folly and madness' (*Mind*, p. 128).

The mind avoids insanity through its continuing dynamism, its ability to move through and to harmonise the varying differentiations of self and other, but when that dynamism is stalled, 'the moment of *difference* can become fixed as a passive, simply affirmative being' (*Mind*, p. 129; 'affirmative' because lacking the 'negation' necessary for dialectical advance). When the division or fissuring which is an inevitable part of the production of the subject becomes fixed into a static position, the subject becomes trapped within a split that it is unable to be overcome. Fissuring is a feature of normal consciousness,[19] but such a feature also allows the possibility of delusion and folly.

Despite, therefore, the promise of the Hegelian dialectic which promotes a dynamic movement of mind towards its goal of harmonised knowing and being, where absolute substance is identified with the subjectivity of its being known, the fruit, as in all organic systems, is not guaranteed for all growth. The Absolute is a conception of speculative philosophy, not a fact of existence. It is a goal not yet achieved for ordinary consciousness, where there are still potential gaps between objective truth and experienced perception.

At the same time such fractures would be a difference between two conceptual forms of consciousness, not between an external reality and an internal idealism as in epistemological discourse, and they would occur at lower levels of consciousness, before philosophical thought had developed its advanced understanding. Gadamer points out, for instance, that, for Hegel, knowing at the stage where consciousness is conscious of the objective world and of itself is not sufficient. Knowing must 'transcend the ontological status of individual subjectivity' in order to become what Hegel calls *Geist* – spirit or mind. This development involves the transition from consciousness to self-consciousness, and the starting point of sense-certainty is where consciousness is 'as yet entirely unconscious of its essential self-consciousness'.[20] That is, the stage of awareness where experience is seen in terms of the blunt distinction between object and self is a lower stage of understanding. It can be transcended by the philosophical mind, but at ordinary levels of experience such transcendence is not so easily attained.

These vestiges of transcendence remind us that the ultimate goal of Hegelian discourse has the appearance of an abstract vision of 'truth' which for deconstruction would be a logocentric delusion. It could appear at first glance that there is a sharp contrast between the non-dualist concept of objective idealism and what that does to the subject (it is part of nature, an aspect of universal consciousness), and the more recent post-structuralist conception that individual experience is decentred and therefore disrupted, breached, not unified. However, I have outlined the concepts of negation and abstraction, and the distinction between levels of consciousness, because it is important to recognise that the Hegelian dialectical model does not mean that all human discourse is a seamless manifestation of universal harmony.[21]

On the contrary, Hegelian discourse registers the dynamics of difference, as I have been stressing throughout. Hegel affirms the dialectical function of the one and the many, of the divisions and the whole, of a consciousness whose unity is developed through and because of its differences. The breaches and openings of differentiation as well as their merging are basic to all ongoing perception and understanding.

Hegel does of course propose at the end of the *Phenomenology* that Absolute Knowledge 'unites the objective form of truth and the knowing self in an immediate unity', a unity which does *not* contain the 'distinction' and 'supersession of distinction' that characterises the text itself. In the text, 'each moment is the distinction of knowledge and truth, and is the process in which that distinction is cancelled and transcended' (VIII.805). But it is precisely the point that the *discourse* of the philosophy, the actual process of articulating the dialectic, does involve differences and distinctions. That is where we are as subjects and readers: defined by the discourse in the act of constituting it, incorporated into its process in the act of incorporating it into ours, and thereby bound to structure and process, fracturing and cancelling.

All this means that in terms of the Hegelian context literary discourses of self are more likely to include gaps than harmonious transcendence.[22] It is not surprising, in this context, that the dramatisation of human figures in dramatic monologues and long poems of the Victorian period involves the discrepancies and differences that occur within the texts of selfhood – the negation of the other, the triumphs of faith and self-certainty, the obsessions and fixities of folly and madness. Nor is it surprising that the tendency of Victorian lyricism to identify poetic discourse with a temporally specific voice, whether in Arnold's lyrics of historical awareness or in long poems of conscious historical anxiety such as *In Memoriam*, leads to a demystification of consciousness and context.

The use of the monologue form by Victorian poets generally presents an experience which is disrupted by irony, so that consciousness is seen as not singular and not authoritative. What for the speaker may be an act of detached observation or conscious self-assertion is seen by the reader as a more complex process of simultaneous production, where self and world are at once demystified – disrupted within themselves and divided between themselves – and fused, joined, conceptually produced within the same discourse. Of course for more sophisticated speakers – Bishop Blougram, for example – the full array of ironic awareness may be part of the dramatic dilemma. However, a poem which does not in fact employ a distinctively defined or named speaker, Browning's 'Epilogue' to *Dramatis Personae*, directly represents the dynamic processes that differentiate subjectivity.

The third part of the 'Epilogue' becomes a virtual paradigm in Victorian poetry for the dialectical production of the self. There, in the voice of the third speaker, an image of Arctic seas is used as a metaphor for the shaping of the individual ego by external forces. Just as waves sweep about some 'central rock', creating the illusion that it is 'The mimic monarch of the whirlpool, king/O' the current for a minute' (81–2), so nature dances 'About each man of us', dividing us, 'each from each, me from you' (88, 95).[23] It is a metaphor for a process of the phenomenal world which impinges on the observer in such a way as to produce the effect of a self as a focus of forces, as the illusion of a solipsistic centre. The person is made by the world, through the pattern of universal action, and yet it is the *personal* world of differentiated consciousness which is formed:

> That one Face, far from vanish, rather grows,
> Or decompose but to recompose,
> Become my universe that feels and knows.
> (99–101)

The face of Christ, the incarnate god, is a paradigm for the process of making all persons and worlds, but the paradox is that from the repetitive process of the pattern emerges personal subjectivity: it is 'his', the speaker's, universe which is the knowable object of consciousness. Browning has produced here the incessant process of change, the continual play of Hegelian difference, of reshaping and transformation. In the impetus towards decomposition and recomposition, it is also the process of Derridean *différance* – differing and deferment – and from this dynamic production there emerges the expression of feeling and knowing. In a quite brilliant description of the volatility of Browning's language in these stanzas, Herbert Tucker stresses the 'intimation of ceaseless becoming, a redemptive vision of imperfection',[24] but what also has to be stressed is that at the point where the universe becomes known, it is inseparable from an experiencing subject.

At the same time, this is not to deny that by becoming the object of a living subject it is nature which brings that consciousness and thereby itself into being. There is a finely balanced interrelationship here that is contained in the final ambiguity of an infinitive (to '-Become') which is also an imperative ('Become my universe').[25] The infinity of becoming is bound to the ceaseless action of the universal pattern which continually reproduces itself, but at the same time that reproduction is inseparable from the subject who participates through possessive self-assertion ('Become *my* universe').

While it may not seem from the discussion so far that in representing the construction of his subjectivity as a passive process governed by external forces the speaker has himself acted, he has, from the outset, posited himself as the evidence for nature's action: 'Take the least of all mankind, as I' (69). He enters the poem at that point as an object within the text (it is convenient to refer to the speaker as male purely by association with the named author; I cannot see that there is anything specifically 'male' about what is said in the poem). He proceeds to explain the existence of that object (himself as I) by providing a metaphor, a conceptual fiction, for the production of separate selves. His account is governed by discourse – the figures construct the effects of his model – but it is also a metafiction, the attempt by a subject to account for its own existence as subject. It is the ability to perform this act of self-mimicry, to posit a metafiction, that is the sign of the speaker's entry into the ongoing construction of his subjectivity.

So far there are two levels of action: the act of nature making men, represented in the metaphor of the sea which models that action, and the act of the speaker in making that metaphor about nature. The second action, however, depends on the speaker's assumption that his making has preceded the utterance; at the point at which he begins, he speaks as if the process is over. Yet the end of the poem shows that there is no closure, as Tucker has so clearly demonstrated. The apparently retrospective account is not, consequently, given from the secure position of a 'made', completed subject, a fixed self who will possess himself through his narrative. Rather, it is from the position of a subject-in-process, of being acted upon as the everchanging focus of ongoing forces, so that the speaker is a subject who will never possess himself utterly. His ego is not, as Hegel would say, something on its own account. At the same time, the speaker still enters the poem through positing that subject-in-process as an object of its own discourse. Through this act, the speaker is able, if not to possess himself fully, at least to locate his position within his own understanding, establish his nature by conceiving of its making, its production through difference.

The speaker whose sense of being a separate self emerges from the process he now describes adds through his conceptual model another dimension to that process. At the end of the poem, he possesses not only a feeling, knowing universe, but also a conception of how he came into that state of possession. This conception is then an additional fact of his subjectivity, part of that universe. He has added the fiction of his becoming to the process of his being, and that is a confirmation of security because a confirmation of the illusion of presence. It is not solely the action of nature which confirms his existence, but also the action of positing himself as his own model, as an object of discourse. Such, then, is the nature of the double action which produces the differentiated subject.

There is also a third level of action: the poet's act in making the discourse. This action is a repetition, within nature, of nature's creativity. At the level of creation, the poet too acts in terms of a double play, an interactive process between nature as object and author as subject. Browning, in providing an aesthetic form which illustrates the world's shaping process, imitates not the product of nature, the result of that process, but the production of nature, the action by which it produces its forms. In this there is an implicit tautology, since the poet is after all himself a part of nature and in imitating the production of nature he is therefore an example, or repetition, of nature imitating itself:

> An infinite circle plays (with) itself and uses human play to reappropriate the gift itself. The poet or genius receives from nature what he gives, of course, but first he receives from nature

(from God), besides the given, the giving, the power to produce . . . .[26]

This circularity does not deny the poet's ability to create. He may receive his power from without, but he can use it to enter the field of nature's making – indeed in his action as author he is already, as acting subject, part of that field.

The implicit tautology is simply the dialectical sense of a unity that exists through its differentiation. The subject is under the power of the object, or consciousness comes to know the indispensable element of itself as other. In this way the self cannot stand outside itself even as a metafiction, and that prospect is enacted at both the level of speaker and the level of author. The speaker's metafiction about his own making is thus contained within a higher poetic mimesis – within the poem as a metafiction written by nature about *its* making.

Self as object and self as subject, therefore, or nature and poet, metafiction and metaphor, all finally conflate into the one process of knowing, the discourse which constitutes the speaker's subjectivity. That conflation is both the point and the paradox of consciousness: that it is made from without, shaped by discourse, and yet what it knows is its own. At the point which it is brought into being, it subsumes all being.

This paradox is a feature of those many Victorian poems which present the triumphs and pitfalls of self-consciousness – usually in some variation upon a monologue. Speakers are subjects to the extent that they are inhabited by what is not themselves, and yet they are also subjects to the extent that they subsume it as their own, possessing the world in order to affirm their existence as subject. They negate the other, in Hegelian phrase: act as if it is their possession. For Hegel, such acts of 'negation' are paradoxically positive, producing dynamic structures of interpersonal action. But if possession becomes pathological or literal rather than actively conceptual, it quickly degenerates into psychological or moral negativity. At the same time, it is the only way the self can act if it desires to retain the psychological rewards of existing as a subject, as a knowing ego that is constituted through division, affirmed through negation and defined by itself as other.

One final point before moving on to the continuities between Hegel and Derrida and to the metaphor of consciousness as writing: in providing a dialectical model for the constitution and inscription of the subject, the 'Epilogue' to *Dramatis Personae* also suggests the ambiguity of subject-world relationships. A subject who claims to possess the world may be equally a subject who is possessed by the world, like the Duke of Ferrara; or a speaker who claims the world has absorbed him, dispossessing him of his humanity, may be equally a subject who attempts to own the world himself, like Mr Sludge. Speakers who appear to be in command of their discourse – Johannes Agricola, Ulysses, Bishop Blougram, the speaker in *Fifine at the Fair* – are usurped by what they fail to control in their text, or restricted by a rhetorical, usually dialectical structure; and speakers who appear to be victims of their discourse or of forces beyond their control – Tithonus, the Bishop of St Praxed's, Andrea del Sarto, the speakers in 'Evelyn Hope' and 'Too Late' – are invariably speakers who would regain sovereignty over their own psychic and physical territory.

Clearly, the human tendency towards onesided (dualist) readings of the interdependence of self and world provides a continuing array of dramatic possibilities. The final point, however, is that this tendency (usually a *desire* for some form of appropriation) also locates the potential for ironic displacement within experience itself – thus challenging the very assumptions of epistemological discourse, whether idealist assumptions about the secure and separate grounds of subjective perception or empirical assumptions about the secure and separate grounds of objective reality.

2
Consciousness as Writing

The discussion of Hegel's objective idealism in Chapter 1 provides a context for reading Victorian poetry which shows how the poetry disrupts conventional assumptions about consciousness as a coherent and controlling unit. It also shows how anti-dualist thinking and post-structuralist ideas are already present in the nineteenth century, particularly the potential for recognising that the human subject does not maintain mastery over its meanings and its consciousness.[1]

I wish in this chapter to define more specifically the continuity from Hegel to deconstruction, and to explain the implications of post-structuralist textualism, notably Derrida's metaphor of consciousness as writing, applying these implications to a reading of Browning's 'Two in the Campagna'. It might, however, help to clarify the concepts that have emerged so far by first comparing another form of nineteenth-century idealism which also theorises the status of division within consciousness – Romantic irony. Romantic irony more overtly than Hegel confronts the Absolute as an unattainable goal.[2] And Romantic irony stresses more overtly the disjunctive nature of opposition and unresolved difference – the ironic dehiscence of the human condition.

I

The main tenets of Romantic irony are usually traced through the aphorisms and paradoxes of Friedrich Schlegel. His propositions appear to develop initially from a sense of the inability of human thought to ascend to the divine. In one typically paradoxical statement, for example, he combines the contemplation of the universe with the impossibility of understanding it: 'You can neither explain nor understand the universe, but only contemplate and reveal it.'[3]

nor understand the universe, but only contemplate and reveal it.'³ In such a formulation there is immediately a gap, in this instance between perception and comprehension.

Irony for Schlegel involves similar structures of conflict. Socratic irony, for example, 'contains and arouses a feeling of indissoluble antagonism between the absolute and the relative, between the impossibility and the necessity of complete communication'.⁴ To be taken to the point of irony is to be 'continuously fluctuating between self-creation and self-destruction'.⁵ In such moments, Schlegel presents the sense of stark oppositions – oppositions, however, that gain their strength and significance from their very relationship of opposition. In this way Schlegel provokes a dialectic which, quite unlike Hegel's, sustains the image of development or becoming through tapping into the energy of 'indissoluble' antagonisms.⁶

There are some passages where he produces a more Hegelian conception of fluent transformation. In the 'Dialogue on Poetry', for example, he says of mythology that 'everything is relation and metamorphosis, conformed and transformed, and this conformation and transformation is its peculiar process, its inner life and method'. But in the very next paragraph he returns to the paradoxes of opposition, where he describes the wit of romantic poetry as 'this artfully ordered confusion, this charming symmetry of contradictions, this wonderfully perennial alternation of enthusiasm and irony which lives even in the smallest parts of the whole'.⁷

From statements like these, readers have taken the sense that Schlegel proposes a view of experience that defines humanly ordered art by its contrast with a chaotic cosmos. It is a view which is inherently ironic, both in acclaiming the 'versatility' that combines 'a comprehensive system' with 'a feeling for the chaos outside that system', and in celebrating the evanescent, unfixed quality of the chaos itself: 'Irony is the clear consciousness of eternal agility, of an infinitely teeming chaos.'⁸

Emerging from the environment of Kant, Fichte and Schelling, Schlegel's position at least in his earlier writings tends to follow the patterns of their subjective idealism. Irony is a process of *self*-creation and *self*-destruction ('Athenäum Fragment', no. 51); empiricism is rejected ('Idea', no. 150); irony is a philosophically artful means of representing a separate nature that, as 'the infinite fullness of life', is unknowable ('Idea', no. 86); and the dialectical aim is to attain personal transcendence over the frightful chasms that are all too apparent in the eternal, unresolved structures of antithesis. Schlegel did also admire Spinoza, who attacked subjectivism, and Gary Handwerk has recently argued that Schlegel's main achievement was to develop a form of ethical irony which aimed to embrace a more collective, *interpersonal* process.[9] Nevertheless, most accounts of Romantic irony tend to stress the subjectivist elements and the epistemological distinction between 'comprehensive system' and chaos 'outside'.[10]

Lilian Furst, for instance, links idealist concepts with the growing eighteenth-century sense of the unreliability of language in order to explain the shift from the fixity of conventional irony to the mobility of Romantic irony: 'The discovery of ambiguities in all words is a potent factor impelling towards more radical and enveloping constructs of irony that mirror the essential paradoxicality of existence.'[11] Undoubtedly it is important to observe this shift in the conceptions of irony: from conventional or fixed irony that is based on a clear sense of the difference between appearance and reality, where ironic ambiguity is grounded in an understood basis of determinate meaning, to an irony of uncertainty, an irony that is 'alert to the plurality of all meaning and the relativity of every position' (Furst, p. 228). But a formulation which refers to the 'essential paradoxicality of existence' or to 'the obdurate paradoxicality of a universe in eternal flux' (p. 229) is a representation that is couched in the language of epistemology. In such a definition the role of irony is to mediate between subject and world, acting as a 'mirror' of consciousness that is supposedly more accurate than previous versions of the Cartesian *cogito*. It is precisely this aspect of Schlegel as subjectivist and epistemologist which distinguishes his dialectic from Hegel and to which Hegel himself objected.[12]

Romantic irony, then, may be seen as another form of nineteenth-century thinking that anticipates deconstructionist thought, particularly that aspect of deconstruction which emphasises the undecidability of aporias, the disjunctions and contradictions inherent in all discourse, and particularly that aspect of Romantic irony which provoked, as in Handwerk's conception of Schlegel's ethical irony, the decentring of self-consciousness. But this form of irony also tends to stress the binarisms of conscious production, allowing opposites to become reified and experience to be defined by their structures – to be defined by opposition and contradiction despite the agility with which they may be manipulated or ironically sustained. It is this sort of dialectic that has been described dismissively as 'polarity-thinking'.[13] In terms of this tendency then, and in terms of the focussed aims of personal transcendence, Romantic irony lacks both the anti-dualism and the unfixed dynamism of Hegel which are more direct precursors to Derrida and post-structuralism.

II

It has to be said that Hegel's *Phenomenology* is too concerned with teleological purpose and too concerned with advances towards totality, through levels or stages of consciousness, to be post-structuralist before its time. It is precisely the Hegelian concept of *aufheben* (literally 'to pick up something', but also to 'move on', keeping what was there before, yet with the sense of improvement or elevation; Solomon, p. 275) from which Derrida detaches himself. Derrida's strategies are deliberately employed to resist reappropriation by that aspect of Hegelian dialectics which desires 'a resolution of contradiction into a third term that comes in order to *aufheben*, to deny while raising up, while idealizing ... while *interning* difference in a self-presence'.[14] At the same time Derrida also agrees that his 'displacement' of Hegel does not take him into an 'exterior terrain' and that 'we will never be finished with the reading or rereading of Hegel'. He also believes that Hegel's text is 'necessarily fissured; that it is something more and other than the circular closure of its representation' (*Positions*, p. 77). A reading which stresses Hegel's 'objective' idealism and dialectical 'transformation' should therefore quite reasonably extract traces of post-structuralist thought.

The main feature of the transition from Hegel to Derrida is probably the removal of any remaining vestige of self-presence as a source or guarantee of knowledge and experience. Hegel already rejects the individual self as the author or origin of meaning. As Derrida observes casually in the extract just cited, Hegel does intern difference within self-presence, even if the act is attached to a process of *aufheben*. But Hegel's texts also retain the terms of traditional epistemology with their potential implications of an idealist metaphysics: consciousness, mind, self. Consciousness remains, even without the connotation of individual mind, as the mode of mediation for meaning and truth. It can certainly be argued that consciousness for Hegel is in effect simply a metaphor, that it has no substantive referent in any conventionally metaphysical or even material sense, no signification outside the contextual implications of Hegel's own text. However, what shifts fundamentally with Derrida, in addition to the rejection of dialectical resolution, is Hegel's structural metaphor of self-consciousness. In deconstruction, it is replaced by the metaphor of text. Textuality rather than consciousness becomes the dominating image.

Derrida rejects any hint of dialectical closure or totality and certainly any binarism which would reify the terms in opposition. Whereas Hegelian discourse may urge the dialectical transformation whereby two terms are shown to contain each other (merging while retaining their difference), deconstruction would stress the undecidability between two contending concepts (Norris, p. 37). However, Hegel's definition of living substance as the process whereby opposite elements are transformed into each other nevertheless anticipates what Derrida has become most famous for – his deconstruction of binary structures, disrupting the privileging inherent in traditionally established dualisms. Both Hegel and Derrida transgress the dualist thinking which defines terms purely through their opposition to each other (Harland, p. 139).

Hegel, for instance, begins the main text of the *Phenomenology* with a discussion of sense-certainty, with the apparently sensuous world, and while he quickly points to the way sense experience is always characterised by a 'fundamental difference', breaking up into two 'thises' (the object and the self as subject), neither is given precedence over the other (I.150). In subsequent passages they become interchangeable. The 'essential nature' of sense-certainty (the apparent certainty of sense-experience) then 'lies neither in the object nor in the I', but in the whole (I.155).

Any epistemological question about the separate reality of the object basically drops away for Hegel as it does for Derrida. Kant had already shifted attention away from experience as revealing the true nature of things to the conditions which allow experience to occur – that is, from ontological to epistemological concerns. Hegel furthers this movement by becoming even more concerned with the forms and processes of experience ('forms of consciousness') rather than with the nature or truth of things-in-themselves. It is not that things-in-themselves, the objects of our supposedly tangible world, disappear, but that their status becomes subsumed into the forms and mediating processes which give them meaning and differentiation.

In post-structuralism what is important are similarly the processes through which meaning is established and the conditions which allow meaning to be produced (the concern follows structuralism's analysis of externalised structures, but post-structuralism, like Hegel, seeks to avoid the rigidity and stasis that is implicit in the structural metaphor). The status of the object or the 'nature' of its independent existence becomes largely an irrelevance, in the sense that the object as object is already a simulacrum, a sign. Those who have reacted with so much outrage to their sense that the world has been stolen from them by a sceptical confidence trick or textual sleight-of-hand are simply, therefore, missing the point – like Dr Johnson when he claimed to refute all idealist thinking through kicking a stone.[15] What is at stake is the power of discourse, the structures which produce meaning and value, not the ontological status of objects.

This point about the conceptualising of 'reality' is contained also in Hegel's recognition that there is no pure, untainted perception, that all sense-experience immediately divides into 'fundamental difference'. Such a view invokes the Derridean proposition that all perception is always already produced. Hegel says that all sense-experience is at once particular and general, 'essential truth and particular example', and both are mediated (I.150). The object cannot be known as immediate perception without also being known at the same time as an 'instance' – that is, as an example of an abstract category or concept. He explains this double conception in terms of the notion of the Now which is never itself, but always what it is not – the immediate past, or the past which maintains itself through contrast with something negative. The 'self-maintaining Now is therefore not something immediate but something mediated'; it is determined *'by means* of the fact that something else . . . is *not'* (I.152, his italics). The proposal that meaning is determined through differences between terms is to become basic for all post-Saussurean thought – except that Derrida is clear that his notorious (non)concept of *différance* (meaning as both differing and deferred) is distinct from Hegelian 'difference' at the point where Hegelian 'difference' becomes contradiction in order to *aufheben*, to lift it into resolution (*Positions*, p. 44).

Hegel says little specifically about language in the *Phenomenology*, but when he answers those who insist on the truth and certainty of the reality of objects of sense, he also anticipates recent concern with the paradoxical qualities of language. Those who make such assertions, he says, state the opposite of what they mean, for when they speak of the 'existence' of external objects, apparently referring to some specific, particular thing, their statement can never mean what they want it to say. They speak of individual things, but they say about them what is universal: 'When I say "an individual thing", I at once state it to be really quite a universal, for everything is an individual thing' (I.160). There is the direct implication here of the deconstructionist sense that to utter the object is to commit it to an already existing series of traces and differences.

Hegel retains the sense of something outside language: the 'This of sense ... cannot be reached by language, which belongs to consciousness, i.e. to what is inherently universal' (I.159). But his focus is on meaning and knowing and it is in relation to them – which he relates to consciousness – that we enter the ambiguities and paradoxes of utterance. The deconstructionist point that there is no outside the text, no meaningful utterance that can stand outside the discourse which gives it existence and sense, is tied by Hegel to consciousness, which clearly plays the role of the universal. Deconstruction replaces consciousness with semiotic structures as the producer of meaning, but Hegel's point about consciousness as the 'inherently universal' still leads quite naturally to Nietzsche's assertion about consciousness as language, as the net of communication that connects people together (see later in this chapter).

It is of course with the production of the self that I am most concerned in this study. And it is here too that Hegel leads naturally to Derrida. Derrida's statement that 'the subject is constituted only in being divided from itself, in temporizing, in deferral' (*Positions*, p. 29), with its several aspects of internal division, temporal process and incompletion, is also already existent in Hegel. The subject, Hegel says, is brought into being through the 'disruption of fluent undifferentiated continuity' which constitutes the 'setting up, the affirmation, of individuality' (IV.223).

Such disruptions and self-divisions occur quite naturally within poetic processes which through intensive foregrounding draw attention to their own rhetorical action; but dramatic monologues in particular enact moments of self-awareness through the speaker's positing of self-images. In such moments there occurs the classic idealist action whereby the subject becomes an object for itself and thus produces the self-division that accompanies its own coming into being: 'Though I stooped/Shrinking, as from the soldiery a nun' ('Pictor Ignotus'); 'I wither slowly ... A white-hair'd shadow roaming like a dream' ('Tithonus'); 'I'm the weak-eyed bat no sun should tempt/Out of the grange' ('Andrea del Sarto'); 'all through the speckled beast that I am' ('The Worst of It'); 'I am become a name' ('Ulysses').

The example from 'Ulysses' is also a reminder that the self in the dialectical model does not exist solely for itself, but is constituted in terms of the other, conditioned by the object (in Hegelian phrase), and Ulysses' claim that he has 'become a name' is perhaps the most significant of all announcements about the self as social and linguistic other. The self and other, however, as I have been suggesting, are not in opposition; rather each is the indispensable element of the other. This means that life itself is defined through the process whereby substance becomes fully subject, conscious of its own action: 'The living substance . . . is that being which is truly subject, or, what is the same thing, is truly realized and actual (*wirklich*) solely in the process of positing itself, or in mediating with its own self its transitions from one state or position to the opposite' (Pref. 80). Herein lies the double action that I have spoken about, whereby the self is at once made through being acted upon and acts itself as part of its own making, and herein lies also the potential for varying levels of awareness that also characterise the drama of the subject in its various stages and forms. We are asked to observe the subtlety and vagaries of unity and difference, external action and internal division, self-mediation, continual transition, dissolution and fusion. According to Hegel, 'the simple substance of life . . . is the diremption [separation, differentiation] of itself into shapes and forms, and at the same time the dissolution of these substantial differences; and the resolution of this diremption is just as much a process of diremption, of articulating' (IV.223).

III

Readers of Victorian literature will be familiar with the difficulty which Victorians felt when required to respond to new evolutionary models of the world, models which provided a view of change and development as intelligible – that is, recognisable and explicable – and yet essentially unauthored, without defined origin or providential plan. Change, transformations, apparently occurred without any determinable cause or discernible intent other than the amoral, pragmatic aim of continuing the existence of organic life. Such a view was a shock to a society dominated by a religious ethos which explained all events in terms of divine origins and teleological purpose. A world without god was a world without an author or plot.

Currently a similar model is being provided for writing, not in terms of evolutionary development, but in terms of a process which exists without beginning or end, without author or reader in their traditional roles as the instigator and receiver of independent messages. What is at stake is no longer god, but consciousness: it is not that consciousness is being denied, but its status and function is being considerably redefined. In one sense, human consciousness in the twentieth century has explored its relationship to language and discovered to its amazement that there is no relationship to explore, since man and language are inseparable. Without separability there cannot, strictly speaking, be a relationship – that is, between man as conceptually constituted and language as the mode of conception. Within this context the post-structuralist metaphor of consciousness as writing becomes an inevitable analogy for explaining such discoveries (or constructions).

I now wish to introduce the implications to be drawn from one example of this metaphor, taken from a passage in Derrida, in order to explain what post-structuralist textualism says about the human subject. It is also my purpose, given the continuities with Hegelian dialectics, to suggest that these implications may provide a means of reading Victorian poetry in terms of the 'representations' of consciousness, without falling back into the traps associated with empirical assumptions. Underlying my remarks are the propositions that the monologue form in particular already contains, thematically and in its epistemological paradoxes, the modern dilemma about the (non)relationship between language and consciousness, and that Victorian poetry in general, insofar as it is concerned even in its larger forms (perhaps most of all in the larger forms) with the existence of a self which is constituted through various versions of poetic language, is dominated by the problems of awareness and knowing – if sometimes not quite consciousness *as* writing, at least consciousness *in* writing.

IV

Consider these two extracts from *Empedocles on Etna*:

Consciousness as Writing

> Before the sophist-brood hath overlaid
> The last spark of man's consciousness with words –
> Ere quite the being of man, ere quite the world
> Be disarrayed of their divinity –
> Before the soul lose all her solemn joys,
> And awe be dead, and hope impossible,
> And the soul's deep eternal night come on –
> Receive me, hide me, quench me, take me home!
> (II.i.29–36)

> But mind, but thought –
> If these have been the master part of us –
> Where will *they* find their parent element?
> What will receive *them*, who will call *them* home?
> But we shall still be in them, and they in us,
> And we shall be the strangers of the world,
> And they will be our lords, as they are now;
> And keep us prisoners of our consciousness,
> And never let us clasp and feel the All
> But through their forms, and modes, and stifling veils.
> (II.i.345–54)[16]

These lines present two anxieties about consciousness: the fear that it may be lost or obliterated in language, 'overlaid . . . with words', and the fear that the speaker may be shut forever within consciousness, imprisoned within its forms and modes. Also, these two contradictory fears involve two assumptions about the status of consciousness: that it is separate from language, and that it is a distinguishing feature of individual knowing whereby it is the means through which the individual is separated from the world. Impelling Empedocles' fears is the desire to find some means of retaining the sense of a consciousness which remains free from the controlling forces of abstract thought or linguistic structuring. This is what remains perhaps of the Romantic desire for an independent selfhood or transcendent ego, the desire for the power of origination, the desire not to be subsumed into a process without authorship or telos. It is one of the devastating ironies of Empedocles' predicament that the only alternative is to commit himself to an external process which is potentially just that. He does not know what death entails, whether an end or merely a repetition, but the crucial difference is the act of death itself, that it be committed by a free individual, an independent consciousness. It is the act, not the product or the significance, the vision accompanying it, which constitutes the fact of independence for Empedocles.

On the other hand, consider these two extracts from Nietzsche:

Consciousness has developed only under the pressure of the need for communication . . . . Consciousness is really only a net of communication between human beings . . . . only this conscious thinking *takes the form of words, which is to say signs of communication,* and this fact uncovers the origin of consciousness.

Consciousness plays no role in the total process of adaptation and systematization.[17]

Consciousness here has been linked totally to language; it has been denied as having any power to authorise action at any significant level in human or social affairs, and it has been assigned only a communicative function. It is through consciousness as language that we are linked, in this model, to other members of the community: it is a 'net' of communication, the web by which we are interwoven. Clearly this proposition is what Empedocles fears, and it has been expanded recently in structuralist and post-structuralist theory, where consciousness is not some entity separate from language, but is inscribed in language, and where it does not originate meaning or thought – it is itself 'written' in and through language.[18] Jacques Derrida, for instance, sustains the corollary of Nietzsche's point about consciousness as a net of communication by saying that writing as an iterative structure becomes 'cut off . . . from *consciousness* as the ultimate authority' and that writing is not therefore 'a communication of consciousnesses or of presences'.[19] If the process of communication is itself constitutive of consciousness, there cannot be separate consciousnesses which perform the communicating.

Derrida's point here is to stress that speakers and their consciousnesses are not required to be present for communication to occur; indeed, quite the contrary is the case. It is the absence of the speaker which is the necessary condition for signs to function as signs. However, while this point involves the absence of separateness, not the absence of consciousness, it is worth noting that the consciousness which Nietzsche and Derrida locate within the process of language as communication is always known as the process within a singular, or seemingly singular, mind. While consciousness may be tied ontologically to language, it is known epistemologically in terms of the combined illusion of singularity and separation. This is an understandable illusion arising from the subject's identification of the web of communication with the weft of his or her biological independence (which is presumably another illusion even in biological terms), and in terms of the context of this discussion, it is the meeting point between the texts of Arnold and Nietzsche. Nietzsche's web of communication is experienced by Empedocles as the location of his separate awareness. This illusion is also a means of explaining why Empedocles is caught in his contradictory fears about consciousness: he experiences consciousness as the defining quality of his separate being and yet he senses that it is constituted in terms of its own modes and 'stifling veils'.[20] The consciousness which is known as an intrasubjective process is yet tied to forms which define intersubjectivity (the point of Hegel's objective idealism).

The increasing post-Romantic recognition of these problematics of awareness and of the sense in which experience is an unreliable source of human understanding (exposed in Browning's and Tennyson's monologues, for instance, through various disjunctions within their speakers' discourse and structures) has led Ann Wordsworth to challenge the reading of Victorian monologues in terms of an empirical base which ties them to speech acts and to assumptions about the originary qualities of character.[21] We are to beware of assumptions about the universality of experience and its necessary meaningfulness and to remain cautious about explaining poems in terms of their apparently referential context when all we have is language and what Ann Wordsworth calls its 'textual mobility'. She points to the dissolution of identity within language and to the way writing may then 'reinvent the self as multiple projections of textuality' (p. 9). There is no need to disagree with these propositions. Victorian monologues, in particular (as well as the long lyric poems), involve a 'textual mobility' which produces a weaving and unweaving of identity, and therefore a precariously realised process of awareness. But this mobility of language, or 'pure unaccountability of writing', need not disallow interpretative acts which read the 'linguistic performance' of a poem as including the action or nonaction of a simulated subject, as the process, that is, by which a consciousness is simultaneously active and passive within the field of its constitution. While it is entirely correct that Ann Wordsworth should challenge prevailing assumptions about the empirical reading of Victorian poetry, there is a point when her method, necessarily polemical, moves towards a reverse privileging of the structures of language over the function of a subject in the act of writing (whether the subject as reader, as author, or as speaker). Writing as the model for speech acts, which is what Derrida suggests may be the case, is a paradoxical process: communication is not a communication of consciousnesses, but communication is not denied (SEC, 181); the subject is situated, but not destroyed;[22] intention no longer governs the whole scene, but intention is not removed or denied (SEC, 192). What is required is a more thorough consideration of what is involved with the image of writing in its (non)relationship to consciousness. The image of consciousness as writing emerges from Derrida's essay on 'Freud and the Scene of Writing', notably from the last section on Freud's piece of wax, or Mystic Pad.

V

In 'Freud and the Scene of Writing', Derrida traces the development of Freud's search for an appropriate model for the processes of memory, a model which would combine the possibility of indefinite preservation with an unlimited capacity for reception.[23] The usual image of writing was inadequate, since a sheet of paper as the receptacle for impressions was limited in size and once filled could not be reused. Eventually Freud explored an analogy between a certain writing apparatus and the perceptual apparatus of the human psyche, and in this analogy Derrida observes the elements of the idea of consciousness as a form of writing. The writing apparatus in question is the child's 'Mystic Pad', a device which consists of a transparent sheet with two layers, one celluloid and one piece of thin waxed paper, which is placed over a block of dark resin or wax. When marks are made up on the top piece of celluloid, writing appears. These marks are etched in the piece of wax, but the waxed sheet can be lifted in order to remove the signs of writing and allow for more writing to be registered. At the same time the marks in the wax are retained and may still be legible under certain conditions. Thus the device includes the requisites of both retention and reception. For my purposes there are four main points to be drawn from Derrida's account of Freud's use of this analogy.

Temporality as Spacing

The image of the Mystic Pad illustrates the interruption and restoration of contact between various layers of the psychic process. Specifically, the image is spatial (the writing occurs on a defined space) and at the same time temporal (the perception exists for the time it remains in that space, until the sheet is lifted, which it inevitably must be in order to allow for more writing to occur). The temporal aspect thus disrupts the homogeneity which would be implicit in a model purely spatial, and the mixed elements are represented by Derrida in terms of a theatrical metaphor: we find 'only the differentiated duration and depth of a stage, and its spacing' (p. 225). Such drama images are worth noting, since they suggest a potential analogy between psychic process and literary staging, the point where psychic action and literary action coincide as a theatrical performance.[24]

Perception as already a Representation

Pure perception does not exist, because what is perceived is what is written on the space of writing. Perception is thus the product of an act of writing which has already occurred, with its complications of spacing, deferring and erasure: '"perception," the first relation of life to its other, the origin of life, had always already prepared representation' (p. 226). All perception is thus located within the already existing structures that allow perception as a meaningfully understood activity to occur, but what is also involved is its essential multiplicity – it is not a singular act. One of the marks of the temporality of the machine of the Mystic Pad, for instance, is that it is operated with two hands; it requires 'a system of gestures, a coordination of independent initiatives', so that it is 'an organized multiplicity of origins' (p. 226). Insofar as the model involves this ambiguity of agencies in its functioning, it represents the fracturing of any belief in writing and perception as a single originary action: 'We must be several in order to write, and even to "perceive." The *simple* structure of maintenance and manuscription, like every intuition of an origin, is a myth' (p. 226).

The Subject as System

It follows from the previous point that neither is the subject of writing a singular entity: the subject does not exist if we mean 'some sovereign solitude of the author' (p. 226). Derrida is careful to refer to the subject of writing, which is to be distinguished from the subject as biological or psychic organism. This subject, then, the subject of writing, is a system, 'a *system* of relations between strata: the Mystic Pad, the psyche, society, the world' (p. 227). It is also a system which is characterised by the paradox of an action, in writing, which is passive, being written: 'We are written only as we write, by the agency within us which always already keeps watch over perception' (p. 226). Jeffrey Mehlman's translation of this crucial passage provides slightly different phrasing: 'we are written only by writing [*en écrivant*], by the instance within us which always already governs perception' (p. 113). The original phrase, *en écrivant*, contains the ambiguity of a process which is both active and passive: we write and are thereby written. The difficulty in English is to capture that ambiguity, but it is important to register its presence, or it may be thought that this passage renders the subject entirely passive, given up totally to the powers of writing as other. That is not the case, however, and the proposition is rather to confront us with the paradox of the active/passive, the action of a subject who writes, and yet who in writing is written as a self produced by the multiple agencies which precede perception. The active and passive elements of this action are not to be conceived as opposite sides of conflicting forces, but as inseparable components of the process of writing, and, in terms of the psychic metaphor which is the concern of this discussion, inseparable components of the process of consciousness. Derrida's paradox here is a version of an earlier attempt by Charles Sanders Peirce to represent the double process of a perception which is at once actively engendered and passively received: 'Every cognition involves something represented, or that of which we are conscious, and some action or passion of the self whereby it becomes represented'. Walter Benn Michaels points out that Peirce's strategy is 'to collapse the distinction between the interpreter and what he interprets', and the consequence is 'not only that the self interprets but that the self is an interpretation'.[25]

The Erasure of Selfhood

An important condition of the machine or tool of the Mystic Pad is that its contents are subject to continual removal, to the raising of the covering sheet from the wax slab. The marks of writing always exist, therefore, under the threat of erasure: 'Traces . . . produce the space of their inscription only by acceding to the period of their erasure' (p. 226). They exist within the conditions of repetition and disappearance. Indeed, traces 'are constituted' by repetition and erasure (p. 226), and the possibility of erasure is a condition of the trace as sign: 'An unerasable trace is not a trace, it is a full presence, an immobile and uncorruptible substance' (p. 230). Writing is characterised by iterability and loss. To be committed to writing is to be committed to the paradox of a constitution which is dissolution, a 'representation' which is 'death' (p. 227). To come into being in the writing which is consciousness is at once to be committed to the repetition and deferral which is the death that is a sign of life. Consciousness as writing involves, therefore, the conception of the self as under erasure: 'The trace is the erasure of selfhood, of one's own presence, and is constituted by the threat or anguish of its irremediable disappearance, of the disappearance of its disappearance' (p. 230).

It should be apparent, then, that the self as constituted in language is attached to images which are part of the temporising and mobility of the trace. The self is attached to itself as always other, to the elusiveness and mobility of the signifier, so that it is attached to a process which guarantees its loss at the moment in which it is brought into being. The threat or anguish of its disappearance may be seen consequently in terms of a fear of nonexistence which leads, paradoxically, to an identification with the very source of the anxiety, with the trace which is the doubling of the self in language, the metaphor which denies full presence, the illusion of a continuity which is bound to process and thus to 'irremediable disappearance'.

VI

The indivisibility of consciousness from the elusiveness and mobility of signifiers provides a useful transition to reading 'Two in the Campagna',[26] a Victorian poem where the elusiveness of signification and the mobility of thought as image become main themes, with devastating consequences for the consciousness defined by their predicament. In part a love poem, it nevertheless moves beyond the traditions of expressiveness in love lyrics to suggest both the underlying lack which impels all desire and the futile attempts of consciousness to understand the source and nature of its own processes. The poem approaches the humiliating discovery of self-consciousness that it can never recover the source or origin which seems always to be implicit in its own utterance. The moment of feeling is lost in the act of its representation which is also the act of its discovery. Bound to the temporality of utterance, thought is irrecoverable, ever absent in the moment of its apparent presence, and the voice in this poem finally confronts the limits of its finitude with the unlimited desire which those limits generate, the yearning to recover lost presence, or the desire of all lovers to obliterate through union with the beloved that absence or lack which makes them lovers. In approaching this moment of crisis, the speaker epitomises the predicament of all those Victorian poems which seek to fix a self within or against the mobility of a discourse which cannot be fixed.

The poem begins with a differentiated consciousness which is able only to speculate about its counterpart ('I wonder do you feel to-day/As I have felt') and which engages immediately in temporal and figurative play: the intermingling of past and present as the speaker places feelings from the immediate past ('As I have felt') against the potential feelings of the beloved in an ongoing present ('Feel to-day'), and the intermingling of literal and figurative (they 'sat down' in order to 'stray/In spirit'), which is also an interfusion of the finite ('sat') with the potentially unrestricted ('to stray'). The second stanza moves even further into a mixing of past and present, and singularity and multiplicity, through recalling the continuing moments of a thought which 'Has tantalized' and the one moment when the speaker apparently 'touched it'. The act is both recollection and repetition. This stanza also introduces the theme of thought as image: the thought which 'tantalized' is 'Like turns of thread' thrown by spiders. It is immediately a problematic image, for it is the tantalising quality of the thought as much as the thought itself which is like the thread that is thrown 'Mocking across our path', and therefore the referent of the image is essentially inseparable from the qualities of the image: the thought does not exist, has no definition, other than as the teasing insubstantiality of a spider's web. The thought is literally the web, and the web is figuratively the thought. The thought is known in no other way than in terms of this conflation of literal and figurative. Such an uncertainty of signification leads 'thought' as signifier to point to its signified not as *a* thought existing outside the utterance, but to thought as indeterminate trace, to signification itself, the process in the poem of attempting to fix the trace, and yet with only an analogy, the analogy of the spider's web, as method. There is, then, no thought, only the image for it, and what these first two stanzas establish is a context where referentiality is undermined, where the literal is continually presented as figure.

The imperatives of present action in the third stanza ('Help me to hold it!') occur, therefore, within a context where the present is not simply itself but is a repetition of the past, and where the literal tracing of the weft among the fennel and brickwork is a figurative retracing of a web which is itself a figure for the traces of a thought that is known only as a figure. We enter thus a network of signifiers. Even the brickwork is not just brickwork, but the sign of 'some old tomb's ruin' (14), and the speaker's attempt to act positively by calling on his companion to help him seize the weft is also paradoxically a sign of passivity in his inability to seize it himself. His active attempt to grasp the thread is thus inseparable from the futility of the effort and from the passive process of following where he is led. He is led to the expansiveness of 'The champaign', where its unending 'fleece/Of feathery grasses' suggests both an enduring possibility of harmony and value, of 'Silence and passion, joy and peace', and a prospect of endless mobility, 'An everlasting wash of air', a future that always contains the past, 'Rome's ghost' (21–5).

Within this context, the process of figuration seems to take on a life of its own, so that the erotic energies of natural processes are the juxtaposed 'naked forms of flowers' and 'miracles' of 'letting nature have her way' (26–8), and the force of this energy and activity leads the speaker to question the freedom of personal action: 'How is it under our control/To love or not to love?' (34–5). Amidst the play of uncertain reference the purpose of this question is ambiguous. One effect of its rhetoric is to urge his companion to relinquish coyness, to be 'unashamed' and submit to the forces and passions of nature – they have no choice; it is not under their control. But it is also a question about origins and may refer equally to the speaker's own sexual desire, his urge to overcome the obstacles of difference. What follows the question, for instance, is not further argument for submission to external forces, but an emphatic statement of desire to fulfil internalised will: 'I would that you were all to me' (36). And these statements of intent are juxtaposed with more questions about origins ('Where does the fault lie?'), questions which make explicit the sense of inevitable failure ('What the core/O' the wound, since wound must be?'; 39–40).

There is a subtle blend of elements here. The lover is caught among forces and desires which seem to take over, leading to the inevitability of sexual union, and yet those desires are accompanied by a sense that they will never be satisfied, so that desire and failure, yearning and futility, already coexist. At the same time, this consciousness also emerges from the rhetoric of persuasiveness, from the attempt to convince the companion that there is no need to be morally restrained, and thus the 'core/O' the wound', the centre of yearning, is quite blurred: what seems to be part of 'letting nature have her way' (29) may simply therefore be the product of a rhetoric which signifies no more than personal need (albeit itself a part of nature).

The origins and signification of concept and feeling are impossible to fix, and the speaker's questions are unanswerable, although that very feature may act as part of their rhetorical persuasiveness. All that seems certain is the repetition of desire – 'I would I could adopt your will' (41) – a desire that is overwhelming, that would exceed the constraints of physical and social inhibition, and yet which is impossible to realise, where the inevitability of the failure is inseparable from the way that desire is conceived. Such desire would also exceed the constraints of knowing through possession. The line 'Nor yours nor mine, nor slave nor free!' (38) may refer equally to the beloved's indeterminate state of being 'just so much, no more' (37), belonging to neither of them, having neither choice nor compulsion, or to the speaker's yearning for an ideal union, where neither of them would be privileged over the other. Read in the latter sense, the consummation of the speaker's purpose would involve the obliteration of all differentiation. But of course the condition of consciousness is that it exists through differentiation; consciousness is brought into being through the separation of the self as subject from the other as object, so that while consciousness remains, such desires can never be fulfilled. He may touch the beloved, kiss her cheek, but inevitably the 'good minute' is lost (50) – temporising intrudes. The speaker is forced back to the earlier confrontation with a process without origin and without end, and the return is signalled through a question which confronts the impossibility of a centre:

> Must I go
> Still like the thistle-ball, no bar,
>   Onward, whenever light winds blow,
> Fixed by no friendly star?
>   (52–5)

The attempt to fix thought fails: 'Where is the thread now? Off again!' (57). To utter the image which represents thought is to gain it and lose it in the same instant. Thus, when consciousness and desire are constituted in language, when they become part of the attempt to pursue meaning, they are alike in their submission to a temporality which allows no fixed moment, no teleological fulfilment.

The last lines finally provide a climactic paradox:

> Only I discern –
> Infinite passion, and the pain
> Of finite hearts that yearn.
>   (58–60)

What is provided here is an overt act of consciousness, a discernment in the sense of its original Latin (*discernere*: to separate), whereby something has been differentiated. In a context of configuration, the speaker finally 'sees' figuratively in a perception that is at once a conception, and what is seen is a concept about his own condition, about its paradoxically divided nature, caught between the desire for infinitude which is realised in consciousness and the inevitable restriction which is at the same time part of that realisation. This is the ironic trap of consciousness: its ability to utter this conception – to become conscious of it – is the condition which renders any attainment of that conception impossible. In this context the process of communication leads to an irony of communication: the discourse which links (we presume) the two people is also able to indicate the basis for their separation. In other words the communicative function which defines consciousness, in Nietzsche's sense, is also a means whereby consciousness is brought to confront its own separation. Or, as stated earlier, consciousness is an intersubjective form which is known as an intrasubjective experience, and that is why the consciousness of a lover, who yearns to escape the bounds of intrasubjectivity and enter entirely the forms of intersubjectivity, is ideally suited to representing such a disjunctive condition.

So far this thematic account of the poem has led to statements about the speaker's awareness of the contradictions inherent in his own condition, where he exists in a precarious state of elusive configuration, ever chasing the disappearing thread of representation. It should be clear by now that the poem in this reading is very close to containing, almost overtly, the elements of Derrida's metaphor of writing, but it remains to indicate how those elements can be traced in the poem more directly, adding a further dimension to the interpretation. The concept of temporality as spacing, for instance, clearly explains the combination of time and space in the image of the thread as thought. Thought is spatially conceived, represented in the image of a web which exists in space, but which also, in being perceived, *moves* through space, and so is subject to process, the conditions of time. Just as the Victorians were thrust by evolution into an organic process without aim or telos, so the speaker in 'Two in the Campagna' is placed within a process of representation, of writing (thought as image), without determinable origin or conclusion – except for the momentary distinction of a paradox of process.

The concept of perception as already a representation is also contained in the image of thought as a spider's thread, an image already available, already written on the mind of the speaker. The various elements of dislocated tenses, shifts between stanzas, entering into a process of thought already begun and the ambiguity of rhetorical questions also suggest the dissolution of singularity. There develops thus a complex interrelationship between several levels and disruptions: recollected feeling, wondering about the companion's feelings, past attempts to capture the thread, present attempts to repeat the process, present desire, the will to aspiration, expectations, confirmation of thwarted desire, statements of intent, statements of abstract questioning, and the movement towards an awareness which attempts to arrest the whole by encompassing it within a philosophical statement about emotional contradiction. Such are the marks of the multiplicity of perception. They are also the marks of the subject as system, and it is clear that varying forces are at work in the production of the subject of consciousness in this text: the speaker's desire for sexual union, the more conceptualised desires for a recovery of lost thought, on the one hand, or for a moment of realised bliss on the other; the imposing atmosphere of the Campagna, with its mixture of 'Silence and passion, joy and peace'; the erotic energies of the natural world and the inexorable temporising which characterises all conscious experience under textual conditions. These forces combine to construct the multiple system of a subject in process.

The double action of a subject which writes and is thereby written is also indicated in the present action of tracing a thread which has already been arranged, by past attempts, in terms of the metaphor for thought, and by the external actions of a spider, in terms of the literal placing of an image within an already existing environment. In tracing the path of the weft, the speaker is being traced by its configuration, both literal and figurative. The same doubleness is contained in the act of 'discerning'. This is the act of consciousness that is constituted in that act by the differentiation which sees (a seeing which is a construction as it is a perception) the nature of its own condition. But the condition and the speaker's awareness of its quality were conditioned by an array of elements, by the experience of the countryside, by the relationship with a lover and by reflection on mental processes, and all these in turn were differentiated through the figurative powers of language itself. These powers are both within the poem in the process of tropes which present and shape all perception, and outside the poem in its antecedents and contemporary contexts. To repeat the actions of the text and trace the origins of the speaker in earlier love poetry is beyond the scope of this discussion, but one obvious instance of this textual writing is the image of the rose: 'I pluck the rose/And love it more than tongue can speak – /Then the good minute goes' (48–50). Richard Altick has already noted that this image echoes Othello's similar sense that the delight of the moment cannot stay:

> When I have pluck'd the rose
> I cannot give it vital growth again,
> It needs must wither.[27]

And as a Petrarchan convention the rose has always been a sign of passion that fades, of beauty that, in Keatsian phrase, 'must die', so that in writing of his brief kiss as a plucked rose, the speaker is thereby written into the texts of all lovers who found that ecstasy did not last.

The speaker must speak – without that action there is no utterance and no constitution of the subject – and the constituted subject interprets, separates off the condition of its feelings. But the subject is also itself an interpretation, a figure within the conditions allowed by utterance itself. In a text such as this it becomes comparatively easy for a reader to observe Peirce's principle that the self is a compromise, for the process of the text is to move through conflicting elements, juxtaposed phrases, towards an abstraction which 'represents' the speaker's consciousness as compromise, as a temporal and spatial conception of opposites that are mutually exclusive and yet mutually sustaining: 'Infinite passion, and the pain/Of finite hearts'.

Of course the commitment to being written is the commitment to temporal dissolution, which is what the text states, and the self under the constant threat of erasure is contained thematically in the futile attempt to grasp the thread which is thought, to seize the moment which is now. Each image is committed to the double process of writing which is both inscription and erasure, the lifting of the paper on the Mystic Pad to clear the space for more writing. There is also in the poem a desire for a life which would mean death, that is, as previously indicated, the desire for a union with the beloved which would mean the loss of the separate self. Such a union would be an identification with the other which would involve loss of identity for the self as separate consciousness: 'I would I could adopt your will,/See with your eyes' (41–2). Such a loss is seen, however, as a potential gain, as physical and spiritual ecstasy, a transportation out of the self which would allow an escape from the threat of erasure through transcending the conditions of that threat. It is the life in death that is the goal of all lovers whose essential lack leads to the desire for reconstitution. It is the paradox of a lover's desire, as indicated in this poem, that it earnestly seeks what would deny its separate seeking. In a sense we are returned to Empedocles, to his desire not for sexual union but for a more elemental union with natural forces which would save consciousness from the dissolutions of language. The paradox of the desire is similar: the way to preserve consciousness from the threat of death is to die. The desired death is not, of course, in either case, read as obliteration; it is read as a transformation, as the loss of an identity which is then reconstituted through a different identification – the transformation of self through sexual union or through union with organic process. Such are the signs of the self as it exists within the conditions which threaten erasure.

VII

If the 'Epilogue' to *Dramatis Personae* is a poetic paradigm for Hegelian dialectical process (see Chapter 1), then 'Two in the Campagna' epitomises all those Victorian poems where speakers confront the failure of the transcendent ego. That failure is provoked through an array of varying contexts, whether through the devastation of grief, as in *In Memoriam*; through the loss of the beloved as the object of identification, as in 'Evelyn Hope' or 'Too Late'; through the suspected failure of personal talent, as in 'Pictor Ignotus' or 'Andrea del Sarto'; through the fragmentation of unity in 'Childe Roland to the Dark Tower Came'; through the inability of Empedocles to resolve the oscillations between society and solitude; through the terrible and inexorable decay without end that is imposed upon Tithonus; through the bitter fancies which threaten to destroy the speaker in *Maud*; or through the dehumanising public identity of 'Mr Sludge, "the Medium"'.

'Two in the Campagna' also epitomises the dramatic production of Victorian poems where speakers use the mediations of language to fix the self against forces which question their authority or centre. In 'The Last Ride Together', for example, the loss of the beloved is replaced by an act of riding, but as the poem unfolds, the act of riding becomes less a literal action and increasingly a trope, a signifier for presence and fulfilment. The threat of failure in 'Pictor Ignotus' and 'Andrea del Sarto' produces in each case a discourse which affirms choice as a means of shoring up the anxious self. In 'The Bishop Orders His Tomb at Saint Praxed's Church' the attempt to arrange the design and materials of the Bishop's sarcophagus is an attempt to manifest quite literally the Bishop's status and power of place. The Bishop's nephews will not accede to his demands, but his figurative speech nevertheless effects the materialisation of self, the fusion of identity with artefact, that he is unable to produce otherwise: 'I . . . stretch my feet forth straight as stone can point' (87–8). Rabbi Ben Ezra seeks to arrest the dissolution of self in old age and death through identifying with the image of a potter's wheel, a metaphor for cosmic process and transformation; such an image explains 'Why time spins fast, why passive lies our clay' (153), allowing Ben Ezra to secure the belief that 'Earth changes, but . . . soul and God stand sure' (159). Or there is 'Caliban Upon Setebos', the quintessential attempt to enter language, to formalise thought, in order to survive in a world which threatens violent destruction – 'there is force!' (213). In each example what matters is not literal action but the discourse which assigns it significance. In Caliban's world, for instance, objects and events are misread signs, signs that gain meaning through being absorbed into his own version of a hermeneutic circle.

The lyrical medium which constitutes such speakers constantly suggests the metaphor of writing for the context of their attempted survival, their attempt to restore the illusion of a singular identity. Perhaps the final moment to list in this connection is 'The Lady of Shalott', where the Lady's linguistic act of inscribing her name upon the prow of her boat returns us precisely to Derridean erasure, to the death of self in writing. In turning from the world of reflection and shadows to the apparently unmediated world of direct perception, the Lady falls unwittingly into the empirical (and dualist) trap, the assumption that the world of 'seen', physical experience is somehow truly real. But she cannot be known without representation even in the flesh; when her body is gazed upon by Lancelot and the others in Camelot, it is still known only as a sign, absorbed, re-presented, by the bland, male cliché of 'a lovely face'. To be known is to enter the divisions and substitutions of discourse; it is, once again, to commit the self to a constitution, in writing, which is the death of the self as origin and presence. Consequently it is entirely fitting that the Lady should die 'Singing *in* her song',[28] since this suggestion of absorption into and by her utterance repeats the death which accompanies her act of self-naming: both acts commit the self to the mobility of signifiers, to the self-proclamation that is self-loss.[29]

Paradoxically, the Lady has a more secure and independent existence when she remains within her world of shadows and reflections, where she has 'little other care' than her weaving. That of course is to be literally unseen and equally unknown, a presence only in terms of the disembodied voice of her song – 'Only reapers . . . Hear a song' – and even that is reflected, a song which 'echoes cheerly' (28–30). Imprisoned within the idealist realm of indirect and private vision, the Lady is cut off from the social world outside, where all reality seems to be defined by Camelot, the aspiration for all movement – the highway winds 'down to Camelot', and damsels, abbot, shepherd-lad, page go by 'to towered Camelot' (49–59). She appears to be trapped by patriarchal convention – 'She hath no loyal knight and true' (62) – but the attempt to break these bonds through leaving the world of personal isolation and entering the public arena of physical and social interaction simply swaps one side of a binary structure for the other (idealism for materialism), one form of discourse for another (the lack of 'loyal knight' for 'a lovely face'). There is no *known* life without representation (since to be 'known' admits the 'other', whether the other as self or the other *as* other). Consequently the Lady's perceptions in both realms are already representations and consequently there is no form of living that is not also a form of death. Hence we may understand the inevitability and tyranny of the sign – the curse, perhaps, of human existence. Perhaps that is also why the Lady's curse is ambiguously placed: 'A curse is on her if she stay/To look down to Camelot' (40–1). For either way, whether she stays from (ceases) weaving in order to gaze directly at Camelot or stays (remains) weaving in order to look *down* to Camelot (remaining aloof, separate from it in her detached idealism), she is doomed to forms of nonexistence, the death-in-life that is a favourite Tennyson paradox and from which there appears to be no escape (see Chapter 3).[30]

All the concepts I have been separating off from Derrida – temporality as spacing, perception as already a representation, the subject as system, the erasure of the self in its utterance – are contained within the metaphor of writing as consciousness. We need to attend to textual mobility and to the unaccountability of writing when reading Victorian poetry, but we should do so with regard to the full complexity of what is involved with such processes. The shifting conceptual context from Hegel to Derrida suggests that linguistic performances in lyric and dramatic poetry can still be read as (re)presentations of the processes which constitute human consciousness, provided that we take full account of the paradoxes and contradictions that are inherent in those processes.

3
Absence and Desire in *Maud*

I

Absence and loss have often been noted as themes in Tennyson's poetry.[1] An oxymoronic 'Death in Life', the presence of absent 'days that are no more', is thus a common effect, where the lyrical present is characterised by a yearning for what is no longer or not yet available. Tithonus' lament for the lost ability to die or Ulysses' sense of insufficiency and of a lost recognition, for instance, along with the accompanying desire to seek fulfilment, respectively, in death or in action, are typical.

It would appear, then, that within the Tennysonian present, completion and fulfilment are not possible. For Ulysses, for instance, experience entails a commitment to process, an attempt to grasp what cannot be grasped – the elusive 'margin' that for ever 'fades' as he moves. Ulysses mourns the disappearance of past selves within social discourse ('I am a part of all that I have met'), and, like Browning's lover in 'Two in the Campagna', yearns for what, if gained, would mean death ('Some work of noble note'). At the same time, he positively welcomes incompletion ('How dull it is to pause, to make an end'), for that is what it means to celebrate life ('As tho' to breathe were life'). As 'a name' he identifies with the textual trace that is always other, with the process that guarantees his loss at the moment that he is brought into being. This, for a man of action like Ulysses, is to identify with the ongoing dialectic, the death in life, that constitutes living. What absence and loss so often mean, then, within Tennysonian discourse is that death characterises the condition of life, not just as past loss or future limit or as the goal of world-weariness, but, more pertinently, as present process, as a psychology of human consciousness.

While Tennyson's poetry appears to stop short of acknowledging the interconnectedness of discourse and self, the preoccupation with loss continually forges the link between absence and desire. That is now a well-established link within Lacanian post-structuralism and is itself tied to the entry of the subject into discourse.[2] The very nature of being human is based, for Lacan, upon a fundamental sense of lack or alienation (the loss of wholeness), but the important awareness of loss emerges with the development of social being – with the child's discovery that the world and its objects are separate (outside, absent), and with the entry into discourse (Lacan's symbolic order) which enables that discovery.[3] Such propositions lead to Lacanian paradoxes about the way the object must be absent in order to be discovered, but they also lead to the sense in which it is absence which impels all desire, the desire to restore the unity which the discovery of absence (and therefore of presence) has broken. The point is similar to the Derridean textualised subject: without absence there is no difference and without difference, division, there is no separate self.

Absence and desire are interwoven since the feeling of loss that accompanies the realization of absence produces immediately the desire to restore the paradise of full presence. In an obvious sense the desire for unity (for Lacan's realm of the imaginary) is a desire for the death of the self – a desire to obliterate the act of differentiation, the entry into language which brings it into existence. At the same time, this desire is no simple death-wish or seeking after oblivion, since there is a less obvious sense in which it is tied to the unceasing movement of the signifier, to the death or loss of self that occurs with every utterance – Derridean erasure (see Chapter 2), or 'the death actualized in the signifying sequence' which Lacan links to the 'subtle body' of desire.[4] Ultimately necessity demands that the repossession of the lost or absent object would entail the end of subjectivity, the death of the self as subject. However, for the life that is constituted through the symbolic order, what is repossessed is not the object but the sign, the signifier which eludes the grasp in the moment that it is seized. Consequently, in appearing to satisfy the need that is outside discourse, possession of the sign merely returns the subject to signification, to the symbolic, the life that is death, to desire.

Once again loss and death are linked to desire and fulfilment, and desire, like death, is both a condition of living and insatiable, impossible to alleviate.[5] Browning's 'Two in the Campagna' proclaims precisely this dilemma with its discernment of 'Infinite passion, and the pain/Of finite hearts that yearn', and Tennyson's repetitive variations on absence and loss hover persistently around the same fundamental concern. What I wish to pursue here is the particular discourse of loss that constitutes *Maud*, a poem which is perhaps one of Tennyson's most intricate presentations of this dialectic of death in life.[6]

II

Maud opens with an excessively horrific sequence of interwoven death and life. This display of the more macabre obsessions that may underpin human alienation serves to introduce a complex dialectic that combines opposites while it disrupts all effects of normalisation. As a poem about love, for instance, *Maud* begins with its absence – 'I hate . . . ' – and if it is about anything it is about what is not there: a dead father, a body, a lost engagement, a duel, an occupant of a beached shell, peace, wealth, love, Maud herself even. Such absences torment the speaker's mind. They are the gaps in his existence which deny wholeness and satisfaction.

The image of the hollow with which the poem begins unfolds as a complex image in the poem, and even in the opening lines it accrues multiple layers of meaning. Literally the hollow is the 'ghastly pit' where the speaker's father died, or, more specifically, where his father's body was found. The hate of the opening lines is therefore the compensating emotion which follows the loss of a father and that father's love. The pit, however, is never merely literal; its very presence, 'there', is the trace or sign of the absent body, of the body which 'had given' the speaker 'life' (I.i.6).[7] Hence it becomes a sign, not just for the death of the absent father, but for the birth of the speaker, and, by extension, for the speaker's identification with the loss that accompanies that birth – the loss which in effect defines birth. Birth and death, then, are already interwoven, as are love and hate, presence and absence, and the speaker's subjectivity is presented from the outset in terms of this fusion of life and death, birth and loss.

The pit's image of emptiness (a sign for the absent father) acts also as a metaphor for the speaker's own loneliness and emptiness. The focus on the hollow and the excessive language of its description ('The red-ribb'd ledges drip with a silent horror of blood'), combined with its clearly figurative function, produce a subject who is obsessed with the macabre nature of his own sense of alienation, fascinated by the web of related images that are woven around the configuration of his father's death. As the impact of the father's death is elaborated through this excess (the body was 'Mangled, and flatten'd, and crush'd, and dinted into the ground'), the loss of the father begins to take on the symbolic significance of the loss of all fathers: the loss of personal origin that accompanies biological authoring (procreation), and the loss of authority in moral order (the questions about whether the father killed himself and about the location of 'villainy') and in law (the corrupted peace in the land).[8] Insofar as the loss of the symbolic father entails the subject's isolation from his society and peers in addition to isolation from his own origins, his alienation is complete, both internally and externally. The result in social terms is 'civil war' and a peace which disparages the past, 'slurring the days gone by' (I.i.27, 33). The result for the person is loss of the human affections, of 'hope and trust', a reduction to inanimate status, to the 'heart as a millstone' and the 'face as a flint' (I.i.31), to a being without signification, 'nameless' (I.iv.119).

In effect this is a reduction of the speaker to the 'rock' which fell with his father's body in the hollow and which lies there yet (I.i.8), so that we are back with the death of self. The death of the father thus authors the death of male (sexual) identity, particularly for the subject who cannot reconstitute the father's role. And indeed an identification with the solidity and fixity of the rock, the reduction of the heart's affections to the static fixity of a millstone, is an attractive prospect insofar as it replaces the threatening turmoil of feelings as strong and as fluctuating as love and hate. The literal rock, which metonymically signifies the father's death, thus becomes a sign also for the attractive fixity and finality of death, for the escape from feeling that is part of the desire for the restoration of wholeness and harmony. To become rocklike is perhaps to regain the strength and order that are lost with the dead father.[9] At the same time any association of the millstone with the positive virtues of strength is rendered ironic by the text's association of becoming flintlike with the passivity of taking the 'print' of the age (I.i.28-9). It would signify the relinquishing of subjectivity, giving up the claims of personal authorship to the power of society to write upon his blankness. He, the written subject, would gain the strength and power of the writing structure, but, for the speaker in this historically conceived context, that means the strength which accompanies a loss of moral authority, the power to 'Cheat and be cheated', and, inevitably, to 'die' (I.i.32). Once again, the obsession with the absent father is an obsession with the loss of social as well as personal signification – the speaker is 'poor' as well as 'nameless' (I.iv.119).

The repetition of images of the body that are related to the hollow and its physical location also lead to another aspect of the speaker's complex of feeling – female sexuality and its covert associations with death and desire. The structure of the hollow, which is 'behind' a 'little wood', which has 'lips' and 'ribb'd ledges' that 'drip' with 'blood' and which is perceived as a 'ghastly pit' where a 'body was found' (I.i.1–5), becomes horrifically and sexually suggestive in its anatomical overtones of the womb which produces still-born life.[10] Such an association is sustained, even confirmed, by 'The shrill-edged shriek of a mother' (not *my* mother, not a *woman*, even though it was the shriek of a wife for her dead husband) which divided the 'shuddering' night (I.i.16). While any direct link between the hatred for this speaker's hollow and King Lear's hatred for the 'hell' or 'sulphurous pit' of female genitalia is heavily suppressed,[11] there are nevertheless signs that this complex of associations (hollow with hate, love with loss, sexuality with death and suffering, dead father with still-born life, mothering with loss of identity) leads also to loss of sexual power – to impotence. The scheme that led to the father's destruction left the speaker 'flaccid and drain'd' (I.i.20), and within the corrupted society sexual energy has become transformed into commercial wantonness – 'lust of gain' – or commercial possession – 'each hand lusting for all that is not its own' (I.i.22–3).

Within this context the fear of repeating the father's suicide and the desire to replace the absent body with a replenishing sexual object, as represented in Maud, come as no surprise. The speaker's attempt to replace the law of the father with his own 'law' (no longer to brood on death and fraud) remains a brittle affair (I.i.55–6). Its very enunciation, with its emphasis once again on mutilation and its repetitions which rhyme 'mood' with 'brood' and 'die' with 'lie', betrays his inability to escape from the structural obsession with 'a horror of shatter'd limbs and a wretched swindler's lie'. The speaker is caught within a discourse which confounds nature, where an 'Echo' does not repeat what is asked, but replies with 'Death' (I.i.4).[12] Even in contemplating his own death there remains the further fear that he would not be mourned, an indication of his desperate need for love – there was at least '*love* in the passionate shriek' (I.i.57). When the only recourse seems to be to flee from 'the place and the pit and the fear' (I.i.64), Maud's image reintroduces the possibility of restoring the absent object, and with it the lost power of sexual potency – male identity as founded upon gender.

Maud is introduced with a flourish of anaphora (I.i.69–72). From the outset emphasising her function as trope, this repetitive and ritualistic device also stresses her role as signifier, as a name whose Germanic origins mean strength, might, battle, strife.[13] She is, then, a highly appropriate object of desire for the speaker: as object she combines the promise of sexual pleasure (the 'sweet purse-mouth') with social approval ('the delight of the village'), and as signifier she offers the restoration of the lost strength and might of the dead patriarch. Since in the context of a bankrupt father, purses become as sweet as mouths (Tucker, p. 411), 'purse-mouth' also incorporates commercial associations. The strength of the lost patriarch is economic as well as sexual.[14]

For this speaker, the ordered rhetoric and abstract delight of stanza 18 cannot stand, however, and he quickly swings back to the fear of being cursed, to the bad dreams which threaten his fancies of full presence. The only solution is to seek oblivion through a solipsistic withdrawal: 'I will bury myself in myself' (I.i.76). The self now becomes another hollow, supplanting the literal hollow in the wood. It is sought as a place of refuge, a source of security within a world that is alien and threatening and where strength and moral law have been lost. As such it is a surrogate womb, where the speaker's restored presence may fill the gap left by the absence of his birth. Yet it is also a burial pit, a surrogate tomb, and the will to self-burial offers a figurative re-enactment, a repetition in discourse, of the father's suicide/murder.[15]

Here once again in nineteenth-century writing is the assumption of the *cogito* and of conventional lyricism, that a speaker only has to look within in order to discover the security and truth of personal presence. But in *Maud* Tennyson shows that looking within reveals a fractured set of discourses, a self which dissolves into myriad moments, moods and textual patterns. Hence the speaker's wish for internal peace is doomed to failure, since absence and loss are fundamentally within, the very condition of subjective existence. His question, therefore, about fleeing place, pit and fear (I.i.64), rests upon a desire to escape the inescapable. The 'ghastly pit' is not merely an external reality; it is a signifier for that internalised state of alienation which constitutes his very being.

Section iv elaborates further this circumstance. Here the speaker desires not only to withdraw from the external world of plunder and lies, but also to withdraw from all feeling, 'For not to desire or admire . . . were more/Than to walk all day like the sultan of old in a garden of spice' (I.iv.142–3). In effect this is a desire not to desire – a desire, in other words, to restore the unity and calm that would be without the divisions that provoke passion: 'let a passionless peace be my lot' (I.iv.151). It is telling, however, that he equates the realm of 'passionless peace' with 'quiet woodland ways', whereas the dominant association so far with a wood is the hated hollow that lies behind – the very source and focus for loss and desire. The desire to be without desire is therefore itself a sign of division, a sign that, in the figurative terms which designate the speaker's psyche, 'the little grove' (I.iv.2) of his rational calm is inseparable from 'the dreadful hollow' (I.i.1) of his hatred and emotional turmoil. It is a sign of division which has its counterpart in the externalised perception of the speaker earlier in section iv that 'the whole little wood' where he sits is 'a world of plunder and strife' (I.iv.125).

III

If necessity dictates that the fulfilment of desire would produce only death, then what can occur is a dream beyond necessity, the dream of a plenitude that would not be death – a society at peace with itself, a love that would transform the self. The speaker's views about the possibility of love to transform fluctuate wildly during the poem, but the dream of a transcendent plenitude (represented as a lost plenitude) echoes persistently. Its main expression occurs in I.v, the well-known episode of Maud's martial song. Here Maud's meaning as strife and battle combine equally with her meaning as strength and might. Strife and battle have often, after all, been the conventional male counterpart to division and loss – glory in battle is the way to retrieve lost honour.

In its general effect, Maud's 'passionate ballad' celebrates heroic action, the authority and honour that can be the glory of male destiny. It is an authority which rewards both men and society with prestige and security; the land and its (male) members act in unison. It is also an authority which embraces the terrible paradox of a self-destructive fulfilment: where young men 'Ready in heart' march 'To the death' that is their honour. At the same time, section v is a tour de force of appropriation – men by battle, battle and death by honour, all three by their 'native land', Maud by the song, the song by the speaker's response, the response by present loss. Of these, the most immediately significant are Maud's absorption within the song and the speaker's appropriation of Maud as the voice of that song. Women do not fight in this model of the golden age, but they may sing of it admiringly. So Maud's function shifts. No longer the ritualised object of sensual and social pleasure, she is absorbed by the song as the voice of male discourse, as the signifier of strength and delight in battle:

> Singing of men that in battle array,
> Ready in heart and ready in hand,
> March with banner and bugle and fife
> To the death, for their native land.
> (I.v.169–72)

The speaker, consequently, although unable to possess the woman as object (she is 'all unmeet for a wife'; I.iv.158), is nevertheless able to possess the woman as sign. Thereby he restores, not lost honour, but the representation of lost honour:

> Maud with her exquisite face,
> And wild voice pealing up to the sunny sky,
> And feet like sunny gems on an English green,
> Maud in the light of her youth and her grace,
> Singing of Death, and of Honour that cannot die,
> Till I well could weep for a time so sordid and mean,
> And myself so languid and base.
> (I.v.173–9)

In this stanza Maud is reclaimed as the enactment of a lost male plenitude: she brings the face and the light and the grace that offer to male fantasising the promise of full female presence; she sings of the Death that produces honour; and, importantly, she sings of the 'Honour that cannot die', the honour that is obtained through death but which is not itself death. Yet the representation cannot reproduce the original. The honour that cannot die can be uttered in language, but that utterance guarantees no literal referent. Indeed, any original referent in historical time is rendered entirely vague by the use of the continuous present and figurative time: men march in 'the happy morning of life and of May' (I.v.168). Time in these first two stanzas is not historical time, but the time of suspended lyricism. Enunciation guarantees no fixity, and Tennyson's grammar in the second stanza underscores this sense in which the attempt to retrieve lost grandeur through fixing it in verse founders upon the necessary temporality of discourse.

The speaker's utterance in stanza two (I.v) remains a discourse without fixed grammatical focus. The appropriation of Maud lifts her into a five-line series of nominative clauses which remain suspended in abstraction, unconnected in any definitive way with the action of the utterance, governed by no finite verb; the continuous action of the speaker's and Maud's celebratory rhetoric then collapses into the weeping which heralds the realisation that the martial song remains but the trace of a plenitude that is irretrievably lost. It is 'a glory' which the speaker 'shall not find' (I.v.183) and he weeps for the present age, 'for a time so sordid and mean' (I.v.178). The celebration of full presence thus collapses into the present absence of social or personal fulfilment, and Maud is firmly established as the symbol of what is missing in both self and society.

Finally Maud's voice must be silenced, for in reinscribing the glory of the past it reinforces the sense that such glory is *lost*, no longer available for a sordid age and a base person. The speaker must reject, therefore, the very thing he desires (the voice), and the command to 'Be still', to silence the discourse which torments him, is the sign once again of his internal division, of the necessity of his separation, not from the song, but from what the song represents. The force of Maud's 'sweetness' which draws him to fall adoringly at her feet is not the force of his desire for Maud as object, but the force of the absence which her song reinstates. He would adore 'Not her, not her, but a voice' (I.v.189).

It is also worth relating this shift in focus, from object to voice, to the separation of Maud at this point from courtly and romance conventions. She is not merely the cruel-fair stereotype of courtly love, idealised and worshipped from afar, nor the sympathetic nurturer of male romance, for she is 'neither courtly nor kind' (I.v.188) – although she is both these things at other places in the poem. These are the conventional and historicised objects of male desire, but Maud is also something more profound within the drama of psychic signification – the signifier of the absent other that accompanies the entry into subjectivity. As physical object, she is always a sign, both sexual and social, within the system of male perception, but in this passage her name is lifted into the realm of pure signification, into a world of entirely textual relationships, where literal reference is entirely tenuous, but where psychic significance is always potent. As woman, Maud represents those female qualities which the speaker seeks in order to replenish the loss that characterises both self and society (and to the extent that she appears to offer a meaning that is outside discourse she functions as a transcendental signified, the ultimate grounding and guarantor, of conventional logocentric discourse). As name and signifier, however, she is absorbed within discourse, functioning both as the continuing sign of the lack that defines all subjectivity and as the particular significance of this speaker's lack – strength, might, battle. Such a signifier is inevitably a powerful presence within the psychodrama of personal identity.[16]

The counterpart to Maud's symbolic function in I.v, with its deeper implications for the lack that characterises both person and society, is most fully contemplated in the so-called epithalamium (I.xviii), the closest the poem comes to an open interweaving of love and death. This section imposes a climactic role upon Maud in terms of her potential to transform loss into fullness, to provide sexual and personal completion.

Maud still functions as signifier, but now the sensual reality of her kiss invokes the strong promise of sexual fulfilment and with that the promise of possessing the other which would hopefully replenish the gap, fill the hollow in the self. The act of possession is clear from stanza seven – 'Maud made my Maud by that long loving kiss' – but hints about possession and assertion are apparent from the opening line, 'I have led her home', and the imagery of blood as river indicates the extent to which her presence offers the ultimate plenitude:

> And never yet so warmly ran my blood
> And sweetly, on and on
> Calming itself to the long-wish'd-for end,
> Full to the banks, close on the promised good.
> (I.601–4)

These lines, with their stress on 'Full'-ness and proximate completion, transform the 'rivulet' which joins Maud's garden to the speaker's wood (I.xiv.517–18) into the sexual excitement of overflowing fluidity and the elated anticipation of 'promised good', the orgasmic closure, the 'long-wish'd-for end', which would satisfy all desires, fill all absences. Indeed, the poem's main trope for absence and death, the hollow, is reiterated as Maud becomes 'The counter charm of space and hollow sky' (I.xviii.641). The trope of the hollow now embraces not only the personal emptiness of the speaker, but also the terrifying cosmic space of an unbounded and pitiless universe (634–8), and such is the potency of Maud's present charm that she has the power to displace, dis-spell, this universal 'nothingness' as well as to integrate both madness (642) and death (644–59).

The culminating stanzas of section xviii (sts. 6–8) integrate the two dominant themes of love and death. In answer to the all-consuming question as to why Love should 'Spice his fair banquet with the dust of death', the speaker implores Maud to reply that '"The dusky strand of Death inwoven here/With dear Love's tie, makes Love himself more dear"' (658–9). Echoing the couplet in Shakespeare's sonnet 73,[17] this couplet provides a dialectical model for the relationship between the two, between love and death. The image of interweaving proposes a fabric that is composed of interrelated yet separate strands (or ties), elements that are exclusive yet mutually sustaining. Once it is realised that they do not compete as opposites to be reconciled, but as components that are dialectically interrelated, each illuminating the other, then death may be incorporated as a good, enhancing the value of love precisely through delimiting its presence.

But the terms of the speaker's discourse act as reminders that the dialectic is itself composed as process, tied to the conditions of temporality and, here, to the subjunctive mood of possibility, not actuality. He 'would' die for the girl, death 'may' give life to love, and Maud's utterance of dialectical resolution is a hypothesis – 'wilt thou not answer this?' His blood was 'close' to the promised good, but that is all. In life, to be close is to be closed from, to be inseparable from the loss which accompanies closure itself:

> ... even then I heard her close the door,
> The gates of Heaven are closed, and she is gone.
> (I.609–10)

Even as the delight of the 'Dark cedar' is perceived as the trace of the delight of its predecessors in 'the thornless garden', and even as Maud is perceived as the trace of her foremother, 'the snow-limb'd Eve' (623–6), the language of the enunciation retains its signs within a temporal present. The cedar and Maud as traces/signs of their forebears remain within a present which is not a thornless garden and which inherited death from Eve as well as Maud's beauty. Even as the narrator claims that Maud has dispelled his forlorn feeling when he preferred not to know about the 'sad astrology' of an empty universe which makes the stars 'tyrants' (634–5), the present tense verb, 'makes', still locates that disturbing and 'boundless plan' within present process.

It should be no surprise, then, that the final stanza within the section dissolves within an uncertainty of reference: 'Is that enchanted moan only the swell/Of the long waves that roll in yonder bay?' (660–1). Maud's disappearance in stanza two would suggest that any hope for a negative answer that might be expressed in this question barely suppresses the disappointment of an affirmative one.[18] Nevertheless, whether the 'twelve sweet hours that past in bridal white' were hours spent in purity (bridal white) or in erotic bliss (hours which 'died to live'), either imagined or actual, the sublime attainment of total possession is yet to come.[19] Maud remains a bride 'to be', and the ideal remains an imagined ideal, just as Maud has always been an imagined ideal – an image of perfection that the narrator represents negatively as an absence of fault, 'Faultily faultless' (I.ii.82).

The lovers part. Maud drifts away, returned not to literal death but to death's second self, the 'false death' of sleep, and the narrator withdraws, once more establishing a gap between them: 'farewell;/It is but for a little space I go' (I.xviii.672–3). All is celebration and delight, 'Blest', and yet the sense of temporal necessity intrudes with the intimation of 'some dark undercurrent woe'. Despite the celebratory mood, the speaker ends up longing to be hopeful – 'Let all be well, be well'. It is a salutary reminder that the poem was originally conceived in terms of unabated yearning, having begun with lyric II.iv, 'O that 'twere possible', which focuses on the hopelessness of desire.[20] Even here, in this climactic section in Part One, when Maud comes closest to fulfilling the terms of her role as desired object, the divisions remain – as indeed they must, since division is the condition of desire as well as the impediment to its fulfilment, to the repossession of wholeness.

IV

As a question about reference and meaning, the question about the location of the 'enchanted moan' (I.660) points to an important feature of Tennyson's methods in this poem. Desires and images frequently merge and subvert each other, as I have explained earlier, and objects are more usually signs than objects. The question about the swell of the waves is precisely a question about whether the waves are merely object or the figure for some other sort of moan. In *Maud*, I think it is axiomatic that the discourse of self develops as a dialectic which exploits the difference while it blurs the distinction between external referent and internalised signification. The two are finally inseparable (though that does not mean they are necessarily or always indistinguishable).

Consider, for comparison, approaches to *Maud* which describe the poem as 'a story of hereditary melancholia and madness; of a father's bankruptcy and suicide; of family feud; of a love which unexpectedly flowers in spite of snobbery and opposition, but which then, expectedly and grimly, is shattered; of death and loss; of brutal Mammonism'.[21] Such approaches are inclined to turn the poem into a narrative of external events, ignoring the brilliance of Tennyson's dialectical and figurative ambiguity which shifts dramatic action away from external event towards signifying process. Despite Tennyson's later additions which attempt to clarify certain issues (the father's death as suicide or the betrothal of the two infants), the proliferation of uncertain contexts, symbolic imagery and absences (father, Maud, duel, love, peace, honour, hollow sky), make *Maud*, like many Victorian poems, a drama of representation rather than the representation of a drama.[22] At best *Maud* is a different sort of narrative: a self-reflexive narrative through which a speaking, signifying subject narrates itself.

The speaker's lyrical perceptions thus suggest quite frequently a oneness with his surroundings. Partly this effect emerges from a conventional and well-established tendency of poetic language to blur the literal and the figurative, usually in an attempt to achieve precisely this sense of an identity of self and world. In *Maud*, however, this process is excessive, always hinting at a potential insanity. As Alan Sinfield notes, 'the symbolic merging of mind and landscape should be consoling, a pleasant delusion of or nostalgia for unity of being', but in *Maud* Tennyson 'pushes it to the point where it denies that comfort' (p. 171).

The threatened insanity in *Maud* is not merely the conventional insanity of loss of reason or inability to distinguish world from mind. It is not merely a matter of the difference between inner feelings (or imagination) and outer reality, although that is what it so often comes down to when critics discuss Tennyson's morbidity or fear of madness.²³ It is an insanity that relates to the mind and self as discourse, where the privileged ability of human consciousness to formulate concepts, to represent its experience in semiotic form, is also Hegel's privilege of madness and folly. Within discourse the tyranny of the self and the tyranny of the sign are potentially one.

In *Maud*, for instance, we are often less than sure whether it is the speaking subject or the spoken object which is being absorbed within the signifying system. We can never be quite sure whether the speaker's specified examples of a corrupt nation are the externalised signs of an internal displacement and displeasure (a view pleasing to middle-class Victorians) or the sharp perception of a detached observer (a view pleasing to intellectuals and reformers: Tucker's 'nostalgically anarchic satirist' [p. 410]) – whether they are the product of a disturbed psyche or a disturbed world, the product of a language that is perverted from within or defiled from without. That is, once attention is drawn to the signifying process, the discourse of the speaker's indictment of the age is never finally separate from the discourse of his cynicism and personal disaffection.²⁴ Nor is this condition to be dismissed as merely an excessive and personalised obsession. Tennyson's absorption and use of lyrical writing in the poem provokes the challenge that perhaps human subjectivity generally, far from achieving a transcendent unity or truth through such specialised language, remains tied in all discourse to dialectical uncertainty, to ambiguous distinctions between reference and signification, to unresolved difference and deferral.²⁵

Maud's several layers of meaning and her role as signifier highlight, then, the way this speaker exists within a network of signs. And to be the focus of this sort of network is to be an ambiguous subject which is both the active agent of its interpretation and the passive agent of continual mediation. It is no wonder that we cannot always determine his degree of awareness about the social implications of his rhetoric (Tucker, pp. 410–11), for, as the product of a discourse that unites subjectivity with acculturation, he is tied not to literal context, but to signifying system. Adept at reading objects as signs, he nevertheless remains trapped within the insecurities of this very process: if all objects are signs, wherein lies any fixed reference that can secure meaning and identity? So he asks impossible questions in an effort at least to articulate the dilemma of understanding.²⁶ Momentarily he admits the conditional status of interpreting the world – in this instance, a matter of reading the garden-rose in his rivulet as a sign from Maud: '(If I read her sweet will right)' (I.xxi.846). But this is a general state of affairs. There is no pure perception. All objects are potential signifiers, realisable only within discourses whose powerful and seductive effects may conceal their own conditionality.

For a subject of this speaker's degree of insecurity and self-consciousness, ambiguities or uncertainties of interpretation frequently induce anxious, fluctuating moods that may swing from hopeful fancy to cynical doubt and back again. In section I.vi, for example, he elaborates a whole series of hypotheses about the meaning of Maud's smile. He wishes she would be a fixed and reliable object producing a world of secure love, but his very discourse absorbs her into a network of possibilities. Was the smile one of passion, 'a delicate spark ... Ready to burst in a colour'd flame' (I.vi.204–8), or one of deception, intended to weave 'a snare/Of some coquettish deceit' (214–15)? Was it 'feign'd' (241) in order to further her brother's political career, or an expression 'of her pitying womanhood' (253)? Such a series of conjectures dramatises the contingent, fictive status of understanding and meaning. The originating smile becomes an event that is lost in a maze of hypotheses, its significance placed at the mercy of the reader/speaker who re-presents the event in discourse, re-creating the intent of the original in terms of his own fears and hopes. In this section the speaker finally rests upon the hopefulness of desire. Despite his fears of being misled, he will posit a reading that knowingly coincides his wish with Maud's intent, that openly constructs his interpretation upon a whole series of conditionals – which is perhaps about all that can ever be achieved within the precarious narrative act of interpreting the absent other:

> Ah well, well, well, I *may* be beguiled
> By some coquettish deceit.
> Yet, if she were not a cheat,
> If Maud were all that she seem'd,
> And her smile had all that I dream'd,
> Then the world were not so bitter
> But a smile could make it sweet.
>   (I.vi.278–84, his italics)

If section vi ends with the hopeful hypothesis of possibility, then section xiv later illustrates the contrary movement, from pastoral calm to shuddering nightmare. As in vi, an ambivalent perception acts as a catalyst for the shift, but also typical is the way scene and mood coexist within a precariously interactive process.

Initially, Maud's garden with its 'roses' and 'lilies fair' invokes a timeless presence where Maud possesses a regained paradise – she 'has' a garden where 'she walks' and 'tends'. But the narrator is outside, able only to gaze upon it, not to participate: he arrived at dawn and 'stood by her garden-gate' (I.xiv.494). Maud's own room also 'looks' upon the garden-gate (the emblem perhaps of their social separation), and this reciprocal gaze leads to the fancy of reciprocal desire: how, if Maud 'Had a sudden desire' to join him, 'There were but a step to be made' (505–10). Such a small step measures the degree of their closeness, but it equally defines their distance, for once again the fancy builds itself upon subjunctives. Paradoxically, the paradisial garden and Maud's room remain unavailable even while the narrator gazes upon them; the timeless present turns out to be another form of absence. And that absence becomes shatteringly apparent as he sustains his gaze: 'I look'd, and round, all round the house I beheld/The death-white curtain drawn' (521–2).

In this act of literal perception, he immediately reads the morning mist (or possibly the house-curtains) as the sign of his alienation, as the 'curtain' which shuts him out. But its whiteness is also written metonymically as 'death-white', so that his alienation carries with it the devastating loss of the absent objects of desire. It is a powerful transformation – he 'Felt a horror' creep over him and 'Prickle' his skin (523–4) – which seems commensurate with the emotional depth of what is suggested. He knew 'the death-white curtain meant but sleep', yet he 'shudder'd and thought like a fool of the sleep of death' (525–6). The way this perception of alienation and death emerges through a network of associations – mist as curtain, curtain as enclosure, enclosure as exclusion, whiteness as death, death as sleep, curtain as shroud – points to its basis within discourse. In effect, the narrator becomes a victim of his own discourse, unwittingly deconstructed, simultaneously woven and unwoven, by its metonymic and metaphoric possibilities.

The speaker's position within a world of signifying and signification culminates in Part One in the famous last section (xxii), 'Come into the garden, Maud'. Again the speaker stands at Maud's garden-gate ('I am here at the gate alone'), but this time he endeavours to participate in the paradise. As he pleads with Maud to enter the garden, he anticipates her presence by himself appropriating the garden, the longed-for symbol of peace and erotic harmony, by gradually subsuming its images and associations within his own discourse.

Hence the garden's contents become notations within his proceedings – 'All night has the casement jessamine stirr'd/To the dancers' (I.xxii.864–5) – or objects to register his versions – 'I said to the lily, "There is but one/With whom she has heart to be gay . . . . She is weary of dance and play"' (I.868–9). Flowers become ciphers within his private emotional fantasy, metaphors for his fervent yearning to believe in Maud's imminent arrival: 'The lilies and roses were all awake,/They sigh'd for the dawn and thee' (900–1). The presence of Venus, 'the planet of Love', becomes a model of the love which seeks fulfilment through absorption within the other: she begins 'To faint in the light of the sun she loves,/To faint in his light, and to die' (859–60). Maud too becomes a sign among signs, as in a sense she always has been; in the garden she will arrive as Queen of the flowers, 'Queen lily and rose in one' (905). Sign and referent merge, weaving an orgy of textual display so complete that Maud's head is not a head but a shining 'sun' for all the flowers (907).

The pathetic fallacy which underlies the whole exercise allows the speaker to think that his perceptions are objective since transferred to an external reality, but the device remains an act of such naive idealism that it is delusory, producing an entirely subjective transference which merges self and world into a circular solipsism. Despite its apparent location within the social world of gardens and dancing, this pyrotechnical display simply enacts a displaced version of the narrator's earlier desire to bury himself within himself.[27] For what begins as the prospect of an immediate and reciprocal fulfilment through Maud's entry into the garden ends as indefinite postponement – amazingly without any loss of exultation. Maud never enters the garden and all the speaker may appropriate are images and words which represent his own feelings, without reciprocation. No wonder the dialogue of flowers in stanza ten produces a lover who is consumed by the anxieties of desire, by the hopes and fears of distraught passion. This is the speech of a lover who longs to possess the absent beloved but whose only recourse is discourse: a fiction of possibility and a dialectic of flower-talk.

Consequently Maud's presence as trope serves only to enforce the sense of her literal absence, intensifying desire. Also, her role subtly shifts within the section. The model of love in stanza two, represented by the desire of Venus to be obliterated within the presence of the sun, presumably sustains the speaker's desire for masculine authority, with himself in the position of the sun (a male figure in the stanza) and Maud as the star whom he will absorb. Later, however, it is Maud who appears in the role of the sun, the object of worship and desire for the flowers (907). In terms of the model provided by Venus, that leaves the speaker in the position of the star to be obliterated, the position where he has always been as a subject whose possession of the object of desire would mean death. His yearning for Maud to come into the garden is thus a desire for the self-completion which would produce self-loss, a covert desire 'To faint in . . . light, and to die' (861).

Section xxii, then, represents the attempt to fill the gap of absence and desire through language, that which has been described as the doomed attempt to increase the density of language in order to create an illusory 'plenitude of the sign' (Sinfield, pp. 83–4). While the intensive lyrical play may produce such an effect, and while the speaker may identify with its rhetoric of anxious and excited hopefulness, with its rapturous claims to future ecstasy, the subjunctives of the last stanza make it clear that the arrival of full presence stands as a hypothesis enacted within a world of signs. The lyrically timeless future of the speaker's emotional resurrection, where his dust would 'hear' and 'beat' in response to Maud's arrival even had he 'lain for a century dead' (920–1), remains therefore the only viable location for the fulfilment of desire, for repossessing the absent object. There is no other substantive reality in this context. The 'woody hollows' in which he and Maud 'meet' and 'the valleys of Paradise' (892–3) have meaning only within the realms of atemporal lyricism, the tropes of the Romantic sublime. There may be flowers in Maud's garden, but their *meaning* is subsumed within a discourse of narrative self-production.This foregrounding of the conditional status of interpretative lyricism entirely governs, in my reading, the poem's apparent celebration of love.[28]

The ultimate culmination within the whole poem of the blurring of reference and signification comes with the madhouse-cell scene (v) in Part Two. This scene also climaxes the theme of self-burial, apparently making literal the incarceration of the self within the hollow of withdrawal and absence. Yet merging these two themes means that any claim to literal burial is rendered entirely problematic, figurative. The figurative burial within himself which the narrator sought earlier (I.i.76) is here introduced as a literal entombment below the ground, 'a yard beneath the street' (II.v.244–5), but according to the rules of normal existence, where dead men do not speak, this claim to literal burial must of course be figurative, shedding doubt on the speaker's sanity.

Within this section opposites coalesce, directions become problematic, and we enter a world of purely dialectical play. The speaker is dead, but not dead, alive to tell the tale. He is buried under the ground, yet the hoofs of the horses beat into his scalp and brain. Their presence above the ground merges with his existence below, so that the world's activity, its 'Driving, hurrying, marrying, burying' (II.250), occurs both above and below: 'here beneath it is all as bad' (252). The dead are alive; and they move in all directions at once – 'up and down and to and fro' (255). So like life is this tomb, that maybe he is not even buried – 'They cannot even bury a man' – which reflects back upon the incompetence of the world above – 'Wretchedest age, since Time began' (259). The speaker identifies with the dead who were improperly buried, cheated by corrupt clergymen, yet he refers also to those whose 'idiot gabble' seems more appropriate to an asylum. There appears to be no precise way of establishing whether the context for this section is a genuine tomb (in which the speaker may have hidden), a real asylum (to which the speaker may have been committed), or the parameters of the speaker's imagination. Partly the problem is a matter of intention. Is the language designed to dramatise the fancies of an 'empty head' (276) or to deliver a satirical indictment that exposes the world of the living as 'but a world of the [presumably moral and emotional] dead' (278)? Or is it not designed? The dialectical play which merges living and dead (without of course losing the differentiation between them) sustains all possibilities.

Such ambiguity of context and intention simply foregrounds what has been implicit throughout – that reference to objects has been more a matter of internalised symbolic action than a gesture towards narrative realism. Once again we are forced back upon what ought to be obvious, at least in this poem – the text itself as context, language as inherently figurative, not transparently referential. Within II.v, where the speaker appears to have finally withdrawn from the world of objects altogether, major images from Part I return, only in ways that now dramatise directly their fundamental and literal absence.

Both Maud and garden, for example, reappear. The narrator

claims that Maud stands at his head. We cannot know directly that this is Maud, since her name does not appear and he refers to her simply in terms of a pronoun of gender – 'she is standing here' (303). But the phrases which deny her value – 'Not beautiful now, not even kind' (304) – help to establish an antecedent for the pronoun in the earlier context of the poem, where Maud's associations with beauty and with being kind were frequent. Now, however, this figure is silent, and the speaker assigns her to some other realm – 'she is not *of* us' (307). In other words, she no longer signifies within his discourse. With no more presence than that of an unsecured pronoun, and without beauty or kindness, she is no longer an object of sexual desire (being un-kind makes her not of his kind). Without name, she is without the signification of strength and might: she is no longer the object whose meaning may redeem this speaker's discourse, nor the voice of patriarchal discourse which may redeem his society's lost honour.[29]

The garden similarly returns in terms of its absence. He knows where 'a garden grows' and the references to its being 'All made up of the lily and rose' (312) unmistakably allude to the garden in Part I. But the speaker is no longer at the garden-gate, whether gazing upon its literal presence (I.xiv) or attempting to appropriate its symbolic presence (I.xxii). Location is indeterminate: he simply knows where it 'grows'. And it is no longer a symbol of plenitude and completion: 'It is only flowers, they had no fruits,/And I almost fear they are not roses, but blood' (II.v.315–16).

In terms of the poem's psychodrama, this is now a speaker who suffers the loss of both the signifier of strength and the signifier of paradisial wholeness. He has become alienated from the signifier of the absence that he sought to replace, from Maud as the sign of all that he lacks. And he has become alienated from the symbol of the replenished order that he sought to regain. Without the real Maud or her garden, he faces the devastating vacuum of personal loneliness and loss. But without Maud or garden as signifiers, he faces the even more terrifying prospect of a language which cannot give meaning to his deepest sense of unease, to the hated hollow within. The possession of such signs at least sustained the illusion of replenishment, even as they simultaneously restored the absences and desires of continuing discourse. But now even that possibility has gone. The speaker may 'know' where a garden grows (310), but all he possesses is its absence and its fruitlessness. Given this predicament, this knowledge of such powerful absences, the understandable and corresponding desire is to escape. Hence he yearns for even deeper burial in an effort to elude the torment of present consciousness, the torment of the self as a discourse that is no longer in possession of the means for transforming its sense of meaninglessness and incompletion:

> I will cry to the steps above my head
> And somebody, surely, some kind heart will come
> To bury me, bury me
> Deeper, ever so little deeper.
>
> (II.v.339–42)

Perhaps we are left with the unanswered question as to whether this cry for what appears to be a total loss of signifying power represents the ultimate insanity – or the ultimate understanding. The very indeterminacy of such a question adds a deeply disturbing undercurrent to the poem.

It should be apparent that the speaker's withdrawal in II.v. from the world of real objects and reference has been accompanied by a corresponding increase in meaning based upon contextual reference within the poem itself.[30] The narrator produces meaning without the security of reference, through images whose sense depends on the context of his earlier discourse.[31] Hence, for example, the apparently absurd question about whether it is 'kind' to have made him 'a grave so rough' (II.335) becomes a question of searing and crushing poignancy once the image of the grave is linked to the metonymic network of hollows and pits. For then it becomes a question about the very condition of consciousness, about what it is to be a human subject, existing not just within, but because of the pit of absence and loss. The madhouse-cell scene thus represents the quintessence of Tennyson's method of dialectical uncertainty: the combination in his method of the potential insanity of human discourse with the very conditions of human subjectivity in discourse.

V

It is an irony of *Maud* that Part II, despite its closer ties with abnormal perception and insane withdrawal into a solipsistic nightmare, may emerge as the more accurate representation in the poem of human meaning and its processes of production. In Part Two perhaps lies the poem's most radical challenge – in its very emphasis on irrational language, on confused, mostly absent referents. Meaning cannot function in its normal social sense through reference to actual objects; it is attained through the associations within a contextualised discourse. By comparison, Parts I and III remain attempts to immerse the speaker in some apparently separate social order – in Part I through the auspices of Maud and her function as social signifier and in Part III through joining that society in actual battle. What is indicated within Part II, however, is that the social order and the separate person are one within discourse and that the insanity of one is potentially the insanity of the other.

The figures within the madhouse in Part II are socially representative – lord, statesman, physician – and they are characterised by generally debased forms of language: chattering, sobbing, betraying, blabbing, wheedling, babbling, whispering, shouting. All participate in 'idiot gabble!' (279). They are incarcerated, it would seem, for 'sins of linguistic deviancy', for violating the social decorum which separates the private from the public (Tucker, p. 426) – the statesman and the physician give away their professional secrets.

This scene subverts oppositions between life and death, above and below, within and without, and private and public. It also, however, promotes the point that language, of whatever form, is the characterising medium of human existence and that there is no escape into a private language of personal thought, no retreat to the hollow of an internalised self which would locate the truth of private insight.

In the previous section the narrator wished to creep into some 'still cavern' (II.iv.236), in a repetition of his desire to return to the womb-like comfort of his buried self (I.i.76), but now he discovers quite directly what has been implicit throughout, that the world within, the 'shallow grave' (II.v.244), is not the realm of peace and comfort which he expected. He thought to gain peace within the grave, but 'it is not so'. He encounters not silence, but language, unceasing utterance. And with that awareness comes the fulfilment of the old 'prophecy' (280),[32] the return of the separate self to the realm of the public:

> For I never whisper'd a private affair
> Within the hearing of cat or mouse,
> No, not to myself in the closet alone,

> But I heard it shouted at once from the top of the house;
> Everything came to be known.
> (II.v.285–9)

This complaint is only partly a matter of meaning not being personally exclusive, of the necessary interpretation of others or of words having social consequences (Schulman, 645). It also points to the more fundamental circumstances of the human subject which exists within a discourse that is by definition socially constructed. The narrator now acknowledges that he is part of this construction – 'See, there is one of *us* sobbing' (268; my italics) – and the terror of everything coming 'to be known' is the terror of losing identity within the discourse of the other. Certainly what is lost is 'the notion of privacy itself' (Tucker, p. 427), but also in that loss lurks the dialectical dissolution of the boundary between self and world, a challenge to Cartesian and idealist assumptions about separate self-presence.

In this scene, the statesman and physician who give away secrets are identified with language that violates the codes of decorum, with the unintelligibility of 'idiot gabble'. But that is not to establish any clear separation between sane world and private idiocy, for the world which does not love the physician (II.v.277), the world of public order, is named by the speaker as also 'a world of the dead' (278), a phrase which echoes and diffuses the earlier 'world of the dead' where dead men chatter and are 'loud' (263). Referents blur; contexts extend. The inner world of 'dead men' in the madhouse cell, a world whose inhabitants are not buried properly, merges with the historical world outside, the 'Wretchedest age, since Time began' (259), the age which fails to bury people properly (260, 334). Separate consciousness and social order would appear to be interdependent, since the dead world inhabited by speaker, lord, statesman and physician is also the historical world where they paid their 'tithes' (261) and where churchmen betrayed their faith (266–7). Hence the failure to bury properly, which begins as a literal, historical allusion (Shatto, p. 212), develops into a trope for the failure to remove the separate, potentially insane, self – the failure, politically, to banish dissenting and satirical perception. Conversely, for the speaker in *Maud*, that means the failure to be accommodated or loved.

But if self and society are interdependent within discourse, then the despairing perception of 'Nothing but idiot gabble' (279) must work both ways, characterising both the realm of personal disaffection and the realm of cultural order. If churchman, statesman, lord and physician may be subsumed within idiot gabble, then the institutions which give them identity may be equally complicit, equally under the threat of moral or linguistic subversion.

The concluding Part III purports on the surface to restore the speaker to sanity by restoring him to society. But identification with the social rhetoric of war is no more fulfilling than any other stage of the poem. That it restores him to a world of literal objects is perhaps why so many have taken this move as Tennyson's support for a jingoistic national policy, as if the poem does indeed herald the wreaking of 'God's just wrath' on 'a giant liar' (III.45).[33] But entry into battle is a socially acceptable way of seeking the death, 'the doom assign'd' (III.59), that will restore personal unity, the death that will remove all psychological absence through the literal absenting of the body.

The intermingling of death and life in II.v meant that the surrogate burial was a form of death-in-life, the passive despair of lost hope. In Part III the departure to war sustains the same dialectic of death and life, although it inverts the relationship, making the commitment to battle and doom a form of life-in-death, a desire for the transfiguration through death which redeems lost love. In context, war legitimises the hate and suicide with which the poem began, but at the same time the desire to be loved remains paramount. If earlier the speaker wondered whether there would be love for him should he kill himself, now he can at least be assured of the admiration of a nation. He can enact Maud's martial song, having identified with the discourse of a nation at war:

> Tho' many a light shall darken, and many shall weep
> For those that are crush'd in the clash of jarring claims,
> Yet God's just wrath shall be wreak'd on a giant liar;
> And many a darkness into the light shall leap,
> And shine in the sudden making of splendid names,
> And noble thought be freer under the sun,
> And the heart of a people beat with one desire.
> (III.43–9)

While Maud herself is no longer present in order to sing admiringly of his effort, her phantom nevertheless points the way by flying to 'the North, and battle, and seas of death' (37). Furthermore, he now displaces Maud's 'voice' (I.v) with his own 'breath' (III.34), replacing her song with the 'battle cry' of 'a loyal people' (35). The desire for intimacy and comfort that lurks in this act of displaced identification (he 'mix'd' his breath with the battle-cry) is finally indicated by his 'embrace' of God's purpose (59).

The rhetoric of war stresses the unity of the nation, the symbolic wholeness which promises to redeem the lack in both person and society. But this speaker's being 'one' with his 'kind' (58) has profoundly ambiguous implications. He is 'one' with the people certainly in the sense that he joins their collective cause, linking his identity to the purpose of a nation and its God. Desire is no longer the personal yearning for a lost plenitude of romance and sexual satisfaction, but the desire of a people determined to pursue the 'light' of freedom, justice and truth. The speaker is also 'one' in his link with universal mortality; his willingness to die in the cause that is 'pure and true' (31) suggests an acceptance of the death which has always been a condition of his birth, but which he earlier half sought and half resisted. He is also one with his kind, however, through his participation in killing (of Maud's brother, or so he believes), which makes him complicit with the civil war from which he earlier detached himself, and through his participation in the madhouse collectivity of Part II, his attachment to the symbolic order of a language which links all public and private utterance. If, then, his separate identity embraces the battle-cry of a nation at war, how much does that battle-cry embrace his insane solipsism through the same act? Is the battle-cry of a loyal people simply the utterance which transforms personal solipsism into collective solipsism?[34]

In Part III the speaker seeks once again, after the unfixed signifiers of Part II, to relate his language and meaning to the external world. In one sense, of course, he has never left that world, since unfixed signifiers are the condition of all human discourse, and the attempt to withdraw into a private fantasy in Part II led only back to public disapproval and gossip. But in Part III the desire to close the gap between self and world can be seen to emerge from the desire to elude the awesome consequences of confronting the absence that characterises subjectivity. Through the speaker's identification with public rhetoric, the gap is closed, and it would seem, consequently, that indeed 'the merciful ground of culture has opened to swallow the hero up, and he has fallen into the bliss of the state' (Tucker, p. 428).

By joining the fight for his country, the speaker can finally pursue the death which would end all desire. Going off to die in battle, to enter the light of 'splendid names' (III.47), becomes a metaphor for the loss (death) of self in social unity, for the public and patriarchal counterpart of fainting and dying in the light of 'the sun' (I.xxii.860), the light of personalised love. Death in battle thus becomes a literal enactment of the entry into language which annuls the self as the father of utterance (see Chapter 2). The only way this speaker can replenish the lost meaning of his father's death is to enact his own, for only in that act does he regain the strength that is culturally assigned to battle. Hence his excitement and delight when the dream-vision of Maud heralds the prospect that 'The glory of manhood' may again 'stand on his ancient height' (III.21).[35] If the narrator could not possess Maud, whether literally or figuratively, in order to restore the lost object as signifier of wholeness, at least he can possess his own body and donate that to the public cause, thereby transforming his own death into a signifier of higher social unity and purpose. Or so it might seem. For the self as separate subject, however, there is only death, an end to its subjectivity and a cessation of discourse.

The poem ends where it began, therefore, with the death that is the condition of life and of living. And the first edition of the poem (1855) ended with a deft echo of the opening images,[36] a poetic re-enactment perhaps of the un-natural nature whose Echo answers Death (I.i.4). In the image of the 'deathful-grinning mouths of the fortress' (III.52), there lurks another repetition of the motif or anatomy of absence – pits, hollows, mouths, lips, grins, gaps that are bloodied and death-ridden.[37] Furthermore, the mouth that offers death is juxtaposed ('by the side') with the rose of passion and plenitude (the 'blood-red blossom'). The flower of desire still signifies the promise of fulfilment, but it is the ambiguous fulfilment of fire, the double action of purifying and consuming, a fulfilment in death and destruction: it is now 'The blood-red blossom of war with a heart of fire' (III.53). In other words, mouth and blossom (metonymic images for hollow and garden, the signs throughout of absence and desire) are brought together in a closure which once again enacts the dialectic of their mutually sustaining and yet mutually destructive relationship.

4
Fact and the Factitious in *Amours de Voyage*

I

Late in *Amours de Voyage*, Claude, the letter-writing protagonist, plays momentarily with the sense that through trusting himself and looking within he might have 'gained a religious assurance' and found in his own 'poor soul' a secure 'moral basis to rest on'.[1] It is a moment of potential comfort, suggesting the solace of a philosophical idealist when he discovers wisdom and authority within the structures of internal feeling. And yet it is not comfort. There was comfort in the previous fragment when he suddenly heard the sound of an English Psalm tune, but in these lines the assurance is only something he could 'almost' believe. In typically self-conscious fashion Claude regards the prospect of belief in an internalised 'moral basis' as mere possibility, as the conceptualisation of a ground he would dearly like to believe in. The assurance is the product of desire and the tone is self-mocking and detached. The moment of grounded belief was therefore never there and even its possibility is rejected: 'Ah, but indeed I see, I feel it factitious entirely' (V.v.98).

Following this rejection of faith in internal self-assurance, Claude determines to confront the objects of external reality: 'I will look straight out, see things, not try to evade them' (V.v.100). He resolves to embrace the truth of the factual world: 'Fact shall be fact for me; and the Truth the Truth as ever'. But the very next line, added without a break, immediately confounds this proposition of fixed reality and knowledge: 'the Truth as ever/Flexible, changeable, vague, and multiform, and doubtful' (V.v.101–2).[2] Truth is therefore unfixed, characterised by flux and fluctuation, and when Claude embraces fact, he equally embraces the factitious. Throughout the poem Claude seeks to unravel the truth from the factitious, but

Fact and Factitious in Amours de Voyage   91

they are finally inseparable, existing not as opposites but as the dialectical transformation of each other. When Claude acts like an epistemologist attempting to separate external truth and reality from internal visions and deceptions, to 'see things' directly without evasion or mediation, he becomes subsumed within a discourse of dynamic, shifting, and textualised process.

The truth of fact is its factitiousness and Claude's emotional and intellectual conflicts in the poem arise from his growing confrontation with the groundlessness of experience and belief. The fixity and certainty he desires are not there. Claude, consequently, is not merely the passive idealist so often constructed by readers, but an idealist who confronts the limits to his own idealism. He confronts, that is, the conditioning power of the object. Hence the poem dramatises the dilemma of the intellectual who becomes aware of the precarious substance of his own intellectualising. Amidst the fluctuations and processes of the poem's discourse, any sense of 'Claude' as a singular, reified consciousness working out its own true destiny increasingly disappears.

Claude's self-conscious and intricate intellectualising has generally been read in terms of Carlyle's praise of anti-selfconsciousness: the view that self-consciousness is a disease which inhibits action.[3] Claude, for instance, is 'incapable of . . . committing himself promptly to a definite course of action'.[4] He suffers from 'intellectual dyspepsia' or mental 'paralysis'.[5] But these readings tend to promote various versions of intellectual conflict which become structured by the opposition of two competing terms: scepticism and idealism, for instance, or outward appearance (sceptical youth) and inner truth (idealistic mind), past and present, action and contemplation, engagement and disengagement, natural and artificial, practical realism and absolute idealism.[6]

In my reading, the poem proposes a world where opposites themselves partake of flux and dynamic process.[7] It is a world, as Robindra Biswas suggests, 'where meaning is in constant process, solidifying, dissolving, re-forming into new shapes, and where large significances have to be painfully extracted from an unremitting flux'.[8] Biswas, employing conventional epistemological terms, also locates this process at 'the vertiginous centre of consciousness' (p. 318). I wish to argue the more radical proposition that this very image of a 'centre' of consciousness is itself displaced. Claude finally has no controlling centre of consciousness: he is imposed upon from without ('I will go where I am led'), any internal spiritual authority is factitious, he leaves 'mere Faith and Love' to chance, and he can only commit himself to a quest for knowledge and the move from Rome to Egypt. The 'conclusion' to go where he is led is no doubt *his* act of mind, and the desire to 'seek Knowledge' is no doubt *his* desire, but this very desire and this very conclusion are themselves signs of displacement, signs of a subject that realises it is not the centre of its own existence.

To some extent this argument has already been made. John Goode has already pointed to the relationship in the poem between the self as subject ('to see with my eyes') and the self as object ('Do I look like that?'), suggesting that the radical feature of *Amours* is that 'there is no assumed *substantial* self to be the source and thus the link between the attributes'.[9] Goode argues that the thematic focus of the poem is 'a search for continuity' and that this search is conducted through three different forms of continuity, each of which is rejected: continuity in time, through the link between social spectator and historical Rome; continuity in space, through the social identity created by love; and continuity in self, through the metaphor of organic growth. As each method fails, the protagonist, in Goode's reading, is thrust back more and more on the sheer flux of empirical phenomena: 'Clough has retreated from the reconstructive rhetoric of Romantic and Victorian poetry to the chaos of the multiform, to the honesty of David Hume' (pp. 290–1).

Goode's article is outstanding, both in elucidating Clough's 'ironic openness' (p. 296) and in making a serious and persuasive claim for the literary importance of *Amours*. However, against his reading which replaces the lack of any demonstrable or reliable continuity of self with 'merely total empiricism' (p. 290), my reading argues that the 'chaos of the multiform' is itself a construct and that the text's thematic empiricism cannot be detached from an equal and inseparable subjectivism. Claude's final embracing of the phenomenal world does nothing to obliterate the involvement of the subject or the abstractions of conceptual discourse.

Certainly Clough eschews the reconstructive rhetoric of much contemporary lyricism, but it is simply not possible to eschew rhetoric altogether, without lapsing into the silence that Claude at one point contemplates. Even then this 'silence' has 'meaning' only insofar as it is known as a conceptual sign, produced within a textual system. Clough's poem, then, does not simply reject reconstructive rhetoric, it actively produces deconstructive rhetoric – and that is to produce a rhetoric which weaves its own fabric of meaningful process in the very act of teasing apart that same fabric. To leave us with 'merely total empiricism' would be to leave us with a poem that is still governed by the binary structure of the material/ideal opposition. *Amours* is more subtle and more radical even than that. The lack of a reliable 'ground' of any sort, including the empirical, confronts us, not only a lack of continuity. It is part of the argument of the context provided by this book that the dialectic of Hegel and the deconstruction of Derrida are more honest and radical (in the sense of fundamental and thorough) even than the honesty of David Hume, and, further, that to pursue the implications of rhetorical structuring towards an unended openness is not a 'retreat' but an 'advance' – at least for Hegel, if not for Derrida.

II

Claude's main roles of identification in the poem – tourist, intellectual, lover and correspondent – are dominated by his philosophical identity as an epistemological idealist. It is that identity, with its Cartesian assumptions of a separate and discrete self, which is most explored and which becomes most problematic.

Hints of the potential for shifting identifications which would undercut the authority of the singular self appear as early as Canto I. The first of these is when Claude momentarily contemplates the shadowy insubstantiality of the social self: 'What our shadows seem, forsooth we will ourselves be./Do I look like that? You think me that: then I am that' (I.iv.85–6). Here already is the displaced self, the self as external sign which decentres all consciousness. However, what provides a more subtle dramatisation of consciousness in Canto I is Claude's play with irony.

In I.vii, for example, he turns back in mock contrition on his own patronising snobbery of the middle-class Trevellyns:

> Ah, what a shame indeed to abuse these most worthy people!
> Ah, what a sin to have sneered at their innocent rustic
> pretensions!
> (I.vii.135–6)

The mocking tone means of course that this rejection of his previous criticism is mere pretence. The self-conscious irony allows him to have his cake and eat it: to repeat his scornful attitude in the very act of appearing to scold himself for it. He then continues to satirise the pretensions of the Trevellyns through a parody of religious ritual, applying the language of religious devotion to their daily social activities:

> Is it not touching to witness these efforts, if little availing,
> Painfully made, to perform the old ritual service of manners?
> Shall not devotion atone for the absence of knowledge,
> and fervour
> Palliate, cover, the fault of a superstitious observance?
> No, the Music, the cards, and the tea so genteel and insipid,
> Are not, believe me, I think it, no, are not vain oblations.
> (I.vii.139–44)

The parody is evident in the fastidiously repeated negatives, in the liturgical terms of 'service', 'atone' and 'oblations', and in the elaborately formal rhetoric. It also has a target other than the Trevellyns, for in addition the passage parodies that stance of tolerant liberalism which would cry 'shame' at his 'abuse': by pretending to scold himself, he also pokes fun at potential scolders. The result is the standard dramatisation of an ironic awareness which is detached from the objects of its irony – in this case these are Claude himself, liberal tolerance, and middle-class pretension. In all this, the implicitly 'real' Claude, the Claude who is responsible for the parody, escapes, standing aloof. The lines project a subject exulting in the ability of his irony to sustain a superior stance, securing in the process a superior intellectual identity.

Claude's next step is to turn yet again on his utterance, glossing yet again his own text and establishing yet another level of detachment. This time he turns on his very irony, admitting its false contrition:

> Dear, dear, what do I say? but alas, just now, like Iago,
> I can be nothing at all, if it is not critical wholly;
> So in fantastic height, in coxcomb exaltation,
> Here in the Garden I walk, can freely concede to the Maker
> That the works of his hand are all very good; his creatures,
> Beast of the field, and fowl, he brings them before me; I
> name them;
> That which I name them, they are, the bird, the beast, and
> the cattle.
> (I.vii.147–55)

So now the mocker mocks his mocking, turns his parody upon himself, makes fun of his very exultation in making fun of the Trevellyns and liberal moralists. But in the act of exposing himself as jester and dandy, he establishes in his tone of exaggerated expostulation yet another level of detachment and irony. In parodying his audacity in taking on the role of Adam, he both separates himself even from that role and at the same time claims that that is exactly what he does. He revels in his power to name and bestow meaning in the very act of detaching himself from its arrogance. There is therefore no need to take his contrition in this passage any more seriously than we took his contrition in the first lines of this letter. The 'real' Claude escapes yet again, even disappears altogether, and the internal divisions propagate.

At the same time, while such divisions question the concept of a unified self, they also function to expose subjectivity, not to deny its production. Distinctions, divisions, the very recognition of limits, still produce the effect of Claude as subject. Indeed, he often uses ironic detachment and intellectual difference as a refuge from vicissitude and fraudulent feeling, areas of experience which he continually associates with the external, phenomenal world of temporality and change.

As a subjectivist, Claude prefers to identify with the potentially infinite and permanent world within. Would we submit to this material world of process and flux, he asks, if we had no 'assurance within of a limitless ocean divine', no truth of 'being' in that limitless realm (III.vi.125–9)? It is not, however, that this limitless world is a reality now which sustains his identity, but the promise that it may become a reality. It is 'the steady fore-sense of a freer and larger existence' to come which permits a commitment to action, which allows 'consent to be circumscribed here into action' (III.vi.123–4). The idealist's dilemma, therefore, is to be caught between a future absolutism and present transience, between the potentially limitless world within, and a material world without that is specific and therefore restricted. To commit himself to 'action' in that world (which is what interpersonal feeling involves) is thus to constrain, to circumscribe, to reduce his personal definition. Within Claude's anxious and epistemological questioning, the oceanic metaphor is an image for the vast depths and spaces of a divine, unbounded existence, and it carries with it the promise of an identity more universal and grand than that offered by the limits of interpersonal commitment.

At least that is how it is for men. For women it is different: 'Ah, but the women, – God bless them! – they don't think at all about it' (III.vi.130). The gender difference appears to be troublesome, however, since Claude repeats three times the comment that women do not see things in this way (122, 130, 138). The unspoken question, which he presumably needs to suppress, is whether they might have a point. He remains stuck therefore within the idealist conceptualising of his desire. Committed to the value of infinite thought and to potential unity with the divine absolute which that brings, Claude finds it hard to accept the challenge of interpersonal value which is provided by women. The relationship with Mary provides several challenges, for instance: to engage with the physical world, to incorporate the world of feelings, to enter the world of interpersonal action, to accept himself as worthy of love, or, in short, to get out of his head. Like all subjectivists, he lives with the continual threat of solipsism, but he prefers to shore up the 'male' world of rationality and thought. Against Mary's world of feeling and phenomenal flux, he wants to believe in a transcendental signified, a reality outside representation that grounds belief and the ultimate meaning and value of his life – a realm where we both 'have our being, and know it' (128).

In the last lines of this letter (III.vi), women are clearly assigned to the external world of phenomena. The ladies would hardly thank us, he says, for telling them that they are not sought for themselves alone, 'as the thing he would wish', but as an interim source of 'solace and pleasure', as 'the thing he must even put up with', until the real goal is attained – 'a perfect and absolute something' (139–44). The absolute will not be forgotten in the interim by the idealist devotee, and devotion will be sustained 'amid fondest endearments' (146). Since reason and truth are supreme values for an intellectual, Claude becomes trapped by his very attachment to them, even to the point where any expression of feeling, any 'endearment', is a lie simply because it is a separate sign, not attached to the absolute which grounds all truth. Women also become signs, since not the thing he would wish; as temporary substitutes for an absolute something, they belong to the world of temporality, to the transient empiricism of physical passion. Only men, in Claude's discourse, have to worry about what they do until they behold the absolute for themselves. The reason Claude's 'truth' might be shocking and revolting to women (149) is because it emerges from a solipsistic self-centredness which banishes all other subjects to the marginalised regions of the objective, and hence insubstantial, world. Women thus become mere objects which sustain his role as central subject. Their nuisance value is that they somehow fail to observe the same system, behaving remarkably like subjects themselves. And of course no thought is given to the reverse possibility – that 'he' might be the temporarily sustaining object of someone else's tyranny as subject (the reader perhaps?).

In passages such as this the discourse of self is attached to male conventions of reason and subjective idealism. The internalised images of oceanic depths enable the subject to identify with the sense of an eternity within, a permanence which can then be set against outside ephemera. The mitigating element is perhaps Claude's sense that the women might well challenge his assumptions, and his propositions are constructed as rhetorical and conditional questions: '*But for* . . . think you we . . . *could* submit . . . , (my italics). If he aspires to believe in the absolute as ultimate truth outside the transience of phenomena, at least that belief is under question.[10]

One of the problems for Claude is that the question about the absolute is also a question about his own identity. If the ocean within is not the limitless divine, then wherein lies his security and definition? In this sense, his anxiety about a future escape clause (the prospect that death is a guaranteed exit from vows and commitments; III.vi.117–21) is implicitly tied to his need for a sense of his own independent will. If he were committed irrevocably to a potentially factitious existence, he would by implication run the risk of being governed by external circumstances. His consciousness would be displaced from its role as the authoritative centre of experience. Such a prospect threatens the illusion of the independent will and the independent ego, and such a threat is the psychological consequence of privileging 'internal' truth, the Cartesian *cogito* as the foundation of experience.

Having spent letter III.vi contemplating his identity in terms of a transcendental absolute which guarantees his idealist status, Claude in the next letter (III.vii) turns this stance of idealist separation on its head. He now contemplates its opposite, his incorporation into all modes and processes – he too is an object in the world of nature and therefore united with all things natural. He is a man by species and by gender and he treats nothing either human or female as alien to him (III.vii.158–9). In this moment he subverts all differentiation and all identity that is established in terms of sexual or human difference: 'All that is Nature's is I, and I all things that are Nature's' (160). Because of this fusion of identity, he 'can be and become anything' that he meets with or looks at (162). It is a moment that conflates the opposition of the natural and the artificial, and the epistemological opposition of internal and external realms. It is also a moment where Claude enacts the identification which would remove all gaps between self and world and therefore all need for yearning or desire. To the extent that he is unified with his surroundings, there is no disjunction between what is experienced and what is conceived, and therefore no basis for yearning for that which is absent.

But for as long as Claude articulates his perception, writing his existence into a letter, he is not unified with his surroundings. The act of representation is an act of differentiation. The sign of this difference remains present in III.vii in the form of Claude's structure that says he 'Fain could demand' to go back to the 'perfect and primitive silence' of the non-sentient world. By being once more 'fixed' in its 'rigid embraces', he would escape the flux of human existence – 'our strivings, mistakings, misgrowths, and perversions' (170–2). The element of the hypothetical in this construction is sufficient to retain the effect of consciousness as implicitly detached. Compare Arnold's Empedocles, for instance, who directly desired to return to the elements which would welcome him home. Claude's statement is the expression of possibility, not direct desire. The point to make is that the collapsing of all difference could only be actuated, attained, in silence, a silence which would be the death of the self as subject (a silence achieved by Empedocles when he leaps into the crater on Etna). The 'articulation' of the collapse of difference, Claude's identification of himself as one of nature's *objects* while simultaneously being the *subject* of all her objects, is also a sign of Claude's existence as the subject of writing. The sign of his consciousness as a self which contemplates the welcome *possibility* of a return to the silence of the rocks is a sign of the division within utterance that produces his separate self – the subject of his discourse. He is at once one with and different from his surroundings.

III

As tourist and protestant intellectual, Claude discovers in Rome a world of shifting images. Signs of Jesuit influence 'overcrust . . . Michael Angelo's dome' (I.v.112) and Christian culture is an overlay upon the 'older, austerer worship' of ancient Rome (I.viii.163). Rome attempts to convert imported Greek statues and an Egyptian obelisk merely through the addition of a Christian cross (I.x). It is a world, consequently, whose transfigured symbols point to the potential groundlessness of change and transformation, and that threat of groundlessness becomes a major impetus to Claude's letter-writing.

In I.ix, for example, he unfolds an elaborate image of transformation in connection with 'feminine presence'. The 'serene coexistence' with women is for some men, he says, a simple necessity:

> Meat and drink and life, and music filling with sweetness,
> Thrilling with melody sweet, with harmonious strange
>   overwhelming,
> All the long-silent strings of an awkward meaningless fabric.
> (I.ix.176–9)

The threads of a meaningless fabric may thus be transformed into the strings of a sounding instrument, producing harmony and grace where there was only silence and awkwardness. It is notable, however, how this rhetoric rests on the flimsiness of metaphor: life as a fabric whose ungainly woof and weave enters into transformation through swapping one metaphor (the thread of fabric, treated figuratively as strings) for another (the strings of an instrument – a metaphor which is presumably both literal, women play the piano or violin, and figurative, the harmonising power of women). The transition is itself a metaphor for the ability of music to produce harmony out of chaos (meaning out of silence) and music in turn is a metaphor for the ability of women to charm men's lives. There is no 'ground' in this process, nothing to pin it down to a specifically material event or fixed symbolic value, only the shifting values of rhetorical relationships, values which are also tied here to Claude's fear about the appeal which such a process has for 'poor soft souls'. Conventionally all this is simply the power of love (as perceived by a man) to make life happy, but the process of transformation is threatening as well as attractive (a 'strange overwhelming').

The oft-quoted letter xii of Canto I provides an even more dazzling account of the fluidity of emotional process. In this letter the world of feeling is a world totally in motion and totally without foundation:

Yes, I am going, I feel it, I feel and cannot recall it,
Fusing with this thing and that, entering into all sorts
    of relations,
Tying I know not what ties; which, whatever they are,
    I know one thing,
Will, and must, woe is me, be one day painfully broken,
Broken with painful remorses, with shrinkings of soul, and
    relentings,
Foolish delays, more foolish evasions, most foolish renewals.
    (I.xii.232–7)

Fusing, entering, tying, shrinkings, relentings, delays, evasions, renewals – it is the language of unremitting flux, where the sentence structure itself enacts the dispersal of the subject as the rhetoric takes over, becoming a series of participial and subordinate clauses, qualifying and accumulating until the list of fluctuating possibilities absorbs any sense of the subject as active agent. It also becomes the language of classical action: Claude quits 'the ship of Ulysses', passes into 'the magical island', receives the *'moly* . . . of Hermes', and enters 'the labyrinth' (238–41). By a contrary figurative movement, the speaker is thus raised to the level of mythical adventurer in the same narrative process which reduces him to the level of personal negation: 'I yield, I am lost and know nothing' (244).

But like any true adventurer, he contains within himself the seeds of success – 'Yet in my bosom unbroken remaineth the clue' (245). There is no secure foothold in the realm he enters: he 'descend[s] through the fissure', he 'sink[s]', he 'swing[s]' from 'shore' to 'shelf' to 'enchanting' floor. Yet he feels 'the strength of invisible arms' above him and remains confident that whatever wounds or deaths he undergoes, he will eventually return to a firm foothold:

    ere the end I
Yet shall plant firm foot on the broad lofty spaces I quit, shall
Feel underneath me again the great massy strengths of
    abstraction,
Look yet abroad from the height o'er the sea whose salt wave
    I have tasted.
    (I.xii.253–6)

Through this narrative, which turns romantic love into the nightmarish and ancient challenge of magic, enchantment and labyrinthine confusion, Claude develops the rhetorical paradox of a ground in the sky. What he expects to feel 'underneath' him again are 'lofty spaces', 'great massy strengths of abstraction'. The metaphor which sustains him, the 'rope' or 'cord' which will 'upbear' him from the seductions of the cavern, becomes the thread of reason and control which finally allows the sentence to establish itself as a sentence and achieve a semantic closure which makes sense (lines 246–56 constitute one sentence). In a way his narrative has produced precisely this effect of order, insofar as it produces, or enables me to produce, the controlling abstraction I have just extracted: love as a mythical struggle with enchantment and death. It is abstraction, conceptual discourse, which supplies the only reassuring ground for Claude and which will enable him to view from a 'height' the 'sea' he has experienced. In this way Claude dramatises his belief in the power of his idealist assumptions (the abstractions) to maintain meaning, and the 'strengths of abstraction' are therefore placed against the fluid uncertainties of the 'sea' below.

Sea or water imagery recurs throughout in varying states of fluidity and movement, acting as one of the main motifs for exploring the concept of change and groundlessness (in its shifting applications within the poem it is itself without ground). A stream working against 'the wave of the tide' may enact a moment of 'poise and retention' (II.vii.172–3). But a fluid reality always contains the potential for transformation – a stream may turn into a flood. Water imagery may thus model a world that is sometimes calm and ordered, but which is also volatile, capable of rapid eruption and transition:

> Order is perfect, and peace; the City is utterly tranquil;
> And one cannot conceive that this easy and *nonchalant* crowd,
> that
> Flows like a quiet stream through street and market-place,
> entering
> Shady recesses and bays of church, osteria, and café,
> Could in a moment be changed to a flood as of molten
> lava,
> Boil into deadly wrath and wild homicidal delusion.
>   (II.ix.237–42)

This is a world, in short, without safe ground or fixed conditions. And it is therefore a world where order and chaos, tranquillity and wrath, are not opposites, but inherent features of the same qualitative process.

Claude of course resists the threat of such amorphous circumstances, attempting, for instance, to maintain a distinction between fixed growth and shifting insecurity:

> There are two different kinds, I believe, of human attraction;
> One which simply disturbs, unsettles, and makes you uneasy,
> And another that poises, retains, and fixes and holds you.
> I have no doubt, for myself in giving my voice for the latter.
> I do not wish to be moved, but growing, where I was growing,
> There more truly to grow, to live where as yet I had
> languished.
> (II.xi.264–9)

As John Goode has observed (p. 289), the phrase 'poises, retains, and fixes and holds you' takes us back to the stream when it met the turning tide, producing a moment of 'poise and retention' (II.vii.173). When Claude gives his 'voice for the latter', he is therefore giving his voice to an image which has already been tainted by the threat of disruption. That which poises and retains may also become flood and transition. The rhetoric of the poem has already shown, therefore, how Claude's attempt to separate attraction which 'unsettles' from attraction which 'fixes and holds' is a delusion of dualist thinking. It may be that he prefers his fluid process to be motionless, but the poem's rhetoric has already indicated how this very conception is bound to the possibility of its opposite.

This false opposition is further disrupted when he adds images of growth. He wants not to move but to grow, and to grow fixed in the spot where he has been growing. Here Claude's rhetoric begins to contradict itself.[11] He wants to avoid change, to remain fixed, and yet he also wants growth, which is change. Claude's attachment to the idea of *bildung* is therefore contradicted by his fear of being disturbed and unsettled. In the following letter he desires merely to 'look', 'watch' and 'wait', to maintain his place in the unchanging and timeless world of 'Eden' (II.xii.274–7). But in Eden, where things do not die and are not born, there is no 'growth' either, and again his rhetoric undercuts his thinking as the indicative verbs turn into participles – 'Waiting, and watching, and looking' – introducing into the stasis of nominal conception the duration of temporality.

Claude's desire for a ground to secure his emotional identity is at odds with the structures and movement of his own discourse, the medium of 'illegitimate process' (II.xi.273).

The most direct subversion of Claude's attachment to growth occurs in Canto III. Romantic organicism and its associated *bildung* tends to presuppose the whole cycle of increase and decay, from birth to fruition to death and rebirth, but that assumption is precisely the target for attack. The letter (III.iv) begins with the metaphoric fusion of the Biblical trees of Knowledge and of Life. There are not two separate trees, Claude says:

> But on the apex most high of the Tree of Life in the Garden,
> Budding, unfolding, and falling, decaying and flowering ever,
> Flowering is set and decaying the transient blossom of
> Knowledge, –
> Flowering alone, and decaying, the needless, unfruitful
> blossom.
> (III.iv.81–4)

The participial repetition in this extract mutates semantic conceptualising into a vertigo of contradictory movement. The periodic sentence structure pushes the adjectival phrases describing the subject (blossom) into a predicative function, so that the garden and the tree of life as well as the blossom of knowledge become caught up in the whirl of incomplete flux. 'Growth' is no longer a smooth development towards fruition, but the double movement of 'budding' and 'falling', 'flowering' and 'decaying'. The process is endlessly repetitive and endlessly inverted, where the rhetorical inversion of 'decaying and flowering' and 'Flowering . . . and decaying' suggests that the two concepts of growth and decay are not opposite, but simply the defining feature of each other. A passage such as this is inherently dialectical in the full Hegelian sense. Also, the main verb ('is set') is casually placed amidst the binary structure of this inversion, effectively rendering any sense of defined placement as merely a moment *within* transience. Any concept of being 'set' (fixed) is thus immediately subverted by its absorption into 'decay'. Similarly, at the 'apex', the summit of aspiration, is futility and fruitlessness. Or at the 'most high' of Life there is implicitly the (Biblical) fall of Knowledge.[12] There is no end, no telos to bestow order and meaningfulness, only collapsing opposites. The 'apex' itself therefore becomes absorbed into the process of flux and decay: the vertex becomes a vortex. All is subsumed into this amazing mutation whereby the Tree of Life as a metaphor of organicism is transformed into a dialectic of contradictory motion – the blossom that flowers while it decays, or falls while it unfolds, the blossom without fruit, the blossom that is both unnecessary ('needless') and highly desirable ('most high'). Life, in short, is subsumed by Knowledge as sheer transience, sheer *différance*.

The second image in this letter, the classical image of Protesilaus and Laodamia, also involves growth without fulfilment or completion. The 'cypress-spires' that emerge in sympathy with Laodamia's grief are left 'Withering still at the sight which still they upgrow to encounter' (III.iv.90). They are thus trapped within a process which again collapses the very opposites which give it meaning – upgrowing and withering, attainment and loss, the goal or 'prospect' of their venture and the sympathetic yearning which impels the effort.

Finally in this letter Claude returns to another oceanic image, being in fact willing to embrace for the moment a life without ground, a life of 'Making your nest on the wave, and your bed on the crested billow' (94). As he calls on the birds of the seas to fill his imagination (96), he submits to this vision of nature as a process of indeterminate flux and groundlessness. It is also a process, as John Goode points out, that diffuses the opposition between wilful self-assertion and government by otherness: the birds '*extrude* from the ocean' their '*helpless* faces' (91; my italics).[13] Therefore it is a process which incorporates the double action of textual production in which subjectivity is both passive and active. Claude identifies here with an image of the subject as an extrusion (specifically an act) which floats helplessly upon the element that allows it differentiation. In this particular letter we are a long way from the grounded ego of Cartesian or subjective idealism.

IV

In the opening letters of Canto II, Claude detaches himself from the discourse of honour and chivalry (II.ii–iv). He queries the assumptions of honour in battle (the requirements of nature rather suggest that he should look after his own life), and he parodies the codes of chivalric behaviour: 'one doesn't die for good manners,/Stab or shoot, or be shot, by way of a graceful attention' (II.iv.69–70). At the comic level these letters act out a parodic confrontation between the Subjectivist Ego and the Behavioural Imperative, but the more serious question is about perception and truth:

> Am I forbidden to wait for the clear and lawful perception?
> Is it the calling of man to surrender his knowledge and
> insight,
> For the mere venture of what may, perhaps, be the virtuous
> action?
> (II.iv.85–7)

This is Hamlet's dilemma. Not the mere simplicity of procrastination and passivity that has been applied to both Hamlet and Claude, but the epistemological problem of knowing what is true and consequently what action is ever justified.

The epistemological theme of 'clear and lawful perception' is an important adjunct to Claude's role as idealist intellectual, but it is also linked with his role as correspondent. Although Claude has avoided the political dispute in Rome (the poem is set during the French intervention against the Roman Republic in 1849), he seems 'fated ... to describe it' (II.i.15). He is thus tied to representation, transforming events into text, and his role as Eustace's 'Own Correspondent' (II.94) reinscribes the metaphor of Adam constituting meaning through naming God's creatures. Adam's act of naming the beasts in the field is embraced by Claude earlier as a metaphor for his textual act of constituting the world through utterance ('That which I name them, they are'; I.153).

What is at stake in this link between the epistemology of perception and Claude's function as writer/reporter is the inseparability of empirical reality from subjectivity and the inseparability of both of these from the mediations of discourse. As a writer of letters, Claude produces biography-in-the-making, an ongoing process of textualising existence.

The link between perception and textual production has profound consequences, for it places Claude amidst a world of signs. His dilemma as a reporter who has to guess dimly at what he reports is indicative, for instance, of the whole epistemological predicament. 'Yes, we are fighting at last', he says, 'it appears' (II.v.95), and 'the sign of a battle' is the lack of milk for his coffee. Or rather the 'sign' itself is 'the answer' of the waiter – '*Non c'è latte*' – so that the presence of this awesome physical event is reduced to a simple verbal gesture of absence. Never was the absent-presence of a textual trace so grandiloquently effective. The fact that there are fewer people than usual in the café also provokes Claude into imagining 'Something is really afloat' (110). That a battle could be 'afloat' is indeed to transform the material into an idealist phantom, but what is really significant is emptiness – absence:

> Ere I leave, the Café is empty,
> Empty too the streets, in all its length the Corso
> Empty, and empty I see to my right and left the Condotti.
> (II.v.110–12)

The factual world is not merely itself, but a sign. Confronted with the stark phenomenon of a naked city, Claude reads its meaning in terms of the 'concept' of emptiness. Streets and shops are themselves signifiers; they become part of a textualised world where objects are signs – signs, that is, for subjects who are able to read. In this somewhat simple scene of mock-epic reporting, we have an example of the inseparable interaction of subject and world. The meaning of this factual scene of emptiness is unproduced without a subject to report it. At the same time, through entering the scene into the world of text and potential factitiousness, through reading the scene as sign, the interpreting subject is brought into existence as subject.

As the day continues it orchestrates a haze of perceptual uncertainty: 'we believe we discern some lines of men' (119), 'we watch and conjecture' (124), 'we watch and wonder; but guessing is tiresome' (132). By dinner time,

> there are *signs* of stragglers returning; and voices
> *Talk*, though you don't believe it, of guns and prisoners taken;
> And on the walls you *read* the first *bulletin* of the morning.
> This is all that I *saw*, and all I *know* of the battle.
> (II.v.141–4; my italics)

Perception and knowledge are absorbed quite literally into a textualised process of signs, readings and bulletins.

There is a similar cloud of unknowing when Claude thinks he has seen a man killed:

> Yes, I suppose I have; although I can hardly be certain,
> And in a court of justice could never declare I had seen it.
> But a man was killed, I am told, in a place where I saw
> Something; a man was killed, I am told, and I saw something.
> (II.vii.163–6)

The effect of the repetition, with a difference, in the last two lines of this extract is quite curious. Both structures play upon the juxtaposition of two actions: the telling (of a man that was killed) and the seeing (of something). In both statements, the two actions are brought together so that they combine objective (in the sense of outside) information with subjective perception in order to give significance to each other. In the first version, however, the simple deduction of significance is reinforced by the link of place: Claude saw something; someone said a man was killed in the same place; so that must be what he saw.[14] In the second version, however, that link is removed and the two actions are presented more starkly as a simple juxtaposition, without any established connection. The additional effect of the repetition, then, is to invoke a hint of doubt about the deduction. It is almost, particularly in terms of the rhetorical impression of narrative order, to suggest that the order of influence has subtly shifted: Claude was told that a man was killed, 'and' (then, as a result?) he saw something. I am suggesting, therefore, that Claude's repetitive musing induces an ambiguity about the causative relationship between his seeing and its status within discourse. Was it merely an indeterminate 'something', or was it, as *reported* by others, a man's death? This brief musing is a further dramatisation of the uncertain boundaries between perception and signification, truth and mediation, fact and the factitious.

The nature of discourse as its own system may also work to Claude's advantage. In Canto III, for example, he resists the demands of duty or obligation as a trap, a conceptual network that establishes its own set of requirements outside his private and internalised freedom. In his determination to be free, he extricates himself from the effects of his own discourse. He declares that he would even dishonour his 'own heart's own writing' and his 'soul's own signature' in order to maintain the separation of a freely choosing ego (III.ix.192–4). The writing images foreground expression as text, as statements that are signs, representations that can be repudiated because they are not the things themselves. This feature of signs is exploited by Claude in his use of metaphors for his engagement with the world (his metaphorical, hypothetical 'engagement' with Mary). He talks of being able to 'fasten ties' as he 'fancied', of being able to 'Bind and engage' himself 'deep', but all the while it is 'like losings in games played for nothing' (III.198–200). The 'deep' binding is purely the construction of signs that have no referent; it is but the momentary identification with a purely semiotic world. As is typical of Claude's predominantly subjectivist discourse, his stance here is constructed through the possibilities provided by semiosis rather than through the configurations of any actual object.

However, Claude is finally returned to the world of objects through a return to the problems of lawful perception. In Canto V, after the disappointments and doomed pursuit of Canto IV, he admits what has been apparent all along: that he wants 'to predetermine the action,/So as to make it entail, not a chance-belief, but the true one' (V.ii.22–3). Action is crucial of course because it is the moment of interchange between self and world, the one moment when the reality of the other cannot be evaded. It is also the moment when the structures and exigencies of that other cannot be avoided, when the subjective self has no guaranteed control. Action which entailed a true-belief would be action that reinforced the conceptions of the subjective ego. But within the epistemological dualism that defines and thereby traps the subjective self, the chances of being wrong are always, by definition, present. Claude is aware of that. It is part of the discourse which defines his consciousness and hence it remains of thematic importance to him – both for his internalised need to develop a secure conception of things (a true belief) and for his social need to establish a socially acceptable identity (his role as intellectual is a means of offsetting his failure as male hero). His admission about his desire, however, is an important step towards incorporating that desire into his conscious identity and thereby confronting the limits to his idealism.

V

The thematic strands which question Claude's subjectivity – self-division, transience, groundlessness, the textualising subject – and his failure in the empirical world (to find Mary) all focus finally on Canto V, where Claude's idealist stance is increasingly under threat.

One of the first consequences is that Claude is forced back onto

Mary's existence as sign, as mere image, for that is all he has left, and the rhetoric of groundlessness (the impossibility of fixing that image) combines with the metaphor of writing:

> . . . it is idle, moping, and thinking, and trying to fix her
> Image more and more in, to write the old perfect inscription
> Over and over again upon every page of remembrance.
> (V.ii.31–3)

The old desire for fixity now confronts the impossibility of satisfaction. The writing metaphor also reinforces the hint in earlier letters that Mary always was an inscription, an image written on his mind, and therefore that she always was a concept caught up among other concepts – the product of his idealist discourse. Now, however, Claude's empirically induced disappointment leads him to accept the power of the other, to 'accept the chances that meet' him. He will 'Freely encounter the world' (V.iv.54–5). He also accepts that the 'old image' would merely delude him, since Mary herself is changing and he too will be 'bold' and change. He subscribes, then, to change and chance in himself as in the world and other people. Such assent is implicitly to recognise the authority of the object (in Hegelian phrase) – that is, to recognise the limits to his idealist epistemology.

Despite Claude's attempts to be self-assertive – 'I will let myself go'; 'I will walk on my way' (53–4) – or to retain some sense of continuity, by resubscribing to the image of honesty and truth, for instance (51–2), the twists and turns of his discourse increasingly threaten to breach the authority of his subjectivity. In letter v the discourse itself literally fragments as the letter breaks into six pieces. Claude is taken even further towards the inadequacies of his idealism – 'Utterly vain is, alas, this attempt at the Absolute, – wholly!' (V.v.63) – and his representations expose the ambiguity of his subjective claims: 'I . . . Have to believe as I may, with a wilful, unmeaning acceptance' (65). This statement in particular incorporates the contradiction basic to his situation: belief is an imposition from without (he *has* to believe) and yet his submission is 'wilful' and 'unmeaning' (as if the power to assign meaning to his 'acceptance' remains with him). Despite the growing sense of a force over which he has no control, then, he clearly does not give up the role of an acting and thinking subject in this implication that the 'acceptance' is meaningless (meaningless, presumably, because imposed and not of his own choosing – meaning for the subjectivist would have to come from the conscious self in order to be meaningful).

Most importantly, however, Claude's role as letter-writer is acknowledged. He directly confronts the conception that his writing is ungrounded by either author (he knows not 'in what wise' he writes) or reader (he writes he knows not 'to whom'). In writing, he turns quite consciously to a 'conception', to his ideal reader – someone in whom 'there is freedom from all limitation'. In Eustace's 'image', then, Claude turns 'to an *ens rationis* of friendship' (V.v.75). Both writer and reader are thus placed within the ungrounded discourse of 'conceived' freedom and 'constructed' friendship. Eustace, as the reader of Claude's letters, is someone whose 'name' (76) is simply a convenient sign for the illusion of an other who will understand, the separate subject whose sympathetic response will confirm the writer's reality and consciousness, but whose fictional and constructed status as sign simply leaves the writer awash in the possibility of solipsism and the factitious. Claude's role or identity as correspondent thus absorbs all other roles and leads in the most fundamental way to his lack of substance, certainty or fixity. Within discourse, nothing has any guaranteed substance or certainty – not meaning, not the reader, not Mary, not the referential geographical or historical context (Claude fails finally to 'see' anything of the French attack on Rome – even that exists in terms of the discourse of local reporting and hearsay), and not Claude as writer. Actuality, belief, subjective consciousness are all subverted as part of the process of corresponding with the fictive Eustace.

At the same time, the double actions of the self/other remain. Claude announces, for instance, that he is giving up belief in the 'choice' of the separate and idealist will. There was a time, he says, when he thought 'choice alone should take, and choice alone should surrender' (79), and then he would not have retired so early from the pursuit. Now all that 'is over' and he accepts that he is 'a coward' (84). But in thus renouncing the prime mover of the individual will, and allowing himself to be written (and written off) by the socialised rhetoric of competition and reward (he has 'slunk from the perilous field'; 82–3), he still clings implicitly to the identity of intellectual honesty and truth: 'Courage in me could be only factitious, unnatural, useless' (85). In the act of giving up identity, therefore, Claude still places himself within the binary formulae of other social and intellectual values: true/false, natural/artificial, utilitarian/useless.

Claude also rejects religious belief based upon internal assurance, as I have discussed at the beginning of this chapter, and commits himself to fact and truth which is flexible, multiform and doubtful. This passage is the intellectual equivalent of his emotional acceptance a few letters earlier of Mary herself being subject to change. He even allowed that he himself could change, 'if it must be' (V.iv.57–8). Both sides of the opposition, self and other, are subject to transition.

In letter vi the singularity of Claude's consciousness is again disturbed as the literal battle for Rome fuses with the figurative battle of his relationship with Mary. As the text of the letter shifts from the language of personal loss ('I . . . sit/Moping and mourning here'; 116–17) to the language of public lament, literal and figurative meanings coalesce in a discourse whose formality and artifice (repetition, rhythm, alliteration) conflate public and private rhetoric. Meaning in this context shifts uneasily among signifiers which merge rhetorical questions with mythic conventions, among signifiers for a whole series of losses: the loss of those who have just died in Rome, Claude's 'loss of a single small chit of a girl' (116), the private loss within self, the loss of his own fictive soul. Nor, within such an artificial construct, does the speaker exist as an author of legitimate meaning. Claude can utter the appropriate laments, but it is empty rhetoric – 'All declamation, alas!' (125) – which prompts the question of when anything has been other than 'declamation' within the context of his letters.

Given such uncertainty of personal location (within the artifice of declamation, wherein lies any real self?), Claude is overtaken by depression and a disturbing sense of dependency. The need for kindness from others is a 'sad self-defeating dependence' (V.viii.149) – where 'self-defeating' plays upon the paradox of a self which overthrows itself. Within the depths ('deeps') of depression (the metaphor of depth echoes the earlier images of ocean depths), he is without support, will, purpose or inner strength (152–3). His consciousness is no longer, if it ever was, a controlling authority in his experience. He now lacks, that is, the traditional support system of subjective idealism – belief in the security of Kant's transcendental ego, in the noumenal self that grounds all action and feeling within the empirical self. Bereft of that belief, Claude is without distinctions between internal and external experience. He can recall no image for Mary, no sign of her existence – all that is left is 'a sort of featureless outline . . . which no recollection will add to' (V.viii.162–3). The final devastation of his belief in the power of reason, or of his identity as intellectual, is to confront the possibility that everything, the whole affair, may have been 'factitious' (164). There was the reality of personal pain; he has 'wept'; but then 'so have the actors' (165). This is indeed Hamlet's problem – how to know 'truth' when even weeping can be simulated.

The poem thus produces the insoluble dilemma. There is no way of separating fact from the factitious when within the discourse of self the two are intertwined. Actuality and simulation, origin and representation are continuous, not in opposition. Consequently, lacking any means of establishing grounds for action, Claude instructs Eustace to take no further measures about Mary: 'Indeed, should we meet, I could not be certain;/All might be changed, you know. Or perhaps there was nothing to be changed' (V.viii.169–70). There is nothing substantial for Claude to grasp – not in the present, the future or the past. At the same time, this does not deny his need to establish some sense of order in this confusion, some way of assigning his place. Hence he turns to the image of fate as an ordering principle, although even then his commitment oscillates and contradicts itself:

> Great is Fate, and is best. I believe in Providence, partly.
> What is ordained is right, and all that happens is ordered.
> Ah, no, that isn't it. But yet I retain my conclusion:
> I will go where I am led, and will not dictate to the chances.
> (V.viii.176–9)

The emphatic structures of 'will go' and 'will not' retain vestiges of the language of the subjective will in the very act of submitting to the imposition of external process. 'I will go where I am led' is a classic expression of the paradox of active submission or submissive action. Claude acts in the process of being acted upon, so that his submission to the empirical outside does not deny his subjective commitment: the distinction simply blurs and becomes the indeterminate double action of post-structuralist subjectivity.

Claude by now has no determinate conclusion, for to commit himself to going where he is led is to commit himself to the indeterminacy of circumstance and chance, whether or not they are the consequence of a fateful plan. In a sense it is also to commit himself to the exigency and plurality of signs: what else will point out the direction he is to follow? Claude's story of love, then, and of his voyage on the fluid medium of his oceanic metaphors provides no Romantic model of growth and development, no movement towards personal transcendence or universal insight, no crowning realisation of some ultimate teleological purpose. It is closer to a dialectical model where opposites dissolve and are continually in a state of transition. Claude does not move towards a moment of fulfilment but simply to a realisation of the way he is a decentred participant in process. All he can do is move on, which he plans to do, 'with the coming of winter, to Egypt' (V.x.205).

Of course Claude as the subject of his letter-writing discourse never loses what is effectively a condition of his very existence as psychological subject – the desire or need to ground his existence in some defining principle which will make sense of the transitions and passing conceptions of life's voyage. So that while he accepts his participation in process, he also clings to his belief in the potential authority of Knowledge: 'Faith, I think, does pass, and Love; but Knowledge abideth./Let us seek Knowledge' (198–9). Unfortunately, the very context of his own discourse has already discredited such a concept. In Canto III, knowledge is merely the 'transient blossom' of the Tree of Life (III.iv.83).[15] The final identification with the quest for knowledge is thus an identification with the transient and shifting relationship between fact and the factitious, and it ironises all romantic quests that rely on the assumptions of subjective idealism. Claude's subjectivism has been displaced and discredited; he has discovered the power of the object, of the other. Yet he does not relinquish the discourse which maintains his position as thinking and observing subject: 'Rome will not do, *I see*, for many very good reasons' (V.x.204, my italics). There can be no resolution. The division and the contradiction are part of the conditions of what it is to be a human subject, and the dramatisation of these circumstances makes this poem an extraordinarily radical work.

VI

As correspondent, Claude's role as subject is attached to a process where self-definition is factitious and where irony subverts any attempt to reify the concepts of self or growth. Feelings of desire, textual instability, sceptical doubt, collapsing opposites, all disrupt any sense of internal order or coherence, and the final attempt to restore some sense of stable ground through the quest for knowledge ('Knowledge abideth') is consistent with the sense of a fluctuating but insoluble conflict that constitutes the drama of Claude's subjectivity. Claude's centrality is further offset by the occasional letters of Georgina and Mary, but there is also another dimension to the poem which counters the authority of Claude's would-be central consciousness – that provided by the lyric passages at the beginning and end of each canto.

Within the letters, Claude's name acts as a sign which confines the sense of identity to a singular subject, countering the contrary movement of the letters whereby they fragment into fluctuating moments of converse responses and shifting images. In fact, Claude's name through its Latin associations – *clausa* (a closing), *claudere* (to close) – directly invokes the attempt to achieve closure, so that his very name signifies the desire to fix identity.[16] At the level of the framing lyrics, however, the subject is dispersed, not named, and in a sense written out. These lyrics (based on formal elegiacs) add a dimension to the poem that reinforces the demystification of subject and world. Even less are these lyrics the engagement of a separate self with a literal world and even less are they the construction of a defined and identified subject. In terms of their relationship to the letters they suggest a shift from the writing of a named subject to an expressiveness that is tied to the foregrounded textualism of lyric verse. This is not to suggest that their function as lyrical framing provides a circumscribed limit which defines meaning and perspective. These lyrics themselves blur the boundaries of perspective, referring both internally to the thematic and narrative content of the letters and outwardly towards the indeterminate continuities of lyrical conventions and figurative meaning.[17] The elegiacs are frames which dissolve frames. Far from dramatising the delimiting action of authorial or subjective consciousness (the ruling perspective of the originating subject), whether as poet or as protagonist, they disperse that frame of reference even further.

If Claude's letters are constrained by their immersion within the actuality/ideality of a historically defined Rome (a Rome that never separates out from his figurative and idealist conception of it), then the elegiacs employ the detached timelessness and indeterminate subject of lyric tradition. Such lyrics remind us of the potential for textual production to establish patterns and conventions of its own, where the subject as controlling authority is absorbed by the structure of the appropriate conventions. Within the poem the link with Claude as protagonist in some passages seems strong, but in most the speaker is far from determinate.[18]

Lyrics at the end of Canto II and the beginning of Canto III are examples where the voice becomes indeterminate. In the former we appear to shift from what is possibly Claude's generalising of his situation (II.339–42), to authorial address to Mary as the 'fair shadow' who is sought after by Claude, to abstract (perhaps also authorial) reference to the Muse who shall follow the going 'forth' from Rome (II.345–6). The whole passage transforms the particular situation of the letters into the generality of all loving quests, whether of male for the female 'fair' or of Muse for the object of inspiration. The opening to Canto III also employs reference to the Roman context, but becomes in effect a generic love lyric, celebrating the traditional desire of all lovers to escape from the mean, phenomenal world into some idyllic realm of idealist union with the beloved. Here the subject is absorbed into the conventions of pastoral and lyric romance, with strong echoes of the Song of Solomon and Goethe's *Roman Elegies*.[19]

At the end of Canto I, on the other hand, the direct address to Alba, the references to Rome and the expressions of a speaker who is caught in the conflicts of sceptical doubt all suggest a subject who is continuous with the 'Claude' of the letters. At the same time, the very nature of the section as an address to Alba, the hills outside Rome, transforms the passage into a text of figurative and symbolic conceptualising that takes the hills out of their literal context into a realm of cultural and lyrical abstraction. Similarly, the series of balanced antitheses ('Is it an idol I bow to, or is it a god that I worship,/Do I sink back on the old, or do I soar from the mean?') refers succinctly to the conflict in Claude's letters, except that here the rhetorical and repetitive structure locates that conflict within a realm of formalised binarisms. It is partly the degree of such formalism which indicates the transformational nature of the lyric, dispersing the distinctiveness of a particular situation, hinting at universality. The dilemma of 'Claude' is now the dilemma of all abstract thinkers defined by similar binary structures.

There is also, however, in the last line of this Canto, a gesture towards dialectical thinking. From the dualist opposition of belief and scepticism we move to the thought of 'Reverent so I accept, doubtful because I revere' (I.288). In this line, doubt is no longer placed as the opposite of reverence, but is its integral feature –

reverence induces doubt. There is also an uncertainty about the function of 'so' (does it mean 'consequently' or 'provided that'?) which makes causation ambiguous. The textual structure of the whole lyric thus enacts the same thematic movement of the letters, both in decentring the individual subject and in subverting dualistic opposition.

In a similar vein the opening lyric to the whole poem can be seen to promulgate from the outset a world of groundless flux that is limited only by the differentiations of subjectivity. The first voice in the lyric calls for travel into a world of external phenomena:

> Over the great windy waters, and over the clear crested
> summits,
> Unto the sun and the sky, and unto the perfecter earth
> Come, let us go.
> (I.1–3)

The journey is committed from the outset to images of fluidity (windy waters), openness (sun and sky) and transition ('every breath even now changes to ether divine'). This voice is countered, however, by another voice which warns of false expectations about the results of travel. The expected new reality, says the second voice, will be simply the same old phenomena: '"The world that we live in,/Whithersoever we turn, still is the same narrow crib"' (I.5–6). To look outwards is to meet 'limitation', where we simply 'measure a cord'.

It is a limitation that is subjective as well as physical. Travel will not reveal the truth about the world, but merely add a further store of falsehood, swapping 'idle fancies' for 'memories wilfully falser' (I.9). Movement within the physical world merely contributes to temporal process: '"'Tis but to go and have been"' (10). This scepticism, however, is the voice of an idealist who counters travel among ephemera with the proposition that whoever would escape and be free should 'go to his chamber and think' (I.8). Here already is a prime case of Cartesian fever, fostering the subjectivist notion that the mind in the confined body is freer and more vast than the unconfined body in a physical world. From the outset, therefore, we have the uneasy juxtaposition of transient phenomena with idealist freedom. Neither the outward journey nor the inward alternative invokes solidity or fixity. There is no ground here, only the elusive continuities of Romantic idealism

Fact and Factitious in Amours de Voyage 117

('the perfecter earth') and idealist subjectivism (thinking in one's 'chamber').

At the other end of the poem, the concluding lyric draws attention to the poem's textual status and to the ambiguities that follow such an awareness. This lyric commits the poem itself, the 'little book', to 'the world', and in this commitment the status of its meaning is left to its fortunes in that world. The text both enters the process of textual uncertainty, '"flitting about many years from brain unto brain"' (V.221; note that the phrase is in the present tense: 'Say, "I *am* flitting about many years"'), and emerges from a defined historical location, '"writ in a Roman chamber,/When from Janiculan heights thundered the cannon of France"' (V.223-4). Textual production thus allows the effects of consciousness, the acknowledgement of artifice ('Go, little book!'), the possibility of reference (historical, social and geographical), and the ambiguities of reading.

For the speaker in *Maud* the last action is a commitment to the 'doom assigned', an identification with social action which provides the image of teleological purpose, a sense of meaningful closure. For Claude, despite his name, there is no such closure, only the commitment to move on to Egypt. At the level of the lyric epilogue there is no closure either, only the commitment to indefinite processes of reading.

In *Amours de Voyage* poetry offers no pretensions about the ideal so beloved by Matthew Arnold of uniting self and world; the relationship between the historical and the imaginative or between the literal and the figurative is demystified, not transcendentally sublime. It is rendered dialectical in the sense of being immersed in the fluidity of textual process where meaning and oppositions shift and transform, but a dialectic which founders on the impasse of insoluble division that characterises subjectivity. Reference to the historical and the literal is not denied, but that reference becomes itself textualised, acknowledged as another mode of representation and mediated through Claude's role as correspondent. The poem is thus textualised at both the level of lyrical timelessness, the illusion of a momentary release from the exigencies of temporality and flux, and the level of the protagonist as letter-writer. Writing, for Claude, is the process of ironic division, the action of differentiation which is the production of a self-conscious and factitious subject-in-process. His attempt to fix the self to knowledge cannot stand. 'Fact shall be fact', he says, but fact is dialectically determined and inseparable from the factitious – 'flexible, changeable, vague and multiform'. At the level of lyrical self-consciousness, the poem was written, it says, in a Roman chamber. But the poem is also, as it says, still flitting about from brain unto brain of 'Feeble and restless youths' – some of them not so youthful anymore.

5
Language and Truth in *The Ring and the Book*

In the context of this study, *The Ring and the Book* is the triumph of dialectical thinking. It is at once the culmination and the demise of romantic epistemology or subjective idealism, providing both the claim and the critique of the transcendental self, of the Cartesian *cogito*. A brilliantly conceived poetic experiment, it acts as a focus for all the thematic and structural issues that have dogged literature and theory during the last 150 years. Here the story of a pitiless, penniless nobleman and his naive, novice bride is told three times in book I and repeated variously and discrepantly through ten separate monologues. Through this series of responses and representations, the poem asserts and subverts the structural oppositions of formalism and reference, fancy and fact, trope and referent, legal fictions and social reality, discourse and event, intrasubjective perception and intersubjective relationship, idealism and materialism, scepticism and belief, dissemination and intention. In its overt questions about the role of language – 'For how else know we save by worth of word?' (I.837) – all issues are textualised and all representations placed within a discourse without a nontextual origin – without, that is, meaning by nontextual referent.[1] As another text, the Old Yellow Book both historicises and textualises the poem's sources. Attention is thus shifted from event as the source of meaning to discourse as the production of meaning: 'There's the irregular deed: you want no more/Than right interpretation of the same' (V.113–14). In short, the poem is an immense literary undertaking, the implications of which have barely been realised, perhaps precisely because it is so immense.

This chapter will focus on the textualisation of meaning in *The Ring and the Book* and thus on the poem as a critique of transcendence. The poem's concerns with both truth and language have often been noted, but generally in terms of a separation between human falsehood (error-ridden language) and divine (transcendent) truth.[2] My point is that this opposition is conflated. There is no separate divine truth in the poem, no dramatised position that corresponds to the position of, for example, Milton's God in *Paradise Lost*, no moment that escapes discourse. Unity, any singular truth, is deferred. A conclusive telos, towards which all events lead, is neither within nor outside the text; it is simply not available. All that is available are textually produced terms whose meaning is derived from an unceasing extension of textual contexts.[3]

I

It has been an axiom of Browning criticism that the grand poetic intention of *The Ring and the Book* is to reveal the truth. This assumption is fuelled by passages in the poem itself, by jocular references in book I to 'whole truth' (117), to truth which is present 'absolutely' (143), to 'lingot truth' (459) and to the proverb that 'Truth must prevail' (413), or by the affirmation in book XII that 'Art may tell a truth/Obliquely' (859–60), a phrase which twice appears in the title of critical discussions about purpose and pattern.[4] But the poem also teaches that 'human speech is naught' and 'human testimony false' (XII.838–9), that language goes 'easy as a glove,/O'er good and evil, smoothens both to one' (I.1180–1), that words 'characterize/Man as made subject to a curse' (X.350–1). It is apparent, therefore, that the poem observes a potential conflict between truth and language, between truth and its mode of representation. If human speech is nought, how does *poetic* speech escape the 'mediate word' (XII.861)?

Mary Sullivan indicates this conflict, and is representative of most established readings, when she observes two basic themes: 'the untrustworthiness of human speech' and 'the power of the creative process to open man's eyes to truth' (p. 172). At one level this discrepancy between human language and poetic truth amounts to a dramatisation of one of the dominant and recurring conflicts in Western thought – between scepticism and belief. Predominantly a clash between doubt and faith in the intellectual life of Victorian England, the opposition is presented to Browning's contemporary readers and their utilitarian biases largely, in book I, through the supposed antagonism of fancy and fact. This contest can also be read in the poem as a division between relativism and essentialism, the form it often takes during the twentieth century.

At another level, however, these themes involve an epistemology of aesthetics. While Sullivan's formulation absorbs many strands related to signification – morality and language, truth and poetic production, perception and creativity – her implication that the poem resolves the inveterate conflict between scepticism and belief depends upon a privileged status for aesthetic discourse. In a similar way, most readers who stress the function of truth in the poem covertly locate it within some version of the powerful Romantic aesthetic of poetic transcendence.[5] Through the splendours of the lyrical sublime or the fusing power of symbol and metaphor, language itself may be transformed, or poets (and readers by proxy) may reach through the exigencies of everyday language to some realm of pure truth beyond, to those temporal and temporary suspensions when we 'see into the life of things'.[6] In the nineteenth century such propositions were attractive to writers and intellectuals seeking ways of defending the truth-value of poetry against a utilitarian hegemony that marginalised and trivialised aesthetic experience. Valorising the value of symbol and metaphor also remained strong at the turn of the century, amidst fin-de-siècle nostalgia for the efficacy of unmediated lyricism.[7]

The language of *The Ring and the Book*, however, is far from pure lyricism, continually being disrupted by the requirements of narrative mimesis. It would rather appear to resist absorption into such an aesthetic. The continual foregrounding of the presence of language through alliteration, assonance and consonantal clusters, would appear to affirm a materialism that is rooted firmly within present temporality rather than encourage metaphysical abstraction. Here moments of lyrical intensity are usually contradicted by their context. In the opening passage, for example, the 'oval tawny pendent tear/At beehive-edge when ripened combs o'erflow' is an image for 'oozings' of raw gold which face not succulent sipping but 'the file's tooth and the hammer's tap' (I.10–14). And the poet's famous personal version of the Franceschini murder in book I (469–678) is so exaggerated in its melodramatic manner as to parody itself, subverting, in the very act of flaunting, its moral absolutism.[8]

Truth in this poem is revealed less through moments of metaphoric or symbolic synthesis than through a structural process of judgement and revelation. Nevertheless, the force of the poet's vision is seen to prevail. Again, Sullivan illustrates the point through her shift in emphasis from the moral or judicial verdict as a product of the poem/trial to the poetic process of arriving at that verdict. Meaning, she says, 'has to do with the process by which the artist sees and shares his vision of truth' (p. 176). This approach inevitably restores the poem to a Romantic aesthetic of creativity, locating truth within the constructive processes of a post-Cartesian consciousness and all which that model assumes about the status of an independent and authoring self. In this instance Browning represents the epistemological problem of discerning truth within a morass of conflicting evidence and testimony, all of which is potentially false, and solves the problem by, in the Pope's word, 'evolving' truth, sifting the contending discourses in order to separate the wheat of truth from the chaff of falsehood.[9] Unlike some critics, Sullivan does not maintain the poet's separate objective stance in this process, but incorporates him as a subjective participant. He is 'excited, emotionally involved, and partial, representing one more viewpoint in the circle of monologues' (p. 177). She reads Browning, then, like many critics, as a neo-Kantian, for whom truth is subjectively conceived and produced.

The plausibility of the reading, however, is affected by an underlying tautology. In attempting to overcome the difficulty of claiming universality or transcendence (p. 174) for a vision that is 'one more viewpoint' in a 'circle' of monologues, Sullivan argues that the poet's viewpoint is arrived at in a 'unique' way: he confirms 'his initial inspiration by re-creating the actors in his own mind and letting them express themselves', and then by 'putting all the resultant differing expressions together', he evolves 'the truth about their motivations' (p. 177). The tautology is revealed by Sullivan's parallel structures: 'confirming his ... inspiration', 're-creating the actors', 'Putting all the ... expressions together', he has 'evolved the truth'. All participial activities blur, so that putting the expressions together is confirming his inspiration and re-creating the actors is putting all expressions together which is confirming his inspiration. The process of evolving truth is one process with confirming inspiration and there can be no sure way of deciding whether the evolved truth is anything other than a solipsistic exercise of self-confirmation (a theme later explored directly by Browning in *Fifine at the Fair*). All that is proven is that the idealist poet can dramatise a world which suitably reflects his own perceptions; and who wants to read a poem that is twice the length of *Paradise Lost* in order to discover that?

The formal problem remains, then, if a singular poetic truth is to be established, of discerning a fixed centre or resolution in a poem whose very method eschews, disrupts, all singular perspectives. Ever since Henry James complained that there was no defined centre of consciousness for the poem,[10] there have been efforts to distil the poet's (singular) meaning. Truth has been located within chosen speakers, usually Pompilia and the Pope,[11] and models of circles, triads and spirals, or all three at once, have been proposed in order to establish patterns which break the mere successiveness of monologues and indicate the poet's controlling design.[12] Alternative readings suggest relativism as a guiding principle, or shift attention from the discovery of truth, an epistemological question, to the struggle for survival of 'being', an ontological issue.[13]

But this poem is too challenging in its multiplicity to be explained by any model of singularity. It encourages a Romantic aesthetic only to betray that aesthetic. There is no hidden form, private code or submerged structural logic which will reveal the secret meaning of *The Ring and the Book*; there is only a long series of discourses directed at a common set of circumstances, each concerned with its own meaning and its own determinate truth; there is only a series of texts which provide the contexts for each other's function and meaning. Poetic method neither eludes nor transforms the conditions of ordinary discourse. Consequently, the poet's own apparent privileging of art over the duplicity of human speech in book XII is both supported and contradicted by the poem itself.[14] Rather than privileging poetic truth over false language, either as a specific meaning to be elicited by the text or as a detached Word to be intuited by the reader, the poem presents truth and language as interdependent, as conceptual themes interwoven through dialectical process. Through foregrounding this thematic interplay, Browning emphasises not truth as product, but truth as process, truth in the making, and in that process truth is both subverted by language and produced by it.

II

There are, then, conflicting aspects of the poem which require further attention. Perhaps the most telling and provocative of these is Fra Celestino's text that 'God is true/And every man a liar'

(XII.600–1), which may be happily cited as evidence for the view that Browning portrays a divine absolutism. But this text is also a version of the paradox of the Cretan liar. If every man is a liar, how can the claim that 'God is true', when made by a man, be a truth? Such paradoxes are playful commentaries on the insoluble contradictions of metatexts. Claims which attempt to transcend the referential field of their own context inevitably fail because their very meaning arises from that context. The claim in this instance that 'God is true' takes its significance from the human context which defines its own condition as one of falsehood. Of course, there is no paradox if the speaker is not a man – a woman perhaps. That is, there is no paradox if the statement is not self-referential. But to avoid self-referentiality the speaking voice has to reside outside both referents, to be neither God nor man. Since the defined speaker, Fra Celestino, does not fit such requirements, the paradox as contradiction is very much active in the poem. At the end of this poem, therefore, is not a transcendent truth, or a resolved paradox, but an insoluble impasse.[15] The grand theme of the poem is not a conclusion about the power of creativity to escape the conditions of human utterance, but a question, perhaps the most startling question of all for the human mind: how can meaning (or truth) transcend context when without a context there can be no meaning/truth at all?

This question also lurks about the Pope's whole monologue, the repository, for most readers, of the poem's most vital truths. The Pope's will to absolutism is exposed at the end of the monologue when, anticipating God's remaking of the soul after death, he adds that the possibility of God's creation being in vain 'must not be' (X.2132). Having invested his life and identity within religious structures, he cannot at the end allow doubt to rule. Yet his discourse is dominated by the fallibility of human perception. Implicitly, the possibility of his being wrong about Guido 'must not be', yet he cannot extract his decision from human imperfection and doubt. Hence the lurking contradiction in his text as he effectively ends his monologue after only 200 lines with the judgement that closes the case and removes all thought – 'there is not any doubt to clear'(233) – but nevertheless continues for a further 2000 lines to explain his 'pause'.

His famous remark about evolving the truth of the Franceschini case, a remark applied so often to the poem's method as a whole, refuses to locate truth in any determinate place:

> Truth, nowhere, lies yet everywhere in these –
> Not absolutely in a portion, yet
> Evolvible from the whole: evolved at last
> Painfully, held tenaciously, by me.
> (X.229–32)

Truth, then, is not fixed, somewhere, but dispersed, 'everywhere' (the Pope refers to the case documents). In being 'Evolvible', truth exists not in any detached state or in any specific location; it exists through its availability for evolving. That which is evolvible is therefore that which is *potentially* available, available in the future, requiring an act of evolving in order to be realised or known and subject always to the process of that act. The Pope contradicts this commitment to deferral and evolution, by claiming, like Celestino's text, to have closed the process, to have indeed 'evolved' truth and located it somewhere (in him), no longer 'everywhere'. The contradiction stands. He is clear about his decision (233–5) and he does not shirk its consequences (2135). But in order to give it meaning and significance he has to extend it into the context of further utterance; even in being claimed as 'evolved', the Pope's judgement, as an act of closure, remains deferred by the doubts and meditations of his own discourse.

While his religious framework, like Fra Celestino's, places divine truth and wholeness of vision outside the limits of human perspectives, the Pope remains aware that his understanding is rooted in this world, given significance by the perceptions of the merely human mind. His image of the convex glass represents God, heaven, the 'known unknown', as the product of human perception, as the 'scattered points' that have been 'Picked out' from the cosmos by the human mind, refocussed by it, reunited and located back 'there', as if in some determinate and fixed place (X.1311–15). God exists 'somewhere, somehow' for the Pope, but in human terms 'there' is a fiction, a word without referent: 'There . . . is nowhere, speech must babble thus!' (X.1318). The 'whole' is 'Appreciable solely by Thyself', he says, addressing God, which makes divine truth unavailable to humankind, except through himself as Pope, as the man chosen to 'represent' God. God, then, remains even for the Pope a representation, a conception formed within the convex glass of human mind.

If Guido is always alert to the possibilities for manipulating meaning through metaphor and trope, the Pope, of all the poem's speakers, is most aware of the way falsehood may characterise human utterance. Even the most innocent of communications, when there is not 'the least incumbency to lie', will 'slip to false' (X.361–7), he observes. Lies are the inescapable circumstances of human discourse:

> Man must tell his mate
> Of you, me and himself, knowing he lies,
> Knowing his fellow knows the same, – will think
> 'He lies, it is the method of a man!'
> And yet will speak for answer 'It is truth'
> To him who shall rejoin 'Again a lie!'
> (X.367–72)

God's 'judgement-bar' escapes such contamination since He is both the Truth and the Word (376–7), the transcendental signified who stands outside discourse and therefore outside all falsehood. But the Pope remains clear that there must 'be man's method for man's life at least' (382). Consequently, he contextualises his judgement of the Franceschini case within the questioning of his human, non-papal self, Antonio Pignatelli (383–98). His procedure as Pope, the spokesperson for divine truth, is thus placed within the context of a 'mere old man o' the world', a context which nowhere eludes the conditions of the world, the 'coil/Of statement, comment, query and response' (373–4).

The Pope's context of query and response incorporates an awareness (which operates throughout the poem) that falsehood in human speech relates to the separation of sign and referent. He is disturbed, for instance, about the exhaustive and destructive energies that have been devoted to the problem of which name to use for God in the Chinese province of To-kien (1589–1604), an obsession with competing signifiers that ignores the importance of the referent. And he is aware that in contemporary Christendom faith in 'the thing' has become faith in 'the report' (1866). The humanist challenge that he represents in the voice of Euripides also plays upon the sign/referent difference: what before Christianity were 'forces and necessity' have afterwards grown 'God' (1766), so that what has changed are the signs, not the scheme – 'parts and whole named new' (1779).[16]

It is this distinction between sign and referent that allows images and terms to shift their application and disturb expectations about fixed meaning throughout the poem. Truth itself, for instance, is a term that is subject to continual repetitions and reversals; it is claimed by speakers in contexts where it is overtly ironic and subject to constant re-formulation (see Altick and Loucks, pp. 23, 121). Within such a process, any sense of a fixed meaning is undercut and the word functions according to context. This is not to say, however, with Altick and Loucks, that 'words originally laden with powerful meaning can be weakened by repetition and abuse' (p. 121). It is not the signified of the signifier 'truth' which is disrupted, but any claimed or implied referent for the sign.[17] Signs still signify within the context of the language which gives them meaning, although signs may point in the wrong direction. A sign is not the thing itself and the word 'truth' can therefore be applied to a range of potential referents, since the meaning as linguistic signification is dependent not upon the nature of the referent but upon the function of the sign among other signs – its function within the semiotic structure which gives it meaning. What Browning does, therefore, is not obliterate the meaning of the word 'truth', but demonstrate and explore the arbitrary relationship between sign and referent. He explores, in other words, the way falsehood is not just a potential feature or result of language but its very condition. The condition for a sign to tell the truth is that it must be able to lie.

This principle is also illustrated by the use of Caponsacchi's name as the password which gains entry into the Comparini household. Guido appropriates the name for his own destructive purposes – the name as sign enables him to lie – and like all signs a proper noun may have its meaning reassigned. As Pompilia claims when referring to the more general appropriation of Caponsacchi's name by a cynical public, 'the name, – /Not the man, but the name of him' is what comes to signify 'mockery and disgrace' (VII.1338–40). Unfortunately she forgot that separation of man and name when she sprang to the door in response to 'the name of him', a name which for her meant 'great heart' and 'strong hand' (VII.1808–10). Meaning in terms of the relationship between sign and referent is relative to context and cannot be assumed to have any fixity.

Indeed, Browning explores the paradox (theorised by Hegel in the nineteenth century and recently by post-structuralism) that truth is not a separately existing essence, but a signifying term whose meaning is interdependent with its supposed opposite, falsehood, and inseparable from its linguistic context. A crucial moment in book I questions the separation of truth from context:

> Are means to the end, themselves in part the end?
> Is fiction which makes fact alive, fact too?
> (I.704–5)

Through such rhetoric Browning offers the Hegelian proposition that there is no end separate from the means which produce it, no meaning outside mediation, no truth outside the falsehood that gives it existence: to re-cite the Pope's remark about evolvibility, 'Truth . . . lies' (X.229). No human is able to confront pure truth, only 'truth with falsehood, milk that feeds him now,/Not strong meat he may get to bear some day' (I.831–2). Pure truth, truth outside representation, is deferred, available 'some day', never 'now'.

Through such rhetoric, then, the poem develops a critique of Romantic epistemology and of the Romantic aesthetic of transcendent lyricism. *The Ring and the Book* locates the function of meaning and knowledge firmly within language – 'For how else know we save by worth of word?' (I.837) – which is to focus attention not on transcendence, but on 'live truth'. This concept is introduced in book I, along with its concomitant, figuration.

III

The opening sections of the poem confront the reader with the figurative function of the images in the title, and through the elaboration of these two images, the ring and the book, the poet introduces the procedures and themes that are to dominate the poem.[18] At the same time, book I is no mere introduction, no frame that sits outside the piece itself; it enacts the conflation of opposites and intermingling of figurative relationships that are the key to the poem's textualism, educating the reader in the manner and theme of the poet's art. Although the figure of the ring has already received more attention than any other image in the poem, it is necessary to unfold this image further in order to stress the role of figuration itself and to explain the poem's disruption of the opposition between live truth and dead fact.

The first line in book I invokes a material referent, the physical presence of a real thing: 'Do you see this Ring?' The reader is thus placed within a literal context, addressed by a speaker existing within a tangible world. The very next phrase, however, significantly qualifies that context, for the ring is no merely natural object; it is 'Rome-work, made to match . . . Etrurian circlets' (I.1–4). The phenomenal object is no purely material 'thing', but is defined by its artificial status, by its function as an imitation, produced by 'Castellani's imitative craft'. The proffered object is therefore immediately entered into a materialist context where it is not merely material, but compounded with mimesis, inseparable from its status and quality as a cultural production. It is thus linked with a cultural context which recedes in time, since it repeats the form and design of Etruscan rings, themselves artefacts from some earlier cultural context. Since it repeats their form it contains the traces of their presence; although absent, they are present within the imitative features of the proffered ring. Again, the designated ring is no merely single or pure object; the referent is itself a sign, a signifier for its intermingling of the material and the artifical and for its link with all previous cultural productions of which it is a repetition.

The Etruscan rings were also found 'alive' and 'spark-like' and the ring which imitates them is 'soft . . . Yet crisp as jewel-cutting' (5–8). Hence two further oppositions are conflated in these opening few lines. The first and most obvious is that the ring intermingles the organic and living qualities of the original, its softness, with the more technical elements of artificial making, with 'jewel-cutting'. The distinction between the natural and the artificial is to feature throughout the poem as speaker after speaker praises the superiority and justifies the virtue of natural behaviour and morality, always tending to ignore the way distinctions between natural and unnatural action are themselves the result of social production, of cultural artifice. The second, and less obvious opposition, is suggested through placing 'alive' in apposition to 'spark-like'. Since the Etruscan rings were found 'alive', the implication is that they are still living, and indeed they are, both as a model for Castellani's ring and as the repetitive design of that ring. At the same time, they were found 'Spark-like', an image for both brightness and ephemerality, combining the quality of life with the condition of a fleeting and fading existence. That which is alive is subject to change and loss. That which has organic existence dies. Yet it can be preserved through repetition and imitation, as Castellani's ring repeats and preserves the originals. The metaphor of the spark will be repeated throughout the poem and in the last book it becomes precisely designated as a metaphor for the sudden rise and decline of Guido's fame, for the growth and loss of his experience in time.

There then follows a sequence which invokes the process of the ring's making, in particular the craftsman's 'trick' through which the 'pure gold' is wrought into an embossed ring. The addition of alloy to the raw metal, an alloy which is then removed once the ring is shaped, has received extensive explication as an allegory of Browning's concept of creativity. That method, critics argue, involves the mixing of imagination with raw facts in order to shape the poem, followed by the withdrawal of the imagination, leaving the truth of the original material available for the reader's understanding. Since the poem rather obviously supports the 'truth' of the poet's own version, this interpretation of the aesthetic process has run into trouble: it seems difficult to accept that the poet's fancy is ever withdrawn, in any manner corresponding to the removal of the alloy from the gold ring, and the poet confuses the issue further by suggesting that the fancy, or 'fiction which makes fact alive', is also 'fact' (I.705) – that ends are never separate from their means.[19]

Here the process of making merges the organic ('ere the stuff grow') with the inorganic ('a ring-thing'), and the natural ('gold') with the artificial ('gold's alloy'). Once the process is complete, however, there is a claimed 'repristination'. But restoration of the original metal is not all that is gained. What readers appear to miss is that the claim of repristination is a claim that there is no *loss* of value in the process, not that there is no *addition*. There is indeed addition: 'you have gained a ring' (30). The aesthetic process therefore loses no worth from the original material and adds to it the 'shape' which allows it to be 'self-sufficient now'; we have gained 'lilied loveliness' and 'The rondure brave'. The climactic point of this brief section is to reinforce the balance and inseparability of nature and artifice: 'Prime nature with an added artistry' (29). The key point, therefore, is not that the artificer removes all signs of his artifice, but that the raw material is enhanced and given a chance for survival, self-sufficiency, which it otherwise lacked. The aesthetic paradox in this fusion of nature and artifice is that the resultant artefact both contains raw existence, the exigencies and temporality of organic process ('Prime nature'), and presents a form (the 'added artistry') which differentiates the object from that process, giving it the illusion of a status that eludes temporality. (Insofar as form exists through differentiation, it appears to step outside temporality, but conceptualising that difference, understanding its presence, remains part of the inevitable temporality of discourse; the point is akin to Hegel's paradox of a totality or unity which is inseparable from its divisions and differences.) The further paradox is that without the artifice, the gold would not have continuing life: without its new shape which defines its difference, bestows self-sufficiency, it would not live. While Browning does not specifically refer to 'life' in the summary of the ring's status as a made and produced object (26–30), the fusion of nature and artistry produces a new meaning for 'living' which begins with the Etruscan rings that were 'found alive'. This new ring is now also 'alive' and it has been given that life precisely through the fusion of nature and artifice, through subverting their opposition.

The produced ring thus contains 'Gold as it was', but also the 'shape' which 'remains' – the 'rondure' and 'lilied loveliness'. At this point it should be clear that the 'Ring' that was first offered the reader is no simple 'thing'. It is a *'ring*-thing' (17; my italics) and that means it incorporates all the combination of qualities and features that have so far been elaborated. Just as its presence invokes the absent 'circlets' which it imitates, so too its presence as made object invokes the processes of its making and the conceptual perceptions of 'shape', 'rondure' and 'loveliness'. As a 'ring-*thing*' it therefore acts already as a visible sign for all the antecedents of design, technique, value and conception that have gone into its making: as a produced artefact, it is the sign of its own production.

The image is given a further and crucial dimension when the speaker/poet turns back self-consciously to his image: 'What of it?' he asks (31). The pronoun refers to the ring in two senses: to the ring in the first line, the offered object, and to the preceding phrase 'you have gained a ring' (30), the process of gaining a ring. What Browning does next, however, is a crucial step in the poem. He overtly enters the ring into language, into semiotic structuring: ''T is a figure, a symbol, say;/A thing's sign' (31–2). By drawing attention to this process of sign-making, the poet reminds us that the ring has all along been not an object, but an image, a sign in language, and it is in language, and specifically the language of this passage (I.1–30), that it has gained its meaning, its definition and signification. To say the ring and its making is a 'figure' is to acknowledge its verbal status and function, without losing anything that has been conveyed, produced in the artifice of this discourse, about its function as a visible and material sign. The mixture of materialism and idealist conception in the ring as literal object now combines overtly with the materialism and idealism of the sign in language, so that the ring becomes a sign like other signs and can function as a signifier for some other signified: 'now for the thing signified' (32), which is 'the square old yellow Book' (33).

Thus the ring is entered into discourse, made part of a language process where all terms are signifiers whose signifieds can become other signifiers, for that is exactly what happens: the signifier 'Ring' now attracts the signified 'Book' (and that signified in turn is about to become another signifier with its own large and developing network of signification). Of course the ring always was part of discourse. For the reader of the poem the ring was never anything other than an image. But by drawing attention to the ring as symbol, Browning draws the reader directly into the very semiotic network of the poem's own process of production. This poem's presence, therefore, as artefact, is also a sign of its own production, like the ring (I shall return to this point later when discussing book XII).

In thirty brief lines Browning has brilliantly set up the subtle processes of signification and sign-making that are the basis of the poem. Signs, like the ring, refer to objects, as referents, and to antecedents, to the designs that they imitate, to the absences whose trace is contained in their presence, but they also signify forwards, to other signifieds which are established through the discourse that gives them meaning. Further, without this discourse, the symbol would have no meaning. It is only within the context of this passage, and this poem, that the ring gains its value as a 'symbol', and only in this context, does a ring come to signify, to *mean*, book. Meaning in this process is textualised, entered into and extended through discourse. Through the referent that is itself a sign, through the sign that becomes a symbol, Browning foregrounds the process of textualisation from the outset.[20]

The Old Yellow Book, to which the poet now moves, is nevertheless a more overt image of textualisation than the ring, and it was retrieved from an array of miscellaneous cultural bric-a-brac through response to a verbal sign: one glance at its 'lettered back' and it must be read (82–3). A ring and a book are incommensurate, but if regarded as artefacts which incorporate the complex set of reconciliations and traces that were indicated in the ring image, then it is easier to see how one might signify the other. It should not be a surprise, therefore, to suggest that the central focus of the poem is on the production of representational form – that is, the poem is continually re-enacting the process whereby 'shape' is given to raw material and meaning to experience, and whereby both shape and meaning (form and content) are fused through figuration, the 'imitative craft' of human discourse.

It is important to observe that, like the ring, the book is also a cultural product which incorporates the process of its production and the imitation of antecedent forms. That is the case both for the book as poem, the book held by the reader, and for the book as Old Yellow Book. Like the ring, the Yellow Book contains both form and raw material: 'A book in shape but, really, pure crude fact/Secreted from man's life when hearts beat hard . . . ' (86–7). It does not, however, contain the pure fact of life itself, but fact 'secreted from' life. Already there has been a process of distillation, of reduction, and the poet's play with mastering the 'contents' and knowing 'the whole truth' (117, 143–4, 364–6) ironises from the outset any crude assumption that reading a book or summarising its contents will possess the whole truth. The Yellow Book contains 'real . . . circumstance', but it is real 'summed-up' circumstance, which is 'Put forth' and 'printed' (146–8). In other words, the life that the Book contains is already inseparable from its discourse, from the productive processes whereby experience and events are summarised and printed.

Further reminders of this process are provided by the need to translate the title (120–1) and by the reference to Latin which is 'interfilleted with Italian streaks/When testimony stooped to mother-tongue' (138–9). Transcriptions of the content and title are 'translations' and even the documents themselves are translations of the language used by original witnesses. The contents of the Yellow Book are therefore signs of an array of antecedent events and utterances, and the lawyers and court procedures emphasise the point by placing the Franceschini case amidst an array of prior legal authorities and precedents (213–40). The text which records the evidence given about the case is thus a sign that a sequence of events preceded the trial, and it is that sequence with its explanations that is part of the signification of the Yellow Book.

Reality in this context disappears into the past. The events that are alluded to in the Yellow Book are lost (in being 'secreted' they are hidden as well as distilled); all that remains are the traces and signs of their presence as recorded by the trial documents and by letters and reports. The Franceschini murder is already textualised when Browning comes to it,[21] and its 'truth' is neither separable from its textual status nor possessable in a summary of its contents. Otherwise, the book could simply be thrown on the fire (375). At the same time, the book cannot speak for itself; the book was lost amidst other cultural bric-a-brac until rescued and read by the poet. In itself, therefore, its content of 'untempered gold' is dead fact – present, but without meaning. Meaning requires textual production. To become alive (known), the facts must be given new shape – read, retold, recontextualised.

The poet (initially the poet as reader, but increasingly the poet as creator, or re-creator) has to fuse his 'live soul' with 'that inert stuff' (469). In telling his fanciful version, the poet does not retell the contents of the Yellow Book, but turns away from the book ('The book was shut and done with and laid by'; 472) in order to 'free' himself and 'find the world' (478). The 'life' in him 'abolished the death of things' (520) and he 'saw' the events once again with his 'own eyes' (523). He has not reconstructed the facts of the Yellow Book, therefore, but textually, in discourse which continually parodies itself, re-enacted the events which preceded them, the events of which they were merely the trace. The textualised version in the Yellow Book, like Castellani's imitative ring, was the sign of a lost set of antecedent processes, the experience that was told and the artifice which made the documents, but from the language of that text, the poet could 'calculate ... the lost proportions of the style' (677–8). Dead signs become alive when re-read, re-spoken, re-contextualised.[22]

The resuscitation of the past is of course Browning's main metaphor for poetic creation in the poem. Through 'Mimic creation' the artist can breathe new life into that which is dead. Each revival is a 'new beginning' which 'starts the dead alive' (733), and since the poet enters the past 'spark-like' (755), the new life is linked to the same image of change and ephemerality that was associated with the life of the Etruscan rings. All imitation is therefore both a revival of the past and a new beginning which moves into the future.[23] The past cannot be recovered as 'the past'; it can only be repeated as an imitation in the living present, and that living present is always subject to the temporality of all discourse – movement, loss, death – just as the poet's fanciful version of the murder story eventually encountered the 'granite' of memory and fact which 'proved sandstone, friable' (667). Dead fact is resident in the unread text, and it becomes live fact only through continuing acts of repetition and resuscitation, through acts of reading, writing and speaking which add the life-giving artifice of discourse. In this sense the poet's act of reading (the Old Yellow Book) is never totally separated from the poet's act of (re)creation (writing this poem). Truth and meaning are not fixed features of the past that are recovered in the present, but fluid features of present discourse, always subject to change and always moving into a never-ending future.

At the end of book I, Browning overtly establishes the relationship of living meaning to change (I.1348–78). He rejects the method of choosing only 'one aspect of the year' to represent the whole 'novel country'. He might 'fix' the land through such a method, but it would be 'dwarfed' to one perspective, life reduced to the death of a singular position ('Life cramped corpse-fashion'). Instead, he proposes to represent the multitudinousness and variegation of living truth:

> Rather learn and love
> Each facet-flash of the revolving year! –
> Red, green and blue that whirl into a white,
> The variance now, the eventual unity,
> Which make the miracle. See it for yourselves,
> This man's act, changeable because alive!
>   (I.1360–5)

Similar to Hegel's speculative philosophy which aimed to represent living reality and not 'inert lifeless understanding' (Pref.110), Browning's poetic method involves the production of living discourse, the shifting, mutable facets of continuing experience. Because the resuscitated past is now alive, it is changeable, and therefore characterised by present 'variance'. Unity is postponed, deferred, always 'eventual'.

Metaphysical readings of the poem tend to regard this passage as testimony for 'an ultimate unification of parts' in the poem, a unity that is usually based upon a Romantic idealist aesthetic that is written into religious discourse: 'Artistic truth duplicates divine truth, whose true unity mystically remains "multiform" in its oneness'.[24] But as far as reading the poem is concerned, an experience that is necessarily temporal, when is there ever a unity which is not also a 'now' that is subject to variance? When can poetic form, as 'known' form, ever escape the temporal conditions of its production? Perhaps nowhere does Browning's text come so close to a definition of Derridean *différance*, particularly in this antithetical structure which places 'variance now' not against, but alongside, in succession with, 'eventual unity', and where *both* (variance and unity) produce the 'miracle' of living meaning.

Through such passages and contradictions, life and truth (as fixed meaning) become incommensurate. The process of living involves an ongoing consumption of past signs and established facts, a consumption which transforms the facts by recontextualising them. Living reality is subject to variation precisely 'because alive'. Unity, once attained, would be dead truth, a fixed form no longer actively engaged with its material. Hence Browning's structure for the poem stresses a continual movement into future texts, an unceasing transition from image to image, statement to statement, a movement which both produces meaning and postpones truth.

Browning's metaphors of the ring and the book provide a model for his art that is also a model for textual meaning. The fusion of natural material and added artistry, which gives a self-sufficient status to shape and raw material, produces the paradox of a fixed form (the ring or the book) that is variegated and shifting (the life and process of making). He confronts the reader with an artefact that contains the contradictions of a product (the completed book) which is inseparable from the process of its production (the text is only alive when being written or read). It combines an eventual unity (a single text) with present variance (the series of competing texts or discourses).

IV

The model of mimic action for poetic creation contains an important structural principle. As resuscitation, poetry may 'appropriate forms' (I.726) in order to restore life to the dead. The poetic act is not an originating event, therefore, but a means of restoring life to what is otherwise without meaning, outside discourse and hence not available for understanding. It is a form of possession, 'owning what lay ownerless before' (I.725), and of colonising, of appropriation ('So find, so fill full, so appropriate forms'), but it is a possession which gives new life to what is repossessed and reactivated, galvanised into new energy ('galvanism for life'). The act of a magician rather than a creator, it is in itself morally neutral and may be performed equally by a Faust or an Elisha, assisted by either Satan or God.

Most pertinently, it is an act of retrospection, re-enacting the past, which is characteristic of all narrative and most speech. Hence every monologuist in the poem in some way or other engages in a retrospective account of events whereby those events are given new life and meaning through the appropriation of 'forms'. When events originally occurred, they may have taken the form of fictions of possibility, where purpose and plan would be uncertain and incidents apparently random; but when told in retrospect, the events are presented as a pattern of purpose and inevitability. When narrated, events are (re)presented in such a way as to confirm the truth and belief of the speaker's perspective (it is no wonder that the poet's view is confirmed by his poem – that happens in all discourse, even this one). This point is illustrated by the way speakers (notably speakers in books II–VII) continually and often at great length cite other speakers, implicitly claiming access to the original evidence. The citation of speeches and conversation is intended by each speaker as a sign of authenticity, to show that their version is based on the true record, and yet structurally what is occurring is an act of possession and reappopriation, an exercise in discourse as power. Even if the quotations are accepted as accurate (testing all credulity), their intention and meaning are altered, subsumed within the speaker's purposes, by being cited within a new context.[25]

Such acts of repossession also extend to socially and historically established images. The intermingling of cultural forms with individual shaping is most obviously illustrated, for instance, by the varying application of the Christian paradise myth in books II–IV. As often noted, the potential cuckold in book II argues for the authority of husbands, and so makes Violante a scheming Eve, whereas the romantic idealist in book III bedecks Pompilia with flower imagery and portrays her as an innocent Eve seduced by a satanic Guido. The more subtly insinuating Tertium Quid prefers to offer Pompilia as a resourceful daughter of Eve.[26] Similar appropriations occur in the use of religious discourse by Caponsacchi, Pompilia and the Pope, in the use of legal discourse by the lawyers, in the use of social conventions such as *honoris causa* by Half-Rome, Guido and the lawyers, and in the use of literary, classical and Biblical allusions throughout.

To possess, however, is to 'know', and each monologuist therefore claims to know the truth, to represent the essence of events by re-presenting, and thereby reinterpreting, their sequence. The pattern of retrospective structuring and absorption thus leads to the claim that it is possible to arrive at a fixed truth – a claim made, explicitly or implicitly, by every speaker. Since these patterns of structuring can in turn be observed by a reader who may extract the patterns from several juxtaposed speakers, it is easy enough to arrive at the possibility of a transcendent truth that incorporates all views. Such procedures have always underpinned readings which privilege Browning's validation of the truth of the murder story – the logocentric view that adding to the number of versions will enable the whole and therefore true view to be obtained (on the model of the divine, detached observer, outside representation and therefore outside mediation).[27]

But this 'transcendent' view will itself be one more act of resuscitation and re-appropriation. As each view is superseded by the one which follows, it becomes subsumed within an ongoing series.[28] All versions, including readers' versions, are trapped within the same pattern. Browning's placement of the Pope's monologue, for instance, effectively locates the 'evolved' truth of the Pope's judgement within the poem's larger discourse.

There is, consequently, another structural principle in the poem which contradicts the truth claims of apparently fixed patterns: the principle of the supplement, or serial textualisation.[29] By placing separate and distinctive monologues after one another, Browning employs a structure which produces a floating irony rather than fixity, indicating the gaps and differences between texts as well as within them. Each new text alters the context and therefore the signification of the previous text and that is a process that can be repeated indefinitely.

'Here were the end', states the poet at the beginning of the last book, employing the subjunctive that dispels all certainty, 'had anything an end'. As each text produces a context which extends and alters the meaning and 'truth' of the previous one, the poem perfectly enacts the deconstructionist point that there is no meaning without context while at the same time that context is boundless, capable of an indefinite number of extensions which proliferate possible meanings, subverting the singularity of statement or judgement.[30]

A serial structure, where differing monologues recite/resite variously related events, also produces a more extreme effect of disruption than a single monologue, since not only is the speaker's position undercut by irony from within his or her discourse, but the single view is also disrupted by the context of plural texts. The single view

Language and Truth in The Ring and the Book   139

is thus shown to be contingent, complicated by the context outside as well as within itself. Also the author himself enters the poem, drawing attention to his own view, parodying his version in the very act of presenting it, and thereby disrupting further the truth-claims and mimetic realism of all speakers.[31]

The point is that these two conflicting structural methods – retrospective narrative and serialisation – produce an insoluble contradiction. To the extent that this contradiction involves the holding together of two conflicting ideas without resolution, the poem repeats the circumstances of Romantic irony (see Chapter 2, n.6). There can be the production of a fixed truth, the meaning generated by each speaker, including the poet in books I and XII, but that truth is inseparable from its production through 'mimic creation', and it is therefore inseparable from the living, re-producing and re-possessing process of that action. As such, it is not fixed at all, but immersed in the fluid temporality of the discourse which re-created it, and in the discourse which is always required to re-enact its meaning – the appropriating, mimic-creative discourse of any reader (see Chell, p. 99). Celestino's paradox both makes its claim for a separate and absolute truth and fails to escape the processes of its production which contradict that claim. There is at once truth and no truth, both the validation of moral judgement (the poet's versions in book I, even if melodramatic and self-parodic, are not seriously contradicted by the rest of the poem) and the critique of all belief.

At the same time, the two structural methods are in conflict only if structure is conceived as a fixed product, as an architectural metaphor for a completed form. Once the implications for 'structure' or 'form' are absorbed from Browning's ring metaphor (about the product which incorporates its production), then a more dialectical conception of the poem's structure emerges, one which more actively incorporates the poem's focus on language and truth. This conception may be modelled by Hegel's notion of content as dynamic form, where content is always in 'transition into a formal shape', or where form is 'the indwelling process of the concrete content itself' (Pref. 115; see Chapter 1).

As already suggested, the form of *The Ring and the Book* is inseparable from temporality (from the fading of experience and the deferral of meaning) and yet provides a shape which appears to resist temporality (the artifice, or 'added artistry' which renders the object 'self-sufficient', and which at one level must refer to the literal text that is held in the hand of the reader). As a poet who resuscitates the past, Browning reclaims the Franceschini murder from historical loss and provides it with an artistic structuring which allows it to survive, to be read. But that, paradoxically, is to rescue the events from time by restoring them to time, to reaffirm their living meaning by assigning them to a structure that is defined by temporal re-enactment (reading) and supplementation (serial texts). Similarly, when individual speakers attempt to use language to weave a fabric of existence that forms a conclusive pattern of truth and justification, their attempt inevitably fails, as language slips away from their grasp, weaving them as much as they attempt to weave it.

Browning also takes the further step, as author, of weaving a pattern of weavers weaving. It is not, therefore, the pattern of any exclusive or singular truth that is the point of the poem, not the establishing of any privileged viewpoint that displays a transcendent truth; but rather it is the pattern of patterning, the process of meaning in process, the form of forming formulations, that is the key to the poem's structural method. In this work, the singularity, the controlling thread, of an omniscient narrative is replaced by the variegated wefts of men and women who view the world through a fabric woven in language.

If speakers are shown by irony and the context of other monologues to fail in their attempts to arrest the flux of experience, to construct a 'whole' for themselves or their auditors, then the poem's 'whole' is a weaving without totality, an unceasing construction of meaning, the inseparability of truth from the textual mobility and differentiations of discourse.[32] Meaning remains elusive, if by meaning we expect some singular, conclusive and verifiable abstraction. But, paradoxically, art may demonstrate both the failure and the success of meaning within these conditions of discourse, provided meaning is conceived as textual, contingent, relative. Patterns and patterning recur, structures remain, but they are redeployed, reappropriated; referents shift and value alters according to context. Browning's poem demonstrates the way meaning is temporal and contingent, subject to the appropriation of forms and the shifting of contexts, but it is also the constructed 'form' of art, the shaped pattern of the ring, the structure of semiotic process, which allows that movement to be 'read', to be 'understood', as theme as well as medium. Indeed, then, the means are inseparable from the ends, in art as in human evidence.

And that, in Hegelian terms, is to formulate content as a dialectic of 'indwelling process'.

One consequence of reading the poem in this way is to revise views about structural development or progression. Established readings of the poem which have located its emphasis in character or judgement have had to face the problem of dramatic climax. The narrative concept of a thematic development that progresses towards 'a revelation of the ultimate significance of event and character' (Altick and Loucks, p. 39) demands a climactic moment when the desired revelation is attained. Most readings have consequently opted for the Pope's speech as the climax, with Guido's second monologue merely confirming the climactic view (or dramatising the potential for human redemption) and the last book as merely an anti-climactic appendage. But once emphasis is placed on language and its epistemological function, any sense of climax is to do with an intensifying of linguistic issues rather than a moment of revelation about significance. In these terms, it becomes preferable to refer to what Douglas Standring has called 'a plateau of intensity' (p. 11). The later monologues of Bottini, Pope and Guido can then be read as a plateau where the recurring, language-related themes of truth, responsibility and identity are pushed to their extremes. Bottini divorces, legally and completely, language from referential meaning; the Pope confronts directly the limits of language, defining the necessity for moral responsibility within those limits; Guido enacts pure amorality, exploiting the equation between utterance and sheer biological survival. Dialectical form does not alter or suddenly transform itself into the fixity of revealed truth: it simply varies in intensity. This plateau, when Guido 'hung at full of fame/Over men's upturned faces' (XII.6-7), then subsides in book XII ('now decline must be') as the poet restores the past he has re-created to the dissipations of time.

In time, meaning and knowing are dispersed: 'live fact' is 'deadened down,/Talked over, bruited abroad, whispered away' (I.834-5). Book X is not a climax of revelation, then, but a contribution to the intensification of discourse which increases with book IX and which in book XI re-enacts the zenith of Guido's 'rocket', when he briefly held heaven 'In brilliant usurpature' (XII.2-5). As a production in discourse, his experience, like a sky-rocket, is subject to temporal loss; it glows and then dies. Similarly, the events of the whole poem glow, fade, become dispersed and dispossessed in a continuation of 'indwelling process' – in subsequent documents –

letters, extracts, reports, accounts of ensuing law cases. Eventually the poet returns us to the poem itself, to the book wherein the dead truth will continue to lie until read – resuscitated and repossessed – when it will lie (tell a fictive truth) once again.

V

Browning's rhetorical question about knowing through 'worth of word' links the themes of truth and language to epistemological discourse. This conjunction would seem to fit the poem into the dualisms of post-Cartesian epistemology, where world and self are separate entities. However, while the proposition about language as the sole means of knowledge leaves open the question of the world as a separate essence (separate, that is, from its representation in discourse), it challenges Cartesian divisions in the sense that in these circumstances the world is not directly known or possessed by mind. If there is no way of knowing other than through 'worth of word', as Browning's rhetoric implies, then there is no meaning without mediation, no knowledge outside discourse. The world is known as it is constituted in *language* (not consciousness, which is a crucial distinction for the poem as a critique of Romantic epistemology), and possession, the act of knowing in poetic resuscitation, is a process, as I have argued, of *linguistic* appropriation. But if words are possessed by their speakers, then speakers may be equally possessed by their words. To know actively, as a linguistically produced subject, is also to be known, in language, as a linguistically defined object. One of the consequences of this double action is to blur distinctions, to allow world and self, belief and desire, to be absorbed into competing discourses, whether institutional or individual. As Simon Petch observes, the competition between legal and religious discourse which Browning found in the Yellow Book becomes intensified in the poem. In its exercise of power, the law, for example, is quite adept at appropriating words, the Bible and even people, assigning them roles in a network of 'semantic relation'.[33] Within such a process further distinctions between means and ends and between process and product also become blurred, as Browning's rhetoric in book I also proposes. Such blurrings, or dialectical transformations, the breaching of terms defined by opposition, allow multiple representations, endless bickering, appropriation and reappropriation, political back-sliding, cheating, expediency, injustice. The two lawyers, for example, exploit the blurring of distinctions between ends and means in order to argue, each for quite different ends, that ends justify means.

Hence the process of dialectical blurring accounts for the poem's frequent observations about the unreliability of human evidence. As explained earlier, the very nature of the sign, which must be able to lie in order to tell the truth, produces the ambiguous 'worth' of all words. At the same time, this process does not deny meaning, for it helps us to 'all we seem to hear' (I.836), confronting us with the inseparability of experience and language: 'For how else know we save by worth of word?' (I.828–9). To foreground the conditions for knowing as simultaneous with the conditions of discourse and with a consequent dominance of linguistic artifice is not at all to give away the possibility of knowledge, as Browning's paradoxes about truth and falsehood make clear. Assumptions about the nature of knowledge and truth are simply redefined in dialectical terms: truth is inseparable from the false medium which produces it.

At the same time, by dramatising the arbitrary relationships between sign and referent, the vast potential for signpost shifting, Browning maintains an epistemological edge, a challenge to all meaning and truth claims. By disrupting all single claims to truth, and exposing the exigencies and discrepancies among institutional as well as individual practices, the poem retains its political bite.

This epistemological critique occurs in several ways. There is the overt challenge of discourse conflict, illustrated, for instance, in book XII, where both Celestino and Bottini juxtapose secular and religious explanations for cosmic cause: Celestino, in referring to the Pope's decision about Guido, says 'What I call God's hand, – you perhaps, – mere chance/Of the true instinct of an old good man' (592–3), and Bottini refers to the new trial brought by the Convertites as 'a veritable piece of luck,/The providence, you monks round period with' (669–70). There is the continual challenge of semantic diffusion, practiced by all speakers in order to manipulate images in their own favour, and practiced by the lawyers as part of their institutional routine. Legal discourse in the poem flaunts a continuing contradiction between linguistic method and institutional truth that is symptomatic of language throughout: 'although . . . legal discourse only manifests what happens elsewhere in the poem's linguistic universe, its tropes and rhetoric exploit the very instability which, in its search for determinate meaning, legal discourse denies'

(Petch, pp. 119–20). There is also the challenge of the Pope's desire, like the lawyers, to exercise epistemological power within contemporary society. His monologue unfolds into a meditation on how to maintain the political force of religious belief and moral teaching, how to control, that is, the language of moral decision-making. Recognising that for himself there is no 'dreadful question' about salvation, since he is defined by his 'circle of experience' with God as its 'central truth' (X.1633–4), he wants to extend the power of Christian witness outside his 'petty circle', and the later stages of his monologue contemplate how that might be done. It may even be necessary, he muses, to disrupt epistemological convention, to deny 'Recognized truths' in obedience to some truth as yet 'Unrecognized' (1869–72).

The central epistemological problem in any discourse – judging what is true perception – is also raised in both legal and spiritual terms. Archangelis introduces the legal version:

> It is enough, authorities declare,
> If the result, the deed in question now,
> Be caused by confidence that injury
> Is veritable and no figment: since,
> What, though proved fancy afterward, seemed fact
> At the time, they argue shall excuse result.
> That which we do, persuaded of good cause
> For what we do, hold justifiable!
> (VIII.429–36)

What Archangelis leaves out is precisely the problem of establishing the reliability of belief in 'good cause', of proving that the supposed 'injury' did indeed seem fact at the time (somewhat crucial in rape trials when the defence is willing submission, or in murder trials when the defence is *honoris causa*). As it stands, this legal authority allows any action to be condoned provided the actor was 'persuaded of good cause' – all that is required, as Archangelis is well aware, is a plausible case for the perception of fact.

The same issue is confronted by the Pope, with virtually the same conclusion. The Pope's hypothetical anecdote about diagnosing a sick man wrongly and thereby bringing about his death (X.243–59) is a means of justifying the need to act regardless of potential misprision – the need, in Archangelis' terms, to 'Act by the present light!' (VIII.441). In the Pope's liturgical language, responsibility is shifted to providence. On discovering the error the Pope would reply:

> 'God so willed:
> Mankind is ignorant, a man am I:
> Call ignorance my sorrow not my sin!'
> (257-9)

Both versions focus on the problem of acting on the basis of limited or imprecise perception. The law accommodates the point by allowing all persons to plead a formal defense, and it should be 'harder to convict', claims Archangelis, than 'to establish innocence' (VIII.456-7). For the Pope, such imprecision is a matter of 'training' and 'passage' (X.1411), developing moral muscle. In neither case is the epistemological question resolved.

Within the Pope's discourse ultimate truth resides within a continuum of levels of transformation, taking various transitional forms; it does not matter whether God's story is 'Absolute' and 'independent truth' or 'only truth reverberate', echoing in the human mind (X.1387-99). What counts is the effect on action, regardless of the explanation of cause, and the epistemological doubt underlying the Pope's pragmatism sustains his decree that what is always demanded amidst the moral cloudiness of human action and perception is 'life's terrible choice', the exercise of 'moral sense' (1238, 1415).[34] But as Adam Potkay explains, the Pope also attempts to overcome any misinterpretation in his choice, to lift his judgement outside human fallibility, by developing the private fantasy of a 'mark' which unequivocally identifies Guido as evil (511-12; Potkay, 147). In effect the Pope argues for a sign that is not a sign, for a characteristic feature of Guido (his belief in the 'vile of life') that requires no reading, no interpretation, and which is therefore outside 'representation'; but the 'black mark' is figurative, without literal referent, gaining its meaning entirely through its absorption into the Pope's discourse. Later Guido parodies the whole idea of a supernatural mark, mocking the sign that requires no reading through the 'brand' which was 'burned' on his brow (XI.502-5).

The poem thus enacts an epistemological critique which becomes, paradoxically, the necessary means towards discerning any truth at all, and that because those means are inseparable, as Browning suggests, from any resulting end of meaning or truth. The poem seems to urge the need, epistemologically speaking, for the Pope's 'terrible choice' – not the discernment of absolute or grounded knowledge and meaning, but the awesome choice between plausible alternatives, a judgement of 'worth of word'. What the poem also urges is the recognition that any such decision or perception is based on nothing more than its own 'present light'. No judgement (including this one) escapes the conditions and processes of its own enactment.

VI

In book XII, the voice of the observing poet reappears in order to show how the events have disappeared into time: 'The act, over and ended, falls and fades' (XII.13). It might be thought that with this fading we at last approach the 'eventual unity', but there is no more a unity of perspective in book XII than there is throughout the poem. The method introduced in book I of textual version succeeding textual version is continued even in the final book through a series of letters and citations and citations within citations that demonstrate the disappearance of the Franceschini murder into a maze of successive texts and statements. Any singular truth remains as unstated as ever, with the exception of the truth about what was clear from the start – the 'restitution' of Pompilia's 'perfect fame' (XII.757). This truth nevertheless remains textualised, recorded and cited as the court's verdict from the trial brought by the Convertites, and approved by the poet: 'Justice done a second time!' (768).

In the concluding section, however, the poet-speaker does claim for art, for aesthetic discourse, the ability to transcend its linguistic limits and convey a truth that escapes the 'mediate word' (XII.861). In introducing this claim he repeats Celestino's admonishment about human falsehood as the lesson of the poem: 'our human speech is naught,/Our human testimony false, our fame/ And human estimation words and wind' (XII.838–40). Like Celestino's text about God's truth, this comment is also a version of Zeno's paradox: while overtly emphasising falsehood as the condition of human utterance, the poet is covertly claiming the opposite – this statement about falsehood is a 'truth' about human speech. But how does *this* 'estimation' escape being merely 'words and wind'? Is it not 'human'?

The poet seeks to escape the limits of human speech by privileging aesthetic production: 'it is the glory and good of Art,/That Art remains the one way possible/Of speaking truth' (842–4). Art is artifice, a medium which foregrounds its own falsehood. But that is the poet's point: 'falsehood' does 'the work of truth'; 'Art may tell a truth/Obliquely, do the thing shall breed the thought', miss 'the mediate word' and so escape misrepresentation, not 'wrong the thought' (857–61). Browning here affirms a 'thought' that is outside discourse, 'missing the mediate word', and points to meaning that is outside representation, to the painting's truth that is 'Beyond' mere imagery (863) and the book's meaning that is 'beyond' the facts (866).

However, in context, to tell a truth 'obliquely' means not to address any defined or specific auditor ('men'), but to address only readers in general ('mankind'). The poet's text, like all language, functions without the presence of author or specified reader; by not being addressed or bound to any particular reader, it yet sustains a meaning that is available for all readers.[35] In this sense meaning may indeed escape the 'mediate word' which is part of the production of meaning by any singular author or reader. But if meaning eludes the production of any single reading, it is never fully available. Since no reader can read as 'mankind', just as no metatext can escape the limits of its textuality, truth is always oblique, never totally present.

What Browning's conclusion amounts to, then, is another paradox, for while he defers to truth, he refers it back to falsehood, to the only place where truth can be located, the poem itself. *He* too may 'write a book shall mean beyond the facts' and thereby claim a meaning outside discourse, a logocentric truth, but that meaning is never directly stated and, according to his own terms, cannot be, for if it were, it would merely appear false and unrecognisable. The speaker in book XII has just explained how the attempt to tell someone he is wrong will fail, for the 'truth . . . when it reaches him, looks false' (854). Language alters during its transmission: once the speaker's words are reappropriated by the listener, their meaning or 'truth' is changed, no longer 'recognizable by whom it left'. Better, the speaker affirms, to have employed 'falsehood', which 'would have done the work of truth' (856–7). Meaning is unfixed, tied to the falsehood of its medium. Any meaning that is 'beyond the facts' is therefore continually deferred, always to be referred back to the text which tells its truth 'obliquely' and always waiting to be stated in some indeterminate future. Once again truth, meaning, is continually present and continually absent, available 'some day', not 'now'.

The poet's statements in book XII, like any other part of the poem, remain bound to their context. In claiming a truth beyond mediate words and imagery on walls, they cannot step outside the medium of their own figuration; their meaning is always to be located back within the text itself and its processes, where 'falsehood' does 'the work of truth'. The poem is about signification, about establishing meaning and truth – 'Truth must prevail, the proverb vows' (I.413). But signification is a process of active making, where the individual sign, like the individual speaker, is a passing locus within a sequence and fluid structure of other signs and speakers. Specific claims may be made for a fixed truth, but they will be 'Life cramped corpse-fashion' (I.1360) and inevitably succeeded by other texts, other claims.

Consequently, as the poem returns, in its concluding lines, to the image of the ring with which it began, the reader is returned to figuration and textuality – in terms both of the ring as a symbol for the book, and of the ring as a figure for process and production. We are returned also to figuration that points both ways, both back towards and further beyond its own discourse. The poet's final play with the ring image (869–74) both refers back to the poem which has produced it – and thence to the creative process and textual shape that it came to designate in book I – and simultaneously extends the image out of the poem into texts and rings beyond, into the poetic texts by Tommasie and Elizabeth Barrett which link Italy and England. The poem's imagery thus gestures towards further texts, with their literal and figurative meanings, their play also with ring imagery, and towards further contexts, the rings on Elizabeth's finger and the physical lands of Italy and England.

Insofar as books I and XII frame the poem, they connect not just to the picture but also to the world, diffusing distinctions between inside and outside. We never leave the process of language; it is simply extended into other representations that differentiate historical and geographical reality. There is no end, no moment of transcendence when text and context are eluded, only the impasse of metaclaims (including the poem's own metaclaims about itself as art) whose meaning is produced by the discourse which they purport to stand outside.

6
The Politics of Self in *The Ring and the Book*

I

To embrace the textualising of truth in *The Ring and the Book* is to render problematic the concept of an unconstituted world. Equally problematic in the poem is the concept of an unconstituted subject, that sense of a separate self-presence that is so beloved of Romantic lyricism and post-Cartesian humanism – an independent and ordering consciousness, an individuality which transcends material mutability, the real self. In *The Ring and the Book*, the self, like the world, is textualised, written into and through the structures of language.

Through the same process of textualising that subverts the human dream of a metatextual truth, Browning offers a remarkable and vital shift in dramatic focus. He transforms traditional dramatic metaphors of human experience, with their focus on human action within an external cosmic plot ('all the world's a stage') and their assumptions of an originating, authenticating playwright outside the play, into a drama metaphor which ties histrionic action to discourse: 'Let this old woe step on the stage again! . . . by voices we call evidence' (I.824–33). The events of the 'old woe' will be restaged, not as sensible phenomena which can be judged by 'sense and sight', but as discourse, as 'voices we call evidence'. The poem provides not direct action or an originating event, but 'Uproar in the echo', not experience as 'live fact', but experience as representation, 'live fact' as it is 'whispered away' (I.834–5).[1] Browning's transformation of dramatic structure thus links 'character' to utterance, to the fluid conceptualising of language process.

For speakers to be speakers ('voices'), they must enter the double process of discourse, becoming 'characters' who both act and are acted. They act through the production of their own rhetoric and they are acted upon by the language (public and institutional) which structures their conceptualising. Hence the drama of voices becomes an interaction of personally assigned concept and socially produced image. And the relationship between self and other is dialectical, a continuing process of weaving and transformation, definition and dissolution. It is a process which characterises the fundamental drama of selfhood in a post-Romantic context – Pater's 'continual vanishing away, that strange, perpetual weaving and unweaving of ourselves'.[2]

The creation of a self-conscious identity that is often hailed as the hallmark of Browning's poetry is not a creation that achieves grounding or self-presence through the structural powers of poetic language, but, on the contrary, it is released into and through the very groundlessness of discourse, its qualities of shifting evanescence. A dialectic of self and other binds the transcendent ego to the conditions of consciousness as writing. Through this fusion of idealist concept and material medium, psychic action and literary action coincide as dramatic staging, as a 'theatre of writing' (see Chapter 2, n. 24).

The image of the stage recurs throughout *The Ring and the Book* and it underpins a general sense of life as a theatrical performance, whether as the literal display of corpses for public edification, or as rhetorical action, deployed for a variety of purposes – the instruction of the court, the advancement of careers, the salvation of the soul, the protection of property, the saving of a life. In this context the main form of enactment is narration – the self as its narrative version of the Guido story. Each speaker exhibits in varying degrees the classic desire described by Paul Ricoeur to establish identity through telling one's own story.[3] Not only do speakers appropriate others in their versions, therefore, but they reappropriate themselves, enacting themselves on the plane of expression, performing themselves in a theatre of writing.

A crucial feature of the metaphor of the theatre, however, is the dimension of temporality which incorporates the continuing sense of incompletion that is attached to the concepts of truth and meaning. For the self this means that there is no governing principle of consciousness which establishes a necessary order or control. The subject, as known, is inseparable from the transient and externalised quality of duration.[4] Just as there is no longer the dramatic guarantee of a divinity who underwrites social and universal action, ensuring causal explanation and the structure of role definitions,[5] so on the psychic level there is no guarantee of the separate self, authenticating judgement or discerning truth.[6]

From this process there emerge two conflicting versions of identity: the self-as-product, created as a fixed, established identity, whether by society or by God, and the self-as-process, a subject tied to the fluid and elusive medium of discourse. Speakers exist within the demands and structures of both these versions; they escape neither, being produced within a dialectic of what Loy Martin has called the person-as-thing and the person-as-process (Martin, p. 106). This dialectic focuses the fusion of psychic action and literary production (writing). The need for emotional security and social acceptance (which in this context also means legal judgement) leads to the structured illusion of a fixed self, a defined identity with an assigned social status and recognition. But the Romantically induced need to internalise that self, a self which is not defined merely by role externals, leads also to expression, to utterance, to the 'voice' which is an elusive effect of linguistic structuring and process. As Nietzsche observed, it is not the 'product' of discourse which is the sign of the self; it is rather the shifting process itself, the ongoing action of speaking or writing.[7] Attempts, then, to represent the ineffable self, to claim what Guido calls 'some nucleus that's myself' (XI.2395), or to attain the psychic rewards of the *cogito*, founder upon the inevitable process and estrangement of discourse.

It is the brilliance of Browning's art in *The Ring and the Book* to show that the claims of personal witness, of the internalised truth of a 'sincere' voice, are inseparable from the processes of their production (see Chapter 5). In this way Browning throws out a challenge to any assumption about the equation of truth or authority with an internalised centre of self. By providing a series of 'voices' which appears to relate 'truth' to an array of centres of being, he disrupts attempts to locate truth in any single centre. That readers still attempt to identify such a location is testimony to the power of Romantic rhetoric and Cartesian thinking; it is also testimony to the force of the desire for univocal meaning which persists within and through, as well as against, the structuring principles of the poem itself. The diffusion of centrality through a multiplicity of narrators does not mean that separate speakers do not act as if they are their own centres of truth. Indeed, that is their very purpose. A feature of the drama within this poem's theatre of writing (a feature of Browning's monologues generally) is the continual struggle by speakers against the forces of dissipation. Speakers desire to fix themselves in their speech; they need to affirm the truth of their self and version.

The desire for self-affirmation also produces a domain where psychic and rhetorical action is inevitably political. In their effort to assert self-presence and truth, speakers direct their speech outwards, only to encounter other discourses – the forces of law, church, class, gossip, anecdote, social myth-making. In this context, personal desire, whether defining itself against or through these external structures, is itself a social force, a social action that necessarily involves other people (both literally and conceptually). Hence the monologues enact political selves, selves who represent relationships with others in order to affirm their own power and place, in order to attain the possession and status that would be the sign of a substantive identity. The politics of self in *The Ring and the Book* is thus an exercise in ordering – in control, representation and survival (both physical and psychological). Its politics of personal power is enacted through a dialectic of self and other; its key features are narrative representation and conceptual possession (or, what amounts to the same thing, identification).

In what follows I shall largely focus on the three protagonists in order to suggest how speakers are structured in terms of institutional and social discourse, how they become attached to the terms and binarisms of these structures, and how their claims to an essential self rest upon an interdependence of self and other. The language of their self-affirming politics is dynamic and dialectical. In this language, the opposites which define identity and the appropriations which establish personal power dissolve into the incompletion of voices whose unity or fixity remains an elusive hypothesis – a fiction of possibility, postponed, deferred.

II

The middle monologues of the three protagonists (books V–VII) repeat strategies in striking ways. Each speaker establishes an early identity in terms of family and social context; each suffers a crisis when that externalised identity proves not to be stable or permanently sustaining; each responds by identifying with various forms of institutional discourse. Each is alert to the possibilities allowed by ambiguous language; each affirms the importance of correctly reading signs. Each monologue deploys passages of rhetorical passivity; each speech dramatises the distinction between the narrated and the narrating self, between the self-as-product, produced through the narrative, and the self-as-process, producing the narrative. Such repetition enhances the impression of a series of mutable selves, all subject to the same potential ambiguities of need and intent regardless of their claimed innocence – Pompilia no less than the others.

Guido's monologue in book V is the first to challenge fully the concept of a fixed self. Like both Caponsacchi and Pompilia who follow, he begins by establishing his identity in terms of family status. Starting from this socially defined self, all three seek to establish a 'real' and separate self which is morally justified.

Guido attempts to do this by attaching himself to external structures, claiming a legitimacy through doing his duty, performing the actions required by his environment – from the duties of eldest son, which prevented him from entering a profession, to the socially imposed demands of *honoris causa* and the cosmically imposing task of acting as an agent for divine good, stamping out evil. Throughout this process, Guido continually presents himself as a passive victim, moulded by circumstances and therefore not responsible for his actions. At times these stances contradict each other, as, for example, when the irrational violence of stamping blindly on 'earth-worms' and 'asp' (V.1667–9) is at odds with the reasoned purpose of performing God's will (V.1702–3). But inconsistency is of little consequence provided the general position of non-responsible action is maintained.

Guido depicts himself as a martyr, then, to his social roles. He was the son who must marry and the cleric who followed the church in humble obedience:

> You know the courses I was free to take?
> I took just that which let me serve the church,
> I gave it all my labour in body and soul
> Till these broke down i' the service.
> (1791–4)

This image is fostered through relating himself to a variety of social discourses: he identifies with the church (as Christ-like martyr), with class (as aristocrat), with the patriarchy (as husband, eldest son and father), with commerce (as both consumer and producer). Thus he becomes, as he might like to claim, absorbed into discourse, textually appropriated. His status as husband, for example, is the 'Text whereon friendly censors burst to preach' (569). As his life takes on public and linguistic existence, its meaning becomes tied, he insinuates, to the symbolic order of his society's ruling institutions. Hence his very birth becomes a signifier within an economy of social value: 'Honour of birth, – /If that thing has no value', and cannot be traded, then the 'social fabric' collapses 'like a house of cards' (439–45). Social and moral order become equated, consequently, with a patriarchal honour that can be fully realised only when husbands are 'once more God's representative' (2043). Hence his effort to restore his honour makes him 'law's mere executant!', the court's 'own defender' (2003–4). Since the structures which give him definition are imperative to the well-being and security of society, it was his institutional (spiritual, moral and legal) as well as personal duty to punish Pompilia when she threatened these structures by leaving her marriage and 'seducing' a cleric.

Although his manipulation of strategies, obvious role-playing and savage vindictiveness provoke easy condemnation, he nevertheless has a point: his identity in this monologue is shaped by social structures, and Pompilia's flight, even if deliberately provoked by him, deeply threatens the identity he received from those structures. He is indeed an eldest son who was manipulated by his brother and by the force of idle gossip. Brought up with expectations that his finances could not support, he suffered the sneers of his father's servants. He can reasonably claim that the law about marriage led him to expect 'loyalty and obedience': 'Father and mother shall the woman leave', and 'Cleave to the husband, be it for weal or woe' (578–82). There may be no moral mitigation, but there is a structural point to Guido's claims, therefore, which is commensurate with his image as passive agent. His technique throughout is to imply that he is merely an agent for other forces, and that the self which is separate from action, the 'real' self, should not be held responsible for the iniquities of those forces. He was merely doing his duty – the joint duty of the man of honour and the man of God.

At the same time Guido also faces something of a continuing crisis, since the structures which give him identity never fully compensate for a sense of deprivation and lack of recognition. Indeed the very expectations which they generate simply serve to emphasise all the more his inadequacies and powerlessness. He drifts aimlessly through poverty-stricken circumstances, never quite succeeding through attachments to church or society affairs. The attempt to retrieve security through the institution of marriage fails, the law fails to retrieve any respect, and in the present speech he throws himself on the mercy of the court in terms of the class unity that is necessary to sustain the hegemony. This too will fail, leading to his final crisis of identification that is enacted in book XI.

Guido's strategy in book V of continually relating himself to social structures means that he maintains an externalised identity. Caponsacchi and Pompilia, on the other hand, through identifying themselves with idealist religious discourse, develop the sense of an internalised centre of being. That is a strategy which Guido later attempts in book XI, when the failure of his institutional definitions provokes the flaunting of an essential self made by God.

Caponsacchi's monologue is characterised by a narrative which continually produces a distinction between the narrated and the narrating selves and by an idealist discourse which structures Pompilia and Guido as moral absolutes. The narrative represents Caponsacchi as a product of growth and spiritual transformation, a transformation that was wrought by the saint-like influence of Pompilia. The implicit result is a self whose purity of intention establishes his own and Pompilia's innocence against Guido's guilt. This self is the subject of the enounced, produced by Caponsacchi's narrative of his past; this, in his eyes, is the authentic self who believed in Pompilia's spiritual value – the Caponsacchi of virtuous action and idealist intention. This self-as-product, or person-as-thing, is disrupted, however, by the aggressive rhetoric of the self as the producer of the present speech – the subject of the enunciation. This is the self whose desires and emotions slide through representations, the self who feels his failure and physical limits. This self intrudes to explain his intentions, to disrupt the narrative, to worry about its effects on his audience, to satirise their past attitudes towards him, to challenge popular and therefore vulgar representations of his relationship with Pompilia. This is the person-as-process who continually slips away, being arrested only by the dualistic cry of the last line: 'O great, just, good God! Miserable me!'

The drama of self in Caponsacchi's monologue is thus enacted on two levels – the drama of his past stages of transition and moral conscience, and the present wrestle with the reconstruction of that past. In the *past* he was appropriated by other roles or discourses.

In the *present* the subject of the enunciation detaches itself from the version constructed by the court, satirising their earlier perception of his role as the coxcomb priest. These two dramatic levels are at the same time interdependent. The present circumstances do not merely frame the narrative, providing some sort of detached boundary in order to define the central narrative (and self), but the present act of speaking is integral to the method (and content) of the narrative, and the narrative impinges upon the responses and attitudes effected by the present speech.[8]

This double drama of the self helps to explain the curious contradiction between aggressive rhetoric and passive action in the monologue. Caponsacchi's address to the court is riddled with harsh invective against Guido and sharp admonishment of the court members for their previous leniency towards Guido; yet Caponsacchi's much vaunted heroism in aiding Pompilia's escape is a series of passive responses rather than positive or self-determined action.[9] Like Guido's version of his passive action after Christmas when he strangely 'did find' himself at the Comparini villa (V.1624), Caponsacchi's responses are transformed by an invading force, and variously he 'found' himself at the theatre (VI.395) or at the front of his church, the Pieve (VI.974–5). As it is presented, the process of Caponsacchi's past transformation is a passive one, but his present mood is aggressive and angry as he confronts his failure to save Pompilia's life. Telling his story is more, therefore, than simply a chance to set the record straight; he desires urgently to affirm *his* truth: 'I need that you should know my truth' (VI.342).

This desire leads Caponsacchi to assert his authority against that of the court. Against their earlier patronising and institutional ambivalence, he places the authenticity of personal experience. When he saw Pompilia directly, for instance, he announces that he was witness to his own self-affirmed truth:

> Pompilia spoke, and I at once received,
> Accepted my own fact, my miracle
> Self-authorized and self-explained . . .
> (VI.918–20)

Yet private authority of this sort cannot produce external or separate evidence to establish its reliability. As a *known* authority, it has no independent status, being open to the charge of solipsism.

The Politics of Self in The Ring and the Book 157

Caponsacchi prevents this accusation by claiming a mutual understanding with Pompilia, but that understanding still depends upon reading signs, as he reports:

> 'As I
> 'Recognized her, at potency of truth,
> 'So she, by the crystalline soul, knew me,
> 'Never mistook the signs.'
> (931–4)

It also depends upon correct interpretation, so that personal experience is entered into discourse as 'fact' and 'miracle', where the juxtaposition of these contradictory terms (terms from different discourses) emphasises their rhetorical function. Within the subjectivity of Caponsacchi's discourse, such opposites absorb each other – the miracle and fact are both *his*, given meaning only within his context – and the dialectical blurring adds rhetorical power to his speech. In similar fashion, recognition and knowing within his discourse are associated with the value-terms of 'truth' and 'soul'. Hence he can later admonish the court for not reading the signs accurately: 'Could you fail read this cartulary aright/On head and front of Franceschini there . . . ?' (1792–3).

But signs are discourse-dependent, often ambiguous, and open to misinterpretation, as Caponsacchi himself urges: Margherita, the 'mistress-messenger', was an agent who 'put her sense into my words', he declares (VI.1803–9). Indeed, Caponsacchi is himself clearly alert to the multiple possibilities of meaning. His defence in the earlier trial was largely based upon alternative readings (1646–1706), and his replies to Guido's letters were openly ambiguous. He claims his purpose was the exposure of fraud, but he is always subject to the objection of the court: what if the letters *were* written by Pompilia? His response is to imply his own purity of intent by attacking the moral condition of those who question spiritual truth: he would reply to a verger's accusation that a scorpion came from the Madonna's mouth by turning it back upon the verger – any reptile came rather from the verger's own dung (667–76). But by attacking the intention of others, he does not clear the ambiguities of his own intention. Indeed his intentions as represented in the text of his letters to 'Guido/Pompilia' were invariably uncertain, so that his claimed innocence rests upon a mixture of *argumentum ad hominem* and self-approving rhetoric.

That rhetoric is largely based upon the claims of natural truth (in interpreting the 'mystery of this murder', he will 'condense/The voice o' the sea and wind'; 72-4) and the language of religious idealism, so that his affirmation of an authentic personal truth is given authority by its attachment to an absolutist rhetoric of good and evil.

Caponsacchi's account of his family context (220-67) shows that his identity as priest was as much an imposed or inherited identity ('Was made expect, from infancy almost,/The proper mood o' the priest') as Guido's identity as eldest son. It is not to be mistaken for any true or natural self. When Caponsacchi showed scruples about entering the church, balking at the required speech act of the vow, he was reassured by the Bishop's soothing rhetoric which showed him that language could be employed for social and institutional purposes without a referential truth – it is merely a matter of substituting one term for another, as the Jews do in order to pronounce the name of their God without actually naming Him (280-9). It is a crucial initiation since it enters Caponsacchi into an institutional structure where language enacts a social fiction, where he is appropriated by the empty formalism of belief without the need for externalised action. As Kris Davis observes, the Bishop 'resolves the gap between the actual and ideal self by denying the ideal'; the Bishop wants the world for the church rather than to take the church to the world (Davis, 58). What is required of Caponsacchi is a double role whereby he plays both priest and man, courting women so that the church might benefit from their wealth and influence. Caponsacchi, then, like Guido, began life as a social identity, as much a puppet of his family background and church as Guido was of his class and patriarchal status. Caponsacchi, however, despite his absorption in the church's duplicitous role-playing, sustains his sense of difference. He rests uneasy in the irony of a discourse that denies the ideal: 'Sir, what if I turned Christian? It might be./The fact is, I am troubled in my mind' (474-5).

After three or four years of empty formalism, Caponsacchi is ready to reinstate an actualised ideal, to embrace some idealised content, and that moment arrives after he sees Pompilia at the theatre. He seizes her image as an abstraction composed of three terms – beautiful, sad and strange – which are repeated compulsively (399, 412, 436, 493), and he responds to her as to a portrait of the Madonna:

> there at the window stood,
> Framed in its black square length, with lamp in hand,
> Pompilia; the same great, grave griefful air
> As stands i' the dusk, on altar that I know,
> Left alone with one moonbeam in her cell,
> Our Lady of all the Sorrows.
>
> (702–7)

Thus his increasingly idealising discourse structures Pompilia as the ideal woman of his church's celibate system, internalising her image as an abstraction, appropriating it as an absolute. The Madonna image provides the love and sexual role for a celibate male – the woman as icon, unavailable sexually and to be worshipped as an internalised other – and embedded in this role is a covert form of self-sacrifice, since in worshipping an unattainable ideal the male must relinquish any fulfilment of personal desire. As a priest, his bride is the church – he pledged to fold his warm heart on the church's 'heart of stone' (979). Yet Pompilia's role as actualised ideal threatens to dissolve the dualistic separation between ideal and real in a way other than the church intended, and Caponsacchi awakens to a form of passion that leads him into conflict over the appropriate action for Christian self-sacrifice.

Through the inspiration of Pompilia, he submits to a transformation of awareness whose dynamic process again conflates opposites ('outside air' and 'inside weight', death and life, harm and wisdom, felicity and annoyance, bitter and sweet) and enters him into 'another state, under new rule' (947–65). The culmination of this process is to produce an ecstasy of spiritual transport, an idealist celebration of timelessness and transcendence. His language employs the conventions of idealised naturalness – the 'nakedness' of primal innocence and the 'shame' which in a fallen world is a sign of conscious virtue; yet neither does it escape its material forms, effecting the barely suppressed 'bitter-sweet' desire of a sexual excitement whose 'proper throe' and 'thrill' may 'outthrob pain':

> the initiatory pang approached,
> Felicitous annoy, as bitter-sweet
> As when the virgin-band, the victors chaste,
> Feel at the end the earthly garments drop,
> And rise with something of a rosy shame

Into immortal nakedness: so I
Lay, and let come the proper throe would thrill
Into the ecstasy and outthrob pain.
(966–73)

So far the church has encouraged Caponsacchi to sustain such ambiguities – he 'both read the breviary/And wrote the rhymes' (344–5). It promoted a dalliance with women, replacing liturgical form with social form: better to 'teach a black-eyed novice cards/Than gabble Latin' (992–3). But Pompilia raises the possibility of actualising an idealised passion, and the church must recall him to his priestly commitment. He discovers that a worship whose form is self-sacrifice makes passion his indisputable mistress (996–9), and the problem is to decide which mistress is to be his master – the church or Pompilia, the spirit or the flesh. And in reminding him of his marriage to 'the mystic love/O' the Lamb' (977–8), the church renders the choice a dualistic alternative. Caponsacchi likens the moment to discovering the richest prize in paradise, the 'apple's self', which makes Pompilia both what he states, 'the thing of perfect gold', and what he suppresses, the forbidden fruit of sexual experience; but that moment of discovery brings a simultaneous awareness of 'the seven-fold dragon's watch' (1002–9). Hence he is led into conflict over obedience.

Having become dissatisfied with an institution that has separated the ideal from the actual, Caponsacchi responds to this conflict between dead church and live passion by transforming passion into an agency for spirit, the potentially physical mistress into an agency for the spiritual Master: 'She it is bids me bow the head: how true,/I am a priest!' (1017–18). In this way he revitalizes his moral identity by attaching it to images of absolute purity – Madonna/Pompilia and God/church – and by identifying with their spiritual level: 'I said/"We two are cognisant o' the Master now"' (1015–16). The result is an idealist discourse which defines Pompilia and Guido in terms of moral absolutes: Pompilia is 'The glory of life, the beauty of the world,/The splendour of heaven' (118–19), or 'The snow-white soul that angels fear to take/Untenderly' (195–6), and Guido is 'the miscreate . . . A spittle wiped off from the face of God' (1478–9), the 'cockatrice' who is one with the 'basilisk', Judas Iscariot (1938–50).

Caponsacchi's life is rescued from futility and moral vacuity by the Pompilia/Madonna figure, and yet he does not emerge content. Apart from his general passivity which meant that it was Pompilia who played the cavalier, not himself, and that he did not finally succeed in saving her, his idealising of her at least maintains the affair's religious value, but the conception produces an absolutism that carries the price of psychological division. His conclusion, for instance, that 'Duty to God is duty to her' leads him to sacrifice desire to the priestly passivity of non-action, but the desire remains, the signs of which Pompilia is clearly able to read:

> 'Why delay help, your own heart yearns to give?
> 'You are again here, in the self-same mind,
> 'I see here, steadfast in the face of you, –
> 'You grudge to do no one thing that I ask.'
> (1067–70)

Caponsacchi is aware that his passions are aroused, but the sexual element of this arousal is sublimated within the iconography of the Virgin and transformed through the language of faith. I have already indicated the example from his passage of moral transformation, but there is a further illustration of the process when the idea of lying with Pompilia is fantasised as an image of two martyrs awaiting the call of the last trumpet in their tomb (1183–92): 'in safety and not fear,/I lie, because she lies too by my side'.[10] He adds, as if to avoid other readings, and yet thereby acknowledging their possibility, 'You know this is not love, Sirs, – it is faith,/The feeling that there's God, he reigns and rules' (1193–4). Through the whole process, Caponsacchi is led into continual play with a passion that divides into the spiritually unattainable and the physically hopeless. He can readily imagine an alternative life lived with Pompilia, but it is merely a dream (2081–97), from which, like a student from visions of Greek and Roman history, he can awaken and 'pass content' (2104). But there is no content. His religious idealism produces a double disappointment. He is given identity by his idealist discourse, but it also condemns him to the insoluble conflicts of a terrible dualism – the division between an unattainable absolute and the suffering victim of finite and material process: 'O great, just, good God! Miserable me!'

If there is no contentment for Caponsacchi, neither is there any resolution into a unified self. Even in a moment of apparently self-determined presence and defiance, when he spurns the court's judgement and gives up all claims to institutional identity (1860–80), he nevertheless exists in terms of Pompilia. His flaunting of the vulgar view that 'The priest's in love' is placed within the context of the liturgical statement of Pompilia's 'revelation', and his rejection of the institutional church as containing 'a crack somewhere' is still given definition and force by his claim that the saintly Pompilia should have churches built for *her*. His rejection of the church authorities is based upon his perception of her as saint and Madonna, as an object worthy of true worship. His stance is never separate, therefore, from his absorption of Pompilia into his self-definition. His spiritual survival has depended on his possession of a purified and idealised image which meant the metaphorical death of her independent reality. Nor is this simply an act of aggressive seizure, but an interactive combination of possession and being possessed. Pompilia possesses him – she reads his intention and admonishes his inaction – and in that act he gains moral and spiritual definition. Ironically, it is Pompilia's real death at the hands of Guido that allows Caponsacchi to enact a more assertive self as confirmation of his identity, since under these circumstances he can possess her image utterly, without contradiction (the court no longer challenges his view). Thereby he sustains both their identities – hers as saint and his as self-sacrificing worshipper (it is not difficult psychologically to give up his role as priest, since his definition in terms of Pompilia is independent of his institutional status).

Caponsacchi's consciousness is therefore never singular, but always doubled, always subject to the invasion or influence of outside rhetoric, just as his moment of personal truth was a moment of *mutual* recognition: 'As I/Recognized her ... /So she ... knew me' (931–3). When he challenges the court to unfrock him (1860–80), he appears to dramatise the self as its own agent, as an independent, authentic consciousness. But, as argued, the self as agent is in this passage a double agent; it acts for the self as other (Pompilia/Madonna) as much as for the self as itself. It is perhaps in moments of greatest intensity – the ritual transformation, the flaunting of the vulgar view of love, the cursing of Guido and its ensuing self-rebuke – that the dialectic of self and other shows most plainly. In such moments the other (Pompilia) displaces the speaker as centre, displaying the heterogeneity of reflection and self-reflection. Caponsacchi's response to the crisis of identity that is provoked by his involvement with Pompilia is not resolved in this monologue, despite his claims to being transformed through her saintly influence, and despite his final claim of passing 'content' from communion with his dream of a life with her. The monologue remains a weaving without totality precisely because being structured within the terms of a dualism which defines value by opposition produces a self that is divided.

III

I have been suggesting that the idealised figure of Pompilia functions in Caponsacchi's monologue to fulfil the speaker's own psychic need. This function repeats that of the earlier, more secular, portrait of her in book III, where Other Half Rome, a sentimental bachelor steeped in the traditions of literary romance, appropriates her as ideal Woman – fragile, passive, innocent, intuitive. These images, which precede Pompilia's own monologue, seem to have predetermined its critical reception.[11] But Pompilia's monologue contains its own ambiguities. She too is produced in terms of a conflict between external structures and an internalised identity based upon religious discourse.

It is notable that Pompilia's initial strategies of self-definition are identical to those of Guido and Caponsacchi: she defines herself in terms of external contexts and claims that her actions were the result of external forces, not of her own volition: 'I started up, was pushed, I dare to say' (VII.1407). Before her marriage, she is a pawn in the play of her adoptive mother and her manipulating future brother-in-law, a 'lamb' which allows itself to be 'clipped' (VII.387–8). After her marriage, she discovers that she is at the mercy of social institutions – marriage, class and church – all of which demand that she submit to the requirements of her husband. Pompilia is thus appropriated by external role requirements – just as God, according to the Archbishop of Arezzo, appropriated Eve in His plan for human procreation (VII.758–68). She begins, then, by uttering the facts of her existence: her age, her name, her marriage and the birth of her child. They are established truths ('All these few things/I know are true'; 35–6) because they are written down, recorded in the church register – the last, the birth of Gaetano, she hopes will be added when they record her death. These are not the truths of an internalised subject, but the truths of historical and social record; she is a series of entries in a book, to which she adds the facts of her murder: 'twenty-two dagger wounds,/Five deadly' (38–9).

The simple directness of Pompilia's manner in these opening lines is typical of a speech that is relatively unadorned – it is perhaps the least rhetorically dense of the monologues. Yet Pompilia's stress on what is 'writ' (3, 8) includes an awareness of the problems of representation. Almost immediately, she notes the incongruities even in this starkly reduced record as she dismisses the long list of six names for 'one poor child' as 'laughable!' (5–7). And the second long section of her monologue is largely concerned with how she will be perceived by her son – that is, with how she will be represented to him (41–107). She even incorporates her inability to write as part of the pathos that she cannot provide her own version of herself, and she is clearly aware that any statement of fact is discrepant with a more subjective truth – if Gaetano were told that his mother was 'Like girls of seventeen', he would think of girls 'who titter or blush', whereas Pompilia prefers to think that she 'looked already old though [she] was young', nearer twenty even (64–75). These discrepancies and Pompilia's awareness of them introduce an incongruity that functions throughout – between the simplicity of the 'few things' that are (literally) 'true' and the sophistication of Pompilia's subjectivity that is alert to the ironies of representation.[12] Already in the opening passages is a potential separation of external fact from internal representation that becomes increasingly apparent as the monologue progresses.[13]

The monologue exhibits a contention between appropriation by external role requirements and a response to those requirements which withdraws into its own internalised domain, an idealist realm that is authenticated and mediated through religious language. While Pompilia's role as victim governs her character as the product of her narrative (the person-as-thing), what dominates her consciousness as the speaking subject (the person-as-process) is the crisis brought about when the external certainties of her existence prove to be illusions, when the objective facts of her world dissolve into what seems 'Sheer dreaming and impossibility' (112).

There is a considerable irony in Pompilia's beginning with the facts of her existence – facts which are established through the discourse of historical and social record, the facts of being born, named, married and giving birth, the roles of daughter, wife, mother – since everything that seems substantial in her life fades and disappears. Her parents are suddenly no longer her parents; her husband is not what everyone told her to expect of a husband ('Every one says that husbands love their wives,/Guard them and guide them, give them happiness'; 152–3); her 'friend' is transformed into 'lover' through an array of gossip ('men will not ask about,/But tell untruths of, and give nicknames to'; 160–1); and finally her child is taken from her, so that 'even he withdraws into a dream/As the rest do' (213–14). Pompilia is made very aware that name and reality do not correspond; concepts, social formulas, turn out to be a series of nicknames, like the associations that Pompilia and Tisbe make as girls with the figures on a tapestry: 'You know the figures never were ourselves/Though we nicknamed them so' (197–8). Hence, Pompilia defines her existence as transient and insubstantial:

> Thus, all my life, –
> As well what was, as what, like this, was not, –
> Looks old, fantastic and impossible:
> I touch a fairy thing that fades and fades.
> (198–201)

Hence also, she is written into the separation of word and object, representation and reality: there is no reality, only a series of representations that fade and disappear.

It is no wonder, then, that she presents her experiences after her marriage as finally 'one blank . . . a terrific dream' (584–5). It is psychologically useful to represent what was already 'representation' as a dream, for in that form it can be emotionally absorbed. You can wake from a nightmare, she says, and after 'a few daylight doses of plain life', the horror is 'Gone!' (586–93). She says she now wakes from the nightmare of her dream, and to dismiss it as a dream that cannot be recalled is a way of handling pain and physical suffering. But she also moves increasingly to reject the real world and develop her own world of spiritual fantasy. Pompilia's politics of self involve the suppression of reality in order to survive internally – an understandable response in the context of suffering, death and institutional appropriation.

The few truths that sustain her 'amid the nothingness' (603–25) are her 'prayer' and its answering 'hope' for deliverance, and her 'fancy' (the signs of her pregnancy). Unlike the social truths with which she begins, these are personal truths, indicating the way her personal reality increasingly displaces social definition. After submitting sexually to her husband, for instance, and finding no change in his behaviour, she rejects any concern with physical appearance in order to focus solely on the idealism of spiritual truth:

> henceforth I looked to God
> Only, nor cared my desecrated soul
> Should have fair walls, gay windows for the world.
> God's glimmer, that came through the ruin-top,
> Was witness why all lights were quenched inside:
> Henceforth I asked God counsel, not mankind.
> (854–9)

She also claims God as her auditor, appropriating Him as her witness – 'I am speaking truth to the Truth's self:/God will lend credit to my words' (1198–9). And eventually she announces the preparation for death which culminates (somewhat necessarily in terms of her literal condition) the internalising process: 'I withdraw from earth and man/To my own soul, compose myself for God' (1769–70).

Notwithstanding this increasing withdrawal, Pompilia learns a great deal about the political realities of a patriarchal society and language. She learns that institutions that are supposedly devoted to moral and spiritual truth support class status and the male role in marriage – '"Since your husband bids,/Swallow the burning coal he proffers you!"' (729–30). She learns about the male double standard which turns blame back on women: how her real mother had to put up with 'every beast/O' the field' who cared to break the 'fountain-fence', turning the 'silver' into the 'mud' which was then blamed on Pompilia's mother – she was the cause, it is said, of the 'plashy pool' which 'Bequeathed turbidity and bitterness/To the daughter-stream where Guido dipt and drank!' (864–73). Pompilia also learns the epistemological lesson that sustains the whole poem, the lesson of difference: 'So we are made, such difference in minds,/Such difference too in eyes that see the minds!' Where she sees a 'dew-drop' in the 'crystal shrine' of Caponsacchi's glory, others 'descry a spider in the midst' (918–29). She understands the subjunctive mood of Don Celestino's psalm: 'Not "If wings fall from heaven, I fix them fast," – /Simply "How good it were to fly and rest" (994–5). And she understands the art of subterfuge: 'Life means with me successful feigning death,/Lying stone-like, eluding notice so' (1004–5). She recognises the paradox of human cognition, that 'such as are untrue/Could only take the truth in through a lie' (1196–7). She learns that words and referents are separate (she thought a cavalier, from the image in the tapestry, was a 'slim young man' with wings and sword, but the cavalier who came to see her was old, 'Hook-nosed and yellow'; 389–98), and that names can be appropriated – it was 'the name' of Caponsacchi, 'Not the man, but the name of him', that had been 'made/Into a mockery and disgrace' (1338–40). And she learns a crucial lesson about human politics: 'Prayers move God; threats, and nothing else, move men!' (1624). Despite, then, her psychological strategy of withdrawing into idealist discourse, there are other aspects to her speech which suggest considerable mental acuity, producing a monologue that is far from the language of a naive innocent.

Pompilia's discourse is also stylistically sophisticated – balanced phrasing, subtle irony, telling metaphor, astute quotations. This is not to suggest that she is a cunning verbal manipulator in the manner of Guido, but it is to observe that she does not avoid, any more than anyone else, the devices and ambiguities of language. She, like any speaker, is produced through her discourse, and she is as adept as anyone else at constructing a version which places herself in the best light. Her desire to internalise a spiritually idealised selfhood is clearly understandable, even necessary, in her circumstances. At the same time it is possible to wonder if her suppression of experience is occasionally too convenient. Certainly the dream effect – sometimes enhanced by lyrical descriptions, of the sun-suffused morning when she guessed she was pregnant, for instance – contrasts with her often acute perception and detailed memory of her interaction with the Archbishop, the Governor, Margherita and Caponsacchi. This is not to suggest that she is a spiritual fraud, but it is to suggest that her monologue is open to reading ambiguous intentions. Her overt intention, for instance, is to defend Caponsacchi: 'I will remember once more for his sake/The sorrow: for he lives and is belied' (944–5). Yet the very next line turns attention back to herself: 'Could he be here, how he would speak for me!' (946).[14] Her unannounced intention, therefore, is to reassure herself about her own qualifications for spiritual transfiguring, to develop a discourse which would allow her to affirm the logic of her own redemption: '*So* shall I have my rights in after-time' (1765; my italics).

The Christian lesson that suffering is God's testing-ground allows her to think of pain as the 'need extreme' which, once endured, will lead to God's intervention (1384–8). But more central to her desire to attain a transcendent peace (369–72) is her appropriation of Caponsacchi as the man who can read the signs, not merely of her salvation, but of her divinity, her saintliness. She prays that he might remain the guide to her special status:

> I did pray, do pray, in the prayer shall die,
> "Oh, to have Caponsacchi for my guide!"
> Ever the face upturned to mine, the hand
> Holding my hand across the world, – a sense
> That reads, as only such can read, the mark
> God sets on woman, signifying so
> She should – shall peradventure – be divine.
> (1495–1501)

Caponsacchi, with his 'face upturned', is clearly Pompilia's worshipper. God's sign is the 'mark' of divinity, and the shift from 'should' to 'shall' indicates the strength of her will to sainthood. She acknowledges the way Caponsacchi needs to interpret, even re-write, the 'print' that is dimmed by human weakness: he 're-writes/The obliterated charter, – love and strength/Mending what's marred' (1504–6). But she also hints at *his* saintliness, apologising if she misuses the term, and citing the external evidence of Don Celestino to sustain Caponsacchi's role as devotee in religious rather than courtly terms: '"So kneels a votarist ... worshipping the while,/By faith and not by sight"' (1506–10).

The higher Caponsacchi's spiritual status, presumably the more authoritative his responses and evidence. Later, for example, he is the 'angel' who 'saved' her, allowing her to announce a spiritual security – 'I am safe!' (1643) – and to claim her own transfigured status through a halo-like image of purity and circular completion:

> Others may want and wish, I wish nor want
> One point o' the circle plainer, where I stand
> Traced round about with white to front the world.
> (1644–6)

In the last lines, Caponsacchi is finally cast as God's agent, through whom God stoops in order to allow Pompilia to 'rise'. Her perception of Caponsacchi's responses, therefore, as verifying the sign of her divinity is crucial to the consummation of her discourse – to the confirmation of her spiritual identity in the form of an apotheosis which finally and literally severs the ideal from the actual. Through internalising Caponsacchi's image – 'He is still here, not outside with the world,/Here, here, I have him in his rightful place!' (1773-4) – Pompilia repeats the interdependence that was fundamental to Caponsacchi's sense of identity. As he absorbed her idealised image into his identity, so she in turn possesses his combined role – 'deliverer' (1409), 'votarist' (1506) and 'lover' (1786) – as fundamental to her need to believe in herself as one of God's chosen.

Less overtly, but equally an act of psychic absorption, Pompilia produces signs of her sainthood through appropriating the image of the Madonna. References to Mary and the claim that Gaetano is fatherless occur early in the monologue. In the opening passages, Pompilia stresses her role as mother – of the first 110 lines, 94 are effectively devoted to her having a child – and associates herself with a statue of the Virgin. She is no more like blushing teenagers 'Than the poor Virgin' who used to adorn her street-corner. The statue was only of 'Thin white glazed clay', but, says Pompilia, 'you pitied her the more' (75–81), exhibiting a clear sense of kinship with this image of unpretentious and fragile innocence. She also proclaims that Gaetano had no father, a point about which she is adamant as she shifts from the literal truth of not knowing his father to the entirely subjective proposition of his never having had a father:

> No father that he ever knew at all,
> Nor ever had – no, never had, I say!
> That is the truth . . .
> (91–3)

Later, she celebrates her sole possession of the child, glad that it 'was, is,/Will be [hers] only' (896–97), and the growing sense of her pregnancy is expressed as her guess that a 'star' would be born (1405), a star which then enacts the Christmas story:

> So did the star rise, soon to lead my step,
> Lead on, nor pause before it should stand still
> Above the House o' the Babe, – my babe to be . . .
> (1448–50)

With this last phrase, Christ's birth is equated with Gaetano's birth, putting Pompilia in the role of Mary. That role is eventually overt – 'This time I felt like Mary, had by babe/Lying a little on my breast like hers' (1692–3) – and while Pompilia can never literally claim Mary's virginity for herself (she admits that she submitted sexually on the advice of the Archbishop), she can claim that Guido never soiled the most valued level of her innocence: 'His soul has never lain beside my soul' (1733). Finally, her fatherless child, born of her love, becomes the evidence that she has fulfilled her task and earned her spiritual 'rights':

> My babe nor was, nor is, nor yet shall be
> Count Guido Franceschini's child at all –
> Only his mother's, born of love not hate!
> So shall I have my rights in after-time.
> (1762–5)

The Madonna image as a model for Pompilia is a contradiction in human terms. Yet it is given authority through the dualist discourse of Christian terminology, where flesh and spirit are separate, allowing Pompilia to avoid the contradiction of a mother who bears a child without a father by emphasising her virginity of soul (1733). In this way the model promotes a mode of idealist existence which Pompilia devoutly desires. Mary produced a child supposedly without intercourse, which is what Pompilia looks forward to in heaven, where the angels are 'man and wife at once/When the true time is' (1836–7). Caponsacchi may be the 'lover' of her 'life' (1786), but it is rather death that is the object of desire for Pompilia, not Caponsacchi, for in death she seeks an identity without division, an idealist resolution to the divisions of the *cogito*. In death there is only spirit.

Pompilia's language of consummation, where angels are both separate and united, may appear to present a dialectical vision of the unity that is difference:

> Be as the angels rather, who, apart,
> Know themselves into one, are found at length
> Married, but marry never, no, nor give
> In marriage.
> (1833–6)

But the point about her conception of heavenly marriage is that it proposes a marriage without marrying, knowledge without carnality. It remains, therefore, a vision produced by Pompilia's commitment to a subjectivist discourse. For her it is a consummation which will resolve her divisions and establish eternal peace, unlike Caponsacchi's tormented existence that remains defined by its separation from God. But that end is achieved through denying the physical, not by dissolving the dualism.

At the same time, within the monologue, the idealist content of the self as redeemed innocent remains a process of interdependence, a dialectic of self and other, as I have already suggested in terms of Pompilia's relationship with Caponsacchi. And it is a dialectic which incorporates Pompilia's husband as well as her rescuer. Guido contributes to her identity, as well as Caponsacchi. The politics of self for Pompilia mean that she achieves her confidence of spiritual power through a combination of absorption and negation. She absorbs the priest: the means by which God stoops that she might be raised. She negates her husband: the opposition against whose hatred she defines her love and saintlike tolerance – 'hate was thus the truth of him' (1727). As part of Pompilia's moral dualism, Guido is damned as not fit for God's presence: 'We shall not meet in this world nor the next', she announces (1719). But Guido's evil is the opposition that defines her saintly self-possession, so that her conceptual relationship with her husband is in practice a dialectic which perceives his ruinous touch as a means of salvation:

> Whatever he touched is rightly ruined: plague
> It caught, and disinfection it had craved
> Still but for Guido; I am saved through him
> So as by fire; to him – thanks and farewell!
> (1736–9)

Despite their proposed separation in heaven and hell, Pompilia cannot elude her interdependence with Guido in her conceptual process, just as her forgiveness is interdependent with judgement and condemnation.[15] She cannot pardon Guido, which she does somewhat reluctantly ('So far as lies in me'), without at the same time implying his guilt. The negation of her husband is thus a dialectical means to identity. The more she rejects everything to do with him, the more she shores up her own piety, just as the more she affirms Caponsacchi as an agent of God, the more she is assured of redemption: 'He is ordained to call and I to come!' (1814).

Pompilia has no self outside discourse: her opening social identity was textually established, and her 'essential' or spiritual self that is marked by God still needs, as a 'mark', a sign, to be interpreted, even re-written (her metaphor), which means that it exists in any meaningful way only in semiotic form. The discourse which separates externalised fact from internalised representation (Pompilia's 'dream'), and which privileges subjectivist over material reality, sustains a self that is an idealist abstraction – an abstraction that remains necessarily a fictional product of discourse, the person-as-thing. Any sense of completion, of established unity, is contradicted by the continuing process of the speech and by shifting moments of feeling and expression. Her final stages in particular are described as being 'most upon the move' (1775). Even her final statement, 'And I rise', is a statement of process, incompletion. As a statement that cannot be literally true, its figurative function is to enact the completion of the redeemed self. In doing that, it makes this monologue the closest in the poem to a portrait, a fixed image, of a completed 'character'. Nevertheless, its function in producing the sense of completion is inseparable from its function as present utterance, so that the self-as-object, or person-as-thing, never escapes the continuing act of its production, the self-as-process.

IV

Guido's second monologue plays openly with the contradictions of an identity constructed in language. Guido parodies the notion of a marked self whose moral identity is plain for all to see. Yet he claims a fixed self made by God to perform God's purpose. The speaker in book XI is a deconstructor of forms, an overt manipulator of language who flaunts a self based overtly upon a trope. Yet he also expresses the desire for a centred self, for a nucleus that is truly himself, which will outlast death. Discourse and desire are thus at odds.

Pompilia's claims to the mark of God (VII.1499) and the Pope's assertions about the mark of Guido's infamy (X.511) are parodied in book XI when Guido mocks the requirements of confession.[16] Not content with being 'the adroiter swordsman', the church wants him to testify, he protests, to a supernatural victory, to its having 'dispensed with steel' altogether and won through sheer 'naked virtue', exposing his branded brow and leading him to self-destruction:

> it was virtue stood
> Unarmed and awed me, – on my brow there burned

> Crime out so plainly intolerably red,
> That I was fain to cry – 'Down to the dust
> 'With me, and bury there brow, brand and all!'
> (XI.488–505)

Just as the earlier references to such marks were placed squarely within a semiotic structure through being dependent upon interpretation and perception, so here Guido, in representing the church's demand and its required 'word', also returns the issue to discourse:

> Did not the Trial show things plain enough?
> 'Ah, but a word of the man's very self
> 'Would somehow put the keystone in its place
> 'And crown the arch!' Then take the word you want!
> (511–14)

Not content with the truth of legal empiricism, the church, in Guido's eyes, chases the truth of Cartesian idealism, the real self within.

It is this 'very self', however, that becomes increasingly uncertain within a discourse which plays openly with the ambiguities of naming – the gospel 'changes names, not things' (362); we 'call things wicked that give too much joy' and 'nickname' reprisal as 'punishment' (531–4) – and which rejects the church's claims to supernatural truth: 'Colly my cow!', Guido exclaims, at the prospect that his fault lay in not recognising God's law above man's law (549–53). And he rejects the church's dualisms, mocking the moral absolutism that would cast him as Satan:

> Abate, cross your breast and count your beads
> And exorcize the devil, for here he stands
> And stiffens in the bristly nape of neck,
> Daring you drive him hence!
> (554–7)

Thus Guido confronts and questions institutional definitions, and through setting himself against 'Civilization and society' – 'Come, one good grapple, I with all the world!' (463–4) – he purports to represent a self which stands apart from social artifice.

He effects this stance through playing with transformations of terms and the blurring of opposites, in order to confound the assumptions of Christian belief and thereby elude its demands. Guilt and innocence, for example, are supposedly opposites. He asserts that to confess his guilt would be a lie (411–15), whereas his innocence is the truth (434); he is the sheep whom the Pope 'calls a wolf' (405). His innocence is therefore based upon guilt, but the 'natural' guilt of the wolf's 'black jaw' which is the shepherd's 'sworn foe'; and the innocent shepherd thieves, so that Guido's naturalised guilt is offset by the shepherd's 'red hand' (434–8), by the Pope's false innocence that belies his title as Innocent (Guido's and the Pope's 'innocence' are linked from the outset: 'innocent am I/As Innocent my Pope and murderer'; 28–9). Later we find that Guido's affirmation of innocence is a ploy to stay alive – 'I thought you would not slay impenitence' (2231) – so that innocence and guilt in this discourse are verbal strategies conceived for the political purposes of Guido's last confrontation with the church's representatives.

Similarly, he undercuts the opposition between faith and unbelief. Faith and unbelief, 'faith's opposite', are interchangeable for all practical purposes; faith is merely played 'as a fancy' and if all Rome were to embrace 'unbelief' as its belief, there would be 'no symptom of an outward change' (595–601). Church members, he argues, also exploit the opportunism required for institutional success, conflating in the process Biblical distinctions between worth and the worthless: 'Gold is called gold, and dross called dross, i' the Book:/Gold you let lie and dross pick up and prize!' (696–7). Further, Christian is simply a 'nickname' given to the world (1917) and the very origins of Christianity are but the shifting terms of pagan belief (1975–9).

Through such dialectical satire Guido reduces his moral error to a game of language, to not using the appropriate 'pass-word' (2014) or the required institutional form:

> '"The fit defence had been, – you stamped on wheat,
> '"Intending all the time to trample tares, –
> '"Were fain extirpate, then, the heretic,
> '"You now find, in your haste was slain a fool."'
> (2036–9)

At the same time, while placing himself as a 'primitive religionist' (1919) against the established church, Guido cannot place himself outside language: 'All's but a flourish, figure of rhetoric!' (851). Hence the 'word' of his 'very self' becomes an identification with a trope: 'the veritable wolf beneath,/(How that staunch image serves at every turn!)' (1178–9). And hence Guido cannot ultimately escape the church's discourse either, despite his rejection of its hypocrisies. He needs it, since it remains finally a means to survival as he begs the Cardinal to employ the appropriate liturgical language, to 'Translate into the Court-conventional' a plea on his behalf (2271–85).

Guido immediately withdraws this appeal (2286), although in defining himself against the church, he remains tied to it. As he subverts the church's oppositions, so his own oppositions of self and world are subverted. The natural man is set against the man of faith, but the natural man is still God-created. Guido's firm ground in the dialectical ocean of his consciousness – 'This something like a foothold in the sea' (2297) – is the belief that God preserves His work and makes all His creatures with a purpose (2301–3). But Guido's final desire for a 'nucleus' (2395), for a fixed, essential self, runs counter to his whole discourse. Faced with the terror of death, he desperately needs to believe in a self that will remain and survive.[17] Unfortunately the 'nucleus' is simply one more metaphor, a hypothesis about what he believes is 'probable' (2393); in Guido's speech, there is only the self as difference, structured within its language.

Guido's most substantial effort to establish an essential self occurs in terms of his masculinity. In another binary formula, he defines himself against femininity and its conventional attributes of weakness and emotionalism. He identifies, consequently, with the conventional masculine attributes of strength and reason: 'Manliness, mind, – these are things fit to save' (2252). In one early passage about being guilty of an 'unmanly' appetite for truth, he justifies the weakness he has been accused of by saying it is his woman self (168–71). He makes opposites coalesce here in a recognition that is amazingly modern in its psychology – the woman is in the man; man does not need to seek what he lacks in a woman (164–6). But he concludes by angrily focussing on his earlier folly of seeking fulfilment through marriage (177). He has the intellectual ability throughout to subvert opposites, to make absolutes non-absolute, but living under an immediate sentence of death prevents the possibility of applying the lessons to his own psychology. He returns therefore to the anger and frustration which he associates with past events and thence to identifying with the strength that he regards as the main sign of his masculinity. The fuss over his murder is 'Because strength, being provoked by weakness, fought/And conquered' (1283–4), and his brawn is an essentialist quality since it is supplied by God:

> God
> Laid down the law: gave man the brawny arm
> And ball of fist – woman the beardless cheek
> And proper place to suffer in the side:
> Since it is he can strike, let her obey!
> (1403–7).

Obedience, then, is the proper role for women in a patriarchal society where men prove their manliness and maintain their political power through controlling wives. Half-Rome's fear of cuckoldry, for example, leads him to use the Franceschini murder as a warning to his wife's potential lover,[18] and Tertium Quid has the first court pronouncement refer critically to Guido as 'a husband who cannot rule his wife' (IV.1218). Guido feels justified therefore in claiming the support of all patriarchal Rome, of all those 'honest' and 'manly' men who have ever 'owned' a woman:

> All honest Rome approved my part;
> Whoever owned wife, sister, daughter, – nay,
> Mistress, – had any shadow of any right
> That looks like right, and, all the more resolved,
> Held it with tooth and nail, – these manly men
> Approved!
> (XI.39–44)

Within this context, Hegelian desire, the urge to negate the independent object, leads frequently to the possession of wives: men achieve identity through their appropriation of women. Through denying the woman's separate subjectivity, objectifying her as a possession, whether figuratively in terms of a literary convention or literally through the ownership bestowed by marriage, they establish their own identity through absorption of the female other. It is a serious threat to Guido, therefore, when Pompilia refuses to submit, or rather submits in an act of such overt passivity that it parodies and undercuts the submission he needs for his identity as strong male.

At the psycho-political level, the Guido/Pompilia structure in book XI is an enactment of the Hegelian Master/Slave structure: 'Here's my slave,/Whose body and soul depend upon my nod' (1420–1). Guido is destroyed by Pompilia's passivity because his desire for mastery requires the reciprocation of her role as slave. While her parents were present, she used to be 'female to [his] male', employing 'her sex's armoury', but then the 'hare' stood 'stock-still', confounding and enraging the 'hound' whose identity is defined by chasing hares (1327–34). Thus Pompilia's passive obedience effectively parodies the role of female slave, mocking Guido's desire for power by her total submissiveness. In wanting a slave, a wife to 'submit herself,/Afford [him] pleasure, perhaps cure [his] bile' (V.718–9), Guido needs also her willingness to perform that role. Thus she is invested with power – the power that is assigned to the slave through the master's psychological dependency. Because the master depends on the slave in order to be master, his negation of her bestows on her the paradoxical power to construct or destroy his identity (as master). Hence Guido returns to Pompilia at the end of the poem. He appeals to her last in his list, not because she is a saint who can intercede with God, but because it is she who has the power to provide him with the interdependence necessary to his identity. There is no essential Guido, only an attempt to identify with a role that cannot be fulfilled because he treats the reciprocal requirements necessary to its function as an act of literal politics: 'We calculate on word and deed' (1394). His understanding of the interdependence within, the woman in the man, comes too late.

Because Pompilia refuses to perform her political function, Guido kills her as an act of appropriate retribution:

> This wife of mine . . .
> Would not begin the lie that ends with truth,
> Nor feign the love that brings real love about:
> Wherefore I judged, sentenced, and punished her.
> (XI.1429–32)

Such punishment, however, is another form of possession, a desperate attempt to regain the power of his identity, to perform an act of appropriation which would establish the self as living and authoritative. Ironically, Pompilia lives on to thwart Guido even after she is supposed to be dead (denying the version that would restore his mastery), and in destroying literally the object of his desire, he also destroys the chance of sustaining the interdependence necessary to his identity beyond the moment of her death. Having become tied to her through his obsession with her gaze, he struggles for psychological survival through internalising her within a discourse that constructs for himself an image of natural strength.

He does this through metaphors which represent his superiority, although, as Lisa O'Connor has argued, the language of those metaphors undercuts him.[19] Images for Pompilia's weakness in book XI frequently show Guido attempting to privilege one term in a binary opposition, but the system keeps overturning and the opposition potentially inverting itself so that weakness and strength swap places. He claims, for instance, that he is 'the wrought man' who is worth 'ten times' the crude and 'untempered iron', and who implicitly contrasts with the weakness of Pompilia's passivity, but her passivity that is 'cold and pale and mute as stone' is 'strong as stone also' (1313–14). He also contrasts the height and vigour of his lava flow with the lowliness and weakness of her 'puny stream' that is fit merely 'to reflect daisies': 'Fire for the mount, the streamlet for the vale'. But water can turn to ice and ice can quench fire, so he must banish her to a 'patch/Of private snow' where she will 'freeze not [him]' (2054–81). Thus the language which assures him of superior strength and security deconstructs that very security.[20] The self indeed is tied to nothing firmer than a metaphor floating in a sea of discourse.

No wonder, then, that he returns to Pompilia in his final desperation. And no wonder that he seeks her aid. In his discourse it is her image which carries the power of his self-definition. It is her image which carries any sense of an essence for Guido, since it is her image and the metaphors he attaches to it which structure his identity. Intelligent enough to challenge the church's assumptions and manipulations, he remains too emotionally obsessed with his anger at women (at Violante as well as at Pompilia) to detach himself from the structural dualism which, ironically, ensures his psychological destruction.

V

There are other forms of definition by opposition in the poem which also deconstruct. Tertium Quid, for instance, sets out to define himself against the mob, against the burgess-life of the Comparini.

He would further his cause with his aristocratic and influential audience by negating the bourgeoisie and claiming possession of the truth which they cannot understand. His meta-discourse, attempting to stand outside the 'rabble's-brabble' of 'reasonless unreasoning Rome' (IV.10–11), is designed to demonstrate his own power of reasoning and reaffirm his status within his circle of the nobility. By placing the Comparini as burgesses ('why seek to aggrandize,/Idealize, denaturalize the class?' IV.65–6) against the nobility ('People talk just as if they had to do/With a noble pair'; IV.67–8), Tertium Quid defines himself by negation of the bourgeois other, with his meta-discourse as the evidence.

The monologue itself leads to a dissolution of that opposition. It does this in two main ways. Firstly, the speaker's detachment and intricate conceptualising, necessary to his stance as intellectual superior to the 'dolts and fools' of the populace, occasionally breaks down. The earliest example is when he refers to what he believes to be the Pope's handout to Pietro. The dole is much admired by the mob, but Tertium Quid perceives it otherwise:

> That is, instead of putting a prompt foot
> On selfish worthless human slugs whose slime
> Has failed to lubricate their path in life,
> Why, the Pope picks the first ripe fruit that falls
> And gracious puts it in the vermin's way.
> Pietro could never save a dollar? Straight
> He must be subsidized at our expense.
> (116–22)

While the sentiments are those which might be expected of intolerant privilege, the language is clearly in excess of that required of political conservatism. The rhetorical overkill suggests a subject who identifies too fiercely with his free-market criticism, a subject who, as his image of the slug takes over, is less than intellectually detached, suspiciously like the 'unreasoning' mob he deplores.

Secondly, the opposition between the self-centred bestiality of the bourgeoisie (the Comparini) and the stylistic finesse of the nobility (represented largely by Guido) also disintegrates, since Guido ends up exhibiting the same qualities of bestial behaviour that Tertium Quid initially attributes to Violante and Pietro. The Comparini are viewed by Tertium Quid as 'gnats' (561), 'selfish beasts' (702) and 'two ghastly scullions' (730). Guido on the other hand has 'touch/O'the subtle air that breeds the subtle wit', blood which is 'thrice-refined' (756–8), and he practices, it is said, 'The finer vengeance' (769). Much later, however, Tertium Quid becomes excited by the powerful anger and furious pursuit of vengeance (1565–79). The passage attempts to retrieve Guido's violent actions as the natural behaviour of a bull-like nature. At the same time, in accounting for 'indiscriminate slaughter' and 'reckless aggravation of revenge', it acknowledges those very qualities, qualities of the 'rude' and the 'brute', which contradict earlier claims for Guido's 'subtle wit' and 'finer vengeance'. Bull-like revenge may be natural to bulls, but it also indicates the 'brute' at the heart of Guido's supposed finesse and style. Hence the difference between the nobility and the bourgeoisie is effectively dissolved rather than secured.

Not unexpectedly, the speaker's auditors are puzzled, and he quickly reverts to the equivocations of a detached intellectual: 'There are difficulties perhaps/On any supposition, and either side' (1581–2). Tertium Quid's attempt to display his wit and agility of reason seems to end up deconstructing all positions and leading to an insoluble impasse, a veritable aporia, which merely reveals his own underlying frustrations, confuses his audience and gains nothing: '(You'll see, I have not so advanced myself,/After my teaching the two idiots here!)' (1639–40). In attempting to establish his identity and social standing through a discourse of opposition and detachment, Tertium Quid founders on the very dialectical nature of his method.

VI

The politics of self in book IV remind us that the pursuit of identity in discourse overlaps continually with the broader politics of social and institutional action. Book IV provides an anecdote, for example, about 'the daily bargain' struck in the marketplace. This anecdote illustrates the way people become stuck in external structures which govern their behaviour:

> Why sells Jack his ware?
> 'For the sake of serving an old customer.'
> Why does Jill buy it? 'Simply not to break
> 'A custom, pass the old stall the first time.'
> (IV.533–6)

The Politics of Self in The Ring and the Book 181

Also, Tertium Quid's very argument is constrained by the structures of his social context. The final impasse, for instance, which illustrates the conflict between his logic and the social inappropriateness of his conclusion is provided by his reference to torture (IV.1621–31). Guido may be innocent, Tertium Quid argues, because of his nobility, and so tortured unnecessarily; yet if Guido be exempted, what crime would ever deserve torture? The obvious solution – to abolish torture – would presumably be too radical for Tertium Quid's hegemonic audience and so he dismisses it as 'the reduction *ad absurdum*' (1631). Thus he refuses to pursue his logic beyond the expectations of his listeners, remaining shackled, consequently, to his political context and further fuelling his anger and sense of personal injustice.

Similarly, in book XI, self and world remain interdependent, despite Guido's attempt to set himself against civilisation for one last fling. Despite his attempt to deny the church's influence by exposing its hypocrisies (the wink about omnipotence, for instance: see XI.2001–3), he has finally to confront the way his appropriation of the church's power over truth and his stance as the natural man outside its institutional role-play do nothing to affect its literal power: in the end it remains the agent of his death (see O'Connor, p. 152).

In book V, Guido embraces the material power of the marketplace by absorbing a social discourse that treats marriage, honour and class as signs whose values (meaning) are assigned through an economy of social structures. It is necessary to maintain this economy, Guido argues, in order to maintain social stability, but of course his external political argument overlaps conveniently with the discourse required for his personal politics as aristocratic male.

The discourse of individuals and the discourse of social structures continually interweave. Individuals appropriate institutional form and institutions appropriate individuals. Legal discourse reconstitutes experience, playing, for instance, with the circumstantial evolution of facts (VIII.139) or with hypotheses built upon a conditional (IX.637–9); and the church teaches Caponsacchi to use both 'breviary' and 'rhymes' in order to exercise secular as well as spiritual influence among social (largely female) circles. Such dialectical interweaving inevitably becomes a problematic. It is a problematic, for instance, which Guido relishes and which Caponsacchi agonises over, as both realise that liturgical discourse loses its moral efficacy through allowing its formalist idealism to be compromised by the personal politics of rank, wealth and ambition. On the other hand a formalist separation is no answer, producing an empty system which offers the comfort of idealist abstractions (the church as bridegroom), but no help to those in literal distress (woman as beleaguered bride). To internalise evidence and act from the heart may be 'correct' for Caponsacchi and Pompilia in this context, but, as the Pope observes, that cannot stand as a model for social morality.

The poem highlights a moral and political dilemma. The processes of discourse which define, and in defining connect, individuals and institutions allow by definition the possibility of fraud and deception. Signs may lie. Dialectical process may blur distinctions. How, then, might truth be established or any subject elude the impurities of the structures which provide meaning and value? There may be attempts to rescue the self from social or institutional corruption – through Caponsacchi's assertion of difference through opposition, for example, or through Pompilia's internalising and idealising of spiritual authority. But such attempts inevitably founder precisely because they cannot escape the medium which enables their very existence. All selves exist personally and politically within a system of meaning which is dynamic and diacritical rather than fixed and referential, and whose processes therefore prevent any speaker, in terms of conceptual identity, from stepping outside its structural demands. Discourse may not be eluded and yet discourse is an impure medium, both conceptually and morally.

I would suggest, then, that the political aim or function of *The Ring and the Book* is not so much to propose a correct political system or to satirise existing ones, as to examine the effects and processes of authority in language. All speakers in some way or other assert an authority of self. Some attach that authority to social formulas like *honoris causa* (Half-Rome, Guido in book V) or courtly romance (The Other Half-Rome), some to the structures of law and family (Archangelis), class (Tertium Quid, Guido) or religion (Pompilia, the Pope), some to the purity of a saintlike counterpart (Caponsacchi, Pompilia), and some to their own powers of reason or explanation (Tertium Quid, Bottini, Guido in book XI). For all, however, a main source of vigour and impetus in their speech is the need to identify that source of authority with their deepest sense of selfhood. For the Pope, for example, the authority of God remains important, since that is the basis of his own sense of worth and purpose after a lifetime devoted to the church and God's Word. For Guido in book

XI, on the other hand, the attempt to stand outside conventional structures as the natural man free from artifice makes the authority of an essential self important. Guido's final desire to believe in 'something changeless at the heart' of himself is equivalent to the Pope's final need to believe that God's creation was not in vain. In all cases, the nature and circumstances of any defined authority are seen to be sustained and produced by the nature and circumstances of the discourse.

My discussion focuses deliberately on a dialectic of incompletion rather than on definitive moral judgements, and some readers may think this emphasis produces a serious dichotomy between the subjectivities of speakers and the realities of violent action. With so much stress on discourse, where all is figuration and textual process, and where judgement is a matter of the most plausible version, what happens to the horrifying brutality of a murder which demands a response of moral outrage? There is no question at all about the portrayal of Pompilia's acute suffering or of Guido's brutality; nor, in the poem's context, about the moral protest which such brutality should elicit. But feelings and attitudes, like events and judgements, gain their meaning and significance from the discourse which produces them. The poem both encourages and dissolves the Cartesian division between internal subjectivity and external reality. It suggests a dehiscence in acts of perception which emerges from the desire to affirm the authoritative self. Yet it locates all perception and acts of judgement within language, where experience is always a construct, always mediated. Only in discourse do events carry such concepts as 'outrageous' and 'brutal' (which is not at all to deny the feelings which promote those judgements or to which those terms may refer).

Through its exploration of textualised experience, the poem shows on one level how truth and value may be taken over by the forces of linguistic indeterminacy. But Browning also ensures that the poem produces no merely formalist hypothesis: in the context of the poem there are serious and quite literal consequences to judgements inferred through discourse (Guido, for instance, loses his head, and the Convertites do not gain Pompilia's inheritance). The dialectical point about the politics of self is that no idea, concept, issue, event, speech or speaker stands alone; all issues and perceptions gain meaning and significance from their interweaving with other issues and perceptions. For some readers, the poem may not relate historically to the Victorian middle-class hegemony as directly as

Maud or *In Memoriam*. But the poem's focus on the role of language as the key epistemological question in all human perception, and in all standard human concerns – social reality, private and public power, belief and morality – means that it confronts the relationships between representation and experience in a more radical way than any other poem in the age.

What I am proposing as the dialectical nature of the discourse in the poem produces a challenge to fundamental assumptions about the status of truth and about the production of the self. Yet people do not exist outside the discourses produced by those assumptions. Nor are there definitive solutions to epistemological questions; indeed, epistemological questions themselves emerge from certain conceptual assumptions. It is rather that the poem dramatises the dilemma that is so peculiar and fascinating to the modern mind: that mankind lives as if on a möbius strip, at once divided and not divided. There is distinctive differentiation, heterogeneous division, and yet a seamless path, absorption within a continuous structure – depending upon which direction you look. Both exist simultaneously, sustaining while opposing each other.

This does not mean that within the context of *The Ring and the Book* there can be no moral difference, but it does mean that emergent differences are inseparable from the structures which allow that difference to occur – structures which include the conditions of reading and readerly judgement. It also means that in terms of the discourse of self, Hegelian difference – the prospect of a unity of consciousness that is constituted through division – is seen in the process of giving way to Derridean *différance*, to a weaving without totality – the unity that is continually deferred, yet necessarily a source of personal and political action.

Afterword: On Poetry as a Significant Discourse

In the popular view, idealist thinking has generally lost ground in the last two centuries to forces of empirical enquiry, and insofar as poetry has been classed in the idealist camp, it has been marginalised by a utilitarian and materialist ethos. At best within this context poetry could be said to explore a special realm of feeling and transcendent truth. But few living in a materialist world are inclined to take that claim seriously. As long as arguments for the value of poetry remain within the established binary structures of post-Cartesian thought, within the dualist separation of idealism and empiricism, then poetry will lose every time. In the context of most materialist and scientific enquiry, poetry will hardly appear to be a discourse that should be taken seriously.

Treating poetry, however, not as a discourse of subjective idealism, but as a dialectic of non-dualist, objective idealism, as a discourse of the sort which I have ascribed to Hegel in this study, might better serve the purpose of claiming poetry as cognitively serious. The point is to elude the either/or tendencies of epistemological thinking, since what Hegel's idealism comes down to is 'the rejection of the distinctions between mind and matter, experience and reality, consciousness and its objects, knowledge and truth' (Solomon, p. 186).

When mind and matter are continuous, knowledge incorporates both object and subject, and the act of knowing affects the object of its knowledge. In Hegel's conceptual philosophy the known object is not external to the knowledge, as is the case for most empirical study. Only fixed, lifeless propositions emerge from studies of what Hegel terms mathematical 'unrealities' – space and numerical units, or, in a word, quantity. Knowledge of that sort, Hegel says, does not arise from the nature of the subject matter itself (Pref. 103).

A similar distinction is used in *The Lucid Veil* by David Shaw in order to distinguish poetic knowledge from scientific knowledge. He describes the knowledge of poets and critics as 'interpretive knowledge', which is 'capable of being "re-presented" in the interpreter's mind'. For the physical sciences, 'there can be no interpretation of physical nature, because physical objects are never an experience as such. They are always the mere objects of experience.' Poetic knowledge on the other hand includes its author: 'the geologist's knowledge of the earth . . . is not a knowledge of the geologist's own self-conscious response or of his own place in geological history'. A poem such as *In Memoriam* thus contains poetic knowledge because Tennyson's 'own response and place are an important part of what he knows' (Shaw, p. 283).

Shaw appears to hit on a useful way of suggesting the value of poetic and liberal education, which is his stated purpose in this passage. But I want to distinguish Shaw's account from what I take to be Hegel's similar distinction, in order to illustrate the difference between a dialectical (Hegel's) and non-dialectical (Shaw's) formulation about poetry and poetic knowledge.

Shaw's presentation occurs within conventional epistemological discourse, incorporating the subject but sustaining its implicit separation from external matter. Tennyson's poem contains a knowledge of chronology and geological time, but it makes that knowledge poetic by adding to it the poet's own response and sense of place – the consciousness of the author. The two, knowledge of time and knowledge of self, remain implicitly distinct, with the crucial point for poetry being the stress on the way geological time is experienced by the poet's subjectivity. Within that experience the concept of time and the concept of self remain untouched by each other; one is simply absorbed by the other and seen in its terms. Such a description, however, is straightforward subjective idealism, and open therefore to all the objections and trivialisations of empirical approaches: for example, the poet's experience may be valuable in poetic and human terms, but it may nevertheless distort the geologist's notion of time which remains attached to the externally verifiable world of empirical perception.

For Hegel, however, such distinctions cannot be made in the same way. There is fixed, essentially dead knowledge of a quantifiable sort, but the knowledge of philosophical understanding involves both object and subject in a process where the two are inseparable, each affecting the other, each incorporating the other. This is a dialectical proposition because the concepts of time and self are transformed through their interconnection, not conceivable outside that relationship and, therefore, not so easily separated into reified categories. It more readily justifies the value of poetic language, not by approving of the incorporation of the subject, but by showing that subject and object are inseparable from true knowledge.

Such a dialectical, non-dualist proposition is similar to deconstructionist thought which challenges relationships or priorities between discourses of origin and discourses of representation – life and art, art and criticism, criticism and philosophy. It is not that distinctions cannot be made between various discourses, but the privileging of any one as a source and repository of knowledge is severely questioned. A more dialectical model for poetry might provide, therefore, a more potent means of validating the cognitive worth of literary discourse. In such a model it is not the self as specific subject which makes poetry important, as Shaw's neo-Kantian phrasing would suggest, but rather the subject as a necessary component of process itself – the process of life, feeling, cognition, consciousness, experience, understanding. This is precisely the point of Browning's 'Epilogue' to *Dramatis Personae*, where the 'universe', as a known universe, is inseparable from an experiencing subject – 'my universe'.

This approach is entirely in accord with the most advanced studies of the nature of matter. Within the new physics of quantum mechanics and particle theory, the world becomes a dynamic whole which always includes the observer. Indeed the observer is no longer a detached onlooker, but a participant whose act of participation brings the universe into existence. The Cartesian partition between self and world is no longer tenable, reality becomes a matter of probability waves, and the tentacles of textuality embrace even the cosmos of space and time. The physicist Mendel Sachs comments, for instance:

> The real revolution that came with Einstein's theory . . . was the abandonment of the idea that the space-time coordinate system has objective significance as a separate physical entity. Instead of this idea, relativity theory implies that the space and time coordinates are only the elements of a *language* that is used by an observer to describe his environment.[1]

Within a relativistic, dynamic universe, where physical material behaves exactly in the manner of a Hegelian dialectic – in terms of movement, process, transformation – poetic discourse which foregrounds the constructions of language functions as a process of legitimate knowledge.

Notes

INTRODUCTION

1. For a recent study which considers these issues in terms of Victorian writing, see John P. McGowan, *Representation and Revelation: Victorian Realism from Carlyle to Yeats* (Columbia: University of Missouri Press, 1986).
2. See, e.g., Vincent Descombes, *Modern French Philosophy*, trans. L.Scott-Fox and J. M. Harding (Cambridge University Press, 1980), chap. 3.
3. Hans-Georg Gadamer, *Hegel's Dialectic: Five Hermeneutical Studies*, trans. P. Christopher Smith (New Haven and London: Yale University Press, 1976), pp. 79–80.
4. Isobel Armstrong, *Language as Living Form in Nineteenth-Century Poetry* (Sussex: Harvester, 1982).
5. So far the closest study to these views is Loy D. Martin's *Browning's Dramatic Monologues and the Post-Romantic Subject* (Baltimore: The Johns Hopkins University Press, 1985); Martin states, for instance, that 'the dramatic monologue, more perhaps than any other literary form, challenges the immense prestige of the Cartesian dualism of the self and the other' (p. 28).
6. Dorothy Mermin, *The Audience in the Poem: Five Victorian Poets* (New Brunswick, N.J.: Rutgers University Press, 1983), p. 9.
7. Tilottama Rajan, 'Romanticism and the Death of Lyric Consciousness', in *Lyric Poetry: Beyond New Criticism*, ed. Chaviva Hosek and Patricia Parker (Ithaca: Cornell University Press 1985), pp. 194–207.
8. See Robert E. Lougy, 'The Sounds and Silence of Madness: Language as Theme in Tennysons's *Maud*', *VP*, vol. 22 (1984), 407–26.

CHAPTER 1: CONSCIOUSNESS AS SELF

1. See Richard Rorty, *Philosophy and the Mirror of Nature* (Princeton University Press, 1979), pp. 3–13, and *passim*.
2. See Lionel Stevenson, 'The Key Poem in the Victorian Age', in *Essays in American and English Literature 'Presented to' Bruce Robert McElderry, Jr.*, ed. M. F. Schulz, W. D. Templeman and C. R. Metzger (Athens, Ohio: Ohio University Press, 1967), pp. 260–89; Alba H. Warren, *English Poetic Theory, 1825–1865* (Princeton University Press, 1950); Lawrence J. Starzyk, *The Imprisoned Splendour: A Study of Victorian Critical Theory* (London: Kennikat Press, 1977); Alan Sinfield's excellent account of the role of poetry within a society governed

by Victorian utilitarianism, in *Alfred Tennyson* (Oxford: Blackwell, 1986); and David Shaw's comprehensive study of poetic theory in the nineteenth century, *The Lucid Veil: Poetic Truth in the Victorian Age* (London: The Athlone Press, 1987).

3. In *The Lucid Veil*, Shaw relates changing theories of language and knowledge to ideological attitudes. See also Howard W. Fulweiler, 'Poetry and the Problem of Language', in *Letters from the Darkling Plain: Language and the Grounds of Knowledge in the Poetry of Arnold and Hopkins* (University of Missouri Press, 1972), chap. 1. Philosophy has always tended to separate its reasoned truth-claims from the contaminations of poetic or figurative language, particularly before Nietzsche's observations about the reliance of philosophy on metaphor and textuality. For a discussion of the present state of the conflict between analytical philosophy and literary theory, see Christopher Norris, *The Contest of Faculties: Philosophy and Theory After Deconstruction* (London: Methuen, 1985).

4. Isobel Armstrong, *Language as Living Form in Nineteenth-Century Poetry* (Sussex: The Harvester Press, 1982).

5. G. W. F. Hegel, *The Phenomenology of Mind*, trans. with an Introduction and Notes by J. B. Baillie (1910, rev. 1931; New York: Harper Torchbooks, 1967), Preface, p. 94. Future references to this text will be documented internally by section and by page number.

6. Richard Harland, *Superstructuralism: The Philosophy of Structuralism and Post-Structuralism* (London: Methuen, 1987), p. 72. Harland distinguishes between three traditions of philosophy: Anglo-Saxon empiricism; the 'I'-philosophy of Descartes, Kant and Husserl; and the Metaphysical philosophy of Plato, Spinoza and Hegel (p. 70).

7. Robert C. Solomon, *In the Spirit of Hegel: A Study of G. W. F. Hegel's 'Phenomenology of Spirit'* (Oxford University Press, 1983), p. 8. Hereafter cited as Solomon.

8. M. J. Inwood's book, *Hegel* (London: Routledge & Kegan Paul, 1983), which appeared in the same year as Solomon's work, offers a methodical study of the Hegelian system as a coherent whole; effectively this is to re-absorb Hegel into analytical discourse.

9. Robert C. Solomon, *From Rationalism to Existentialism: The Existentialists and Their Nineteenth-Century Backgrounds* (1972; rpt. Humanities Press/Harvester Press, 1978), p. 49.

10. Frank Kermode's discussion of the teleological structure of narrative in *The Sense of an Ending: Studies in the Theory of Fiction* (Oxford University Press, 1966) is of course well known.

11. In the *Phenomenology* Hegel posits life as 'the *whole* which develops itself, resolves its own development, and in this movement simply preserves itself' (IV.224). The aim of simple preservation hardly seems to justify the notion of teleological absolutism.

12. See Solomon, p. 277.

13. See also Solomon: 'Since consciousness ultimately recognizes itself as Spirit, that is, as everything, "consciousness" is not actually opposed to anything else; in fact, it is Hegel's whole aim to show that there is nothing "outside" of or opposed to consciousness' (p. 277); and

Armstrong: 'Reality is not outside the self' (p. 21), and 'if the distinction between external and internal is eliminated by the fact that both are aspects of consciousness because nothing lies outside the self, then all categories are wrought out of mind which subsumes them' (p. 32).

14. Jacques Derrida, *Of Grammatology*, trans. Gayatri Spivak (Baltimore: The Johns Hopkins University Press, 1972): 'il n'y a pas de hors-texte' (p. 158). The phrase is usually translated as 'no outside-text' or 'no outside the text'; it should not be read in the manner of some literary critics as 'nothing but the text', as if it were a new critical slogan for pure formalism.

15. Hegel also says that 'Being is entirely mediated' (Pref. 97) and that mediation 'is reflection into self, the aspect in which the ego is for itself, objective to itself' (Pref. 82). The covert element here, which Hegel does not draw out, is the way this act of reflection implies some sort of semiotic process, or act of representation. If so, then it also implies the post-structuralist proposition that reality, being, is always already a conception, already a mediated presentation: there is no outside representation.

16. Solomon, p. 444. For Solomon's account of the Master/Slave parable and its application to everyday life, see pp. 443–55. He observes, for instance, that it is an asymmetrical relationship that can take many forms: 'Master–slave is but an extreme; domination and submission are common in a great many interactions – on the basis of who's smarter, who's neater, who's more mechanically inclined, who's more charming, who's more angry, who's more sexually demanding, who's more insecure, and so on' (p. 444).

17. Solomon illustrates this reciprocal interaction through R. D. Laing's notion of 'knots': 'I see you, you see me, I see you seeing me, I see you seeing me see you . . . .' (p. 447).

18. See Hegel's *Philosophy of Mind*: being Part Three of the 'Encyclopaedia of the Philosophical Sciences' (1830), translated by William Wallace, together with the 'Zustze' in Boumann's text (1845), translated by A. V. Miller, with a Foreword by J. N. Findlay (Oxford: Clarendon Press, 1971), p. viii. Hereafter cited as *Mind*.

19. See *Mind*: 'mind in spite of its simplicity is distinguished within itself; for the "I" sets itself over against itself, makes itself its own object and returns from this difference . . . into unity with itself' (p. 11).

20. Hans-Georg Gadamer, *Hegel's Dialectic: Five Hermeneutical Studies*, trans. P. Christopher Smith (New Haven and London: Yale University Press, 1976), p. 36.

21. Perhaps the distinction about different levels of consciousness helps to explain why Victorian poetry encourages readings which suggest Hegelian dialectical unity as well as deconstructive disrupted centres and textual self-consciousness. See, for example, Sinfield's distinctions in *Alfred Tennyson* (notably chap. 4) about Tennyson desiring a transcendent absolute, but being unable to attain it.

22. See, for example, Kris Davis, 'Browning's Caponsacchi: Stuck in the Gap,' *Victorian Poetry*, vol. 25 (Spring 1987), 57–66.

23 All quotations from the 'Epilogue' are taken from *Browning: Poetical Works 1833–1864*, ed. Ian Jack (London: Oxford, 1970).
24. Herbert F. Tucker Jr., *Browning's Beginnings* (Minneapolis: University of Minnesota Press, 1980), pp. 185–6.
25. The syntactical ambiguity of 'Become' was pointed out to me by Lisa O'Connor, a graduate student at Massey University, New Zealand.
26. Jacques Derrida commenting on Kant's aesthetic of pure mimesis, in 'Economimesis', *Diacritics*, vol. 11 (1981), 11.

CHAPTER 2: CONSCIOUSNESS AS WRITING

1. Such ideas are already present in most periods of thought going back at least to Plato, Heraclitus, Sextus Empiricus and Pyrrho of Elis. What Hegel provides, however, is a historically produced moment when certain suppressed or barely conceived notions that run counter to the dominant discourses of the last three hundred years re-emerge, becoming transformed and refined in the process. Such a process still continues.
2. There is some ambiguity about whether Hegel regards Absolute Knowledge as attainable. Solomon suggests there are two Hegels: one who wants to establish a total all-embracing system, and the other who accepts that movement and transformation need not have an attainable goal in order to have a goal at all (p. 15). He claims that for the second Hegel 'the Absolute is only the distant goal, never to be reached, or else, if one does reach it, it will turn out to be . . . the motivation for a grand and dangerous journey . . . a fraud, or at most, just another stage on the journey' (p. 16).
3. Friedrich Schlegel, from 'Ideas' (1800), No. 150, in *German Aesthetic and Literary Criticism: The Romantic Ironists and Goethe*, ed. Kathleen M. Wheeler (Cambridge University Press, 1984), p. 59. Hereafter cited as Wheeler.
4. From 'Critical Fragments' (1797), no. 108; Wheeler, p. 43.
5. From 'Athenäum Fragments' (1798), no. 51; Wheeler, p. 45.
6. See Anne K. Mellor, *English Romantic Irony* (Cambridge, Mass. and London: Harvard University Press, 1980): Romantic irony can appear 'as two opposed voices or personae, or two contradictory ideas or themes, which the author carefully balances and refuses to synthesize or harmonize' (p. 18); and Clyde de L. Ryals, *Becoming Browning: the Poems and Plays of Robert Browning, 1833–1846* (Columbus: Ohio State University Press, 1983): 'It is the function of philosophical irony as [Schlegel] expounds it to permit an individual to hold the two contrary states of being and becoming in mind at the same time and to recognize that they cannot be harmonized' (p. 5); Ryals' excellent application of the concepts of Romantic irony to the early works of Browning contains provocative implications for the reading of Victorian poetry in general.
7. From the 'Dialogue on Poetry' (1799–1800), in Friedrich Schlegel,

Dialogue on Poetry and Literary Aphorisms, trans. Ernst Behler and Roman Struc (University Park and London: the Pennsylvania State University Press, 1968), p. 86.

8. 'Ideas', nos. 55 and 69; Wheeler, p. 56.
9. See Gary J. Handwerk, *Irony and Ethics in Narrative: From Schlegel to Lacan* (Yale University Press, 1985). Handwerk argues that what is central to Schlegel is not the humanity-nature or subject-object opposition, but rather a concern with communication and its consequent intersubjectivity. He agrees that Schlegel did start from the position of irony as heightened self-awareness on the model of the individual ego, but shows how Schlegel went further, 'to analyze the dynamics of the transition between the subject and the other subjects that compose community' (p. 5). In this reading, Schlegel's ethical irony destabilises self-consciousness itself, adding as purpose 'an intentional decentering of the subject that operates as an opening out to the other' (pp. 42–3).
10. See, e.g., Janice L. Haney, '"Shadow-Hunting": Romantic Irony, *Sartor Resartus*, and Victorian Romanticism,' *Studies in Romanticism*, 17 (Summer 1978): 'Schlegel's irony is a version of that subjective idealism that offers triumph to the self' (p. 313); and Paul Hamilton, 'Romantic Irony and English Literary History,' in *The Romantic Heritage: A Collection of Critical Essays*, ed. Karsten Engelberg (Copenhagen: University of Copenhagen, 1983): 'Romantic irony can be provisionally defined as a self-awareness which is always in excess of any means chosen to express it' (p. 14).
11. Lilian R. Furst, *Fictions of Romantic Irony* (Harvard University Press, 1984), p. 42.
12. See Furst: Hegel attacked the subjectivist foundations of Romantic irony, arguing that 'the authority of the object' had been replaced by 'the boundless vanity of the enthroned ego' (p. 32).
13. See Peter L. Thorslev, Jr., *Romantic Contraries: Freedom versus Destiny* (New Haven: Yale University Press, 1984), p. 159. Thorslev characterises all dialectical thinking in this way, claiming that for 'the Romantic dialectician' the 'opposition alone is real' (p. 68). The reason for not excluding Hegel from this blanket claim seems to be that Hegel is equated by Thorslev with the subjectivism that says 'things have no reality apart from our knowledge of them, and the mind itself ultimately creates this knowledge which is the only reality' (p. 71). As I have argued, Hegel's writing refutes that form of subjectivist thinking as another crude dualism.
14. Jacques Derrida, *Positions*, trans. Alan Bass (London: the Athlone Press, 1981), p. 43. I am inclined to think that Hegel's resolution of oppositions into a 'third term' is not as consistent or as frequent as Derrida and tradition suggests.
15. It is a nice irony that contemporary physics now shows idealism to be basically correct about the nature of materialist reality, particularly that idealism which argues for the inseparability of object and subject, observed and observer. See also the Afterword, below.

Notes to pp. 47–52   193

16. Matthew Arnold, *Selected Poems and Prose*, ed. Miriam Allott (London: Dent, 1978).
17. Friedrich Nietzsche, *The Gay Science*, trans. Walter Kaufmann (New York: Vintage, 1974), pp. 298–9 (section 354); *The Will to Power*, ed. Walter Kaufmann (New York: Vintage, 1967), p. 285 (section 526). All italics here and elsewhere are Nietzsche's.
18. Nietzsche also anticipates such a proposition: 'In brief, the development of language and the development of consciousness (*not* of reason but merely of the way reason enters consciousness) go hand in hand' (*The Gay Science*, p. 299, section 354).
19. Jacques Derrida, 'Signature Event Context', *Glyph*, vol. 1 (1977), 181. Hereafter cited as SEC.
20. Again this conception can be found in Nietzsche: 'Fundamentally, all our actions are altogether incomparably personal, unique, and infinitely individual; there is no doubt of that. But as soon as we translate them into consciousness *they no longer seem to be*' (*The Gay Science*, p. 299, section 354).
21. Ann Wordsworth, '"Communication Different"', *Browning Society Notes*, vol. 13, no. 1 (n.d.), 4–18. This essay in *BSN* is part of a growing concern among critics with the importance in Victorian poetry of language as theme, the textualisation of experience, consciousness and the self as illusion: see also, Harold Bloom and Ann Wordsworth in *Robert Browning*, eds. Harold Bloom and Adrienne Munich (Englewood Cliffs, N.J.: Prentice-Hall, 1979); Tucker, *Browning's Beginnings*; E. Warwick Slinn, *Browning and the Fictions of Identity* (London: Macmillan, 1982); Armstrong, *Language as Living Form in Nineteenth-Century Poetry*; Timothy Peltason, 'Supposed Confessions, Uttered Thoughts: The First-Person Singular in Tennyson's Poetry', *Victorian Newsletter*, no. 64 (1983), pp. 13–18; Tucker, 'From Monomania to Monologue: "St Simeon Stylites" and the Rise of the Victorian Dramatic Monologue', *Victorian Poetry*, vol. 22 (Summer 1984), 121–37; Slinn, 'Some Notes on Monologues as Speech Acts', *BSN*, vol. 15, no. 11 (1985), 1–9. Clyde Ryals'book, *Becoming Browning*, in its use of Romantic irony and F. Schlegel's dialectics as a context for reading Browning is also directly relevant.
22. Derrida, in *The Structuralist Controversy*, eds. Richard Macksey and Eugenio Donato (Baltimore: The Johns Hopkins University Press, 1972): 'The subject is absolutely indispensable. I don't destroy the subject; I situate it' (p. 271).
23. In *Writing and Difference*, trans. Alan Bass (London: Routledge & Kegan Paul, 1978), pp. 196–231. In this section of the discussion, references to this essay will be cited within the text by page number.
24. In the notes to his own translation of 'Freud and the Scene of Writing', Jeffrey Mehlman observes that 'Derrida presses in the direction of a theatre of writing', in *Yale French Studies*, vol. 48 (1972), 73.
25. Walter Benn Michaels, 'The Interpreter's Self: Peirce on the Cartesian "Subject"', *Georgia Review*, vol. 31 (1977), 401. The quotation from

Peirce is cited on the same page in Michaels' article. The role of interpretation within self-conception or self-understanding is receiving increased philosophical attention; see, for example, Anthony Paul Kerby in 'The Adequacy of Self-Narration: A Hermeneutical Approach', *Philosophy and Literature*, 12 (1988), 232–44, where he argues that 'we must recognize interpretation as an integral part of the subject's very being' (233).

26. All quotations from 'Two in the Campagna' are taken from *Browning: Poetical Works 1833–1864*, ed. Ian Jack (London: Oxford University Press, 1970).
27. Richard D. Altick, 'Lovers' Finiteness: Browning's "Two in the Campagna"', *PLL*, vol. 3 (1967), 79.
28. 'The Lady of Shalott', 152, my italics; cited from *The Poems of Tennyson*, ed. Christopher Ricks (London: Longmans, 1969).
29. The Lady becomes indeed Geoffrey Hartman's 'floating signifier'; see his chapter on 'Psychoanalysis: The French Connection', in *Saving the Text* (Baltimore: The Johns Hopkins University Press, 1981), p. 110. Hartman also makes the point about her attempt to place herself 'in an unmediated relation to whatever "really" is', adding that this wish 'means a desire to be defined totally: marked or named once and for all, fixed in or by a word' (p. 97). For further discussion of the semiotic possibilities of this poem, see Anne C. Colley, 'The Quest for the "Nameless" in Tennyson's "The Lady of Shalott"', *Victorian Poetry*, vol. 23 (1985), 369–78, and Gerhard Joseph, 'The Echo and the Mirror *en abîme* in Victorian Poetry', *Victorian Poetry*, vol. 23 (1985), 403–12.
30. I take the point about the ambiguous curse from Herbert F. Tucker, *Tennyson and the Doom of Romanticism* (Cambridge, Mass.: Harvard University Press, 1988), p. 108; Tucker also notes, echoing Hartman, that the Lady 'confronts not the world, but the impossibility of her confronting the world' (p. 114).

CHAPTER 3: ABSENCE AND DESIRE IN *MAUD*

1. See, e.g., Arthur J. Carr, 'Tennyson as a Modern Poet', in John Killham, ed., *Critical Essays on the Poetry of Tennyson* (London: Routledge & Kegan Paul, 1960), pp. 41–64; Dorothy M. Mermin, 'Tennyson's *Maud*: A Thematic Analysis', *TSLL*, vol. 15 (1973), 267–77; Simon S. Petch, 'Tennyson: Mood and Myth', *Sydney Studies in English*, 4 (1978–79), 18–30; Samuel E. Schulman, 'Mourning and Voice in *Maud*', *SEL*, 23 (1983), 633–46; Alan Sinfield, *Alfred Tennyson* (Oxford: Blackwell, 1986), partic. pp. 98–102.
2. The appropriateness of Lacanian theory for Tennyson's poetry has already been explained by Sinfield (pp. 98–102). For an excellent account of the development of the subject in Lacanian terms, see Kaja Silverman, *The Subject of Semiotics* (New York: Oxford University Press, 1983), pp. 149–93, and for another application of

this theory to Victorian writing, see Steven Connor, *Charles Dickens* (Oxford: Blackwell, 1985), chap. 6.

3. There is a clear sense in which the well-known 'mirror stage' in Lacanian development is never entirely separate from retrospective conceptualising within the Symbolic order, or at least from some sort of socialised mediation, through the interpretations of a parent perhaps or contextual paraphernalia (see Silverman, pp. 160–1).

4. Jacques Lacan, *Écrits: A Selection*, trans. Alan Sheridan (London: Tavistock, 1977), p. 265.

5. Desire is impossible to satisfy in Lacanian terms precisely because it derives from the divisions through which the subject is constituted. It is 'fueled by drives which can never be satisfied because they have been denied any expression within the subject's psychic economy', and it is 'directed toward ideal representations which remain forever beyond the subject's reach' (Silverman, p. 176). Sinfield defines Tennyson's particular brand of melancholy in terms of this impossibility of desire: where the loss of the imaginary wholeness coincides with the inability of language to restore that wholeness (p. 102).

6. After Herbert Tucker's outstanding and absorbing account of *Maud*, in *Tennyson and the Doom of Romanticism*, where he explains the appropriations of social discourse, the way social codes are implanted within the strongest forms of personal lyricism, it may appear that I am merely restoring a psychological reading. It should be observed, however, that the context of Hegelian and post-structuralist discourse within which I am placing the poem makes all personal discourse a process of social appropriation – for Lacan, for instance, the self exists as a signifer within the discourse of the Other, and for both Hegel and Derrida the self is situated within a dialectic of self *and* other. Tucker's challenging point that 'the overdetermination of imagery . . . throughout *Maud* seems to call for not just a Freudian but also a social psychology' (p. 411) is encompassed, I would claim, by the Lacanian model, since within this model it is the signifying process itself which provides the means of identification. All references to Tucker's work in this Chapter refer to his book on Tennyson.

7. All quotations from *Maud* are taken from *Tennyson's 'Maud': A definitive edition*, ed. Susan Shatto (Norman and London: University of Oklahoma Press, 1986). Textual references will be given to Part, section and line number.

8. Lacan follows Freud in stressing the affinity between the signifying relations of the symbolic father, the father who represents law and authority, and of death: Freud was of necessity lead, Lacan claims, 'to link the appearance of the signifier of the Father, as author of the Law, with death, even to the murder of the Father' (*Écrits*, p. 199).

9. The biblical texts to which these images allude reinforce this association; see Job 41.24 and Isaiah 50.7 (Shatto, p. 168).

10. Jonathan Wordsworth, in '"What is it, that has been done?": the Central Problem of *Maud*', *Essays in Criticism*, 24 (1974), 356–62,

observes that 'once it has been pointed out it is difficult not to see the details of the first two lines . . . in terms of the female body' (358).
11. See *King Lear*, IV.vi.123–30.
12. The addition of stanzas 14–16 to section i in 1856 may remove some of the ambiguity about the father's suicide, but they also reinforce the sense of the speaker's psychological entrapment, enclosed within a dialectic that equates love with death and loss.
13. Shatto, p. 33; see also Shatto's source, E. G. Withycombe, *The Oxford Dictionary of English Christian Names*, third edition (1977), pp. 212–13.
14. Tucker demonstrates quite brilliantly the interweaving of erotic and cultural power in the poem's language and narrative (see partic. pp. 415–22).
15. The speaker's suicidal impulse has been frequently discussed; see, e.g., Jonas Spatz, 'Love and Death in Tennyson's *Maud*', *Texas Studies in Literature and Language*, vol. 16 (1974), 503–10, and Frank R. Giordano, Jr., 'The "Red-Ribbed Hollow", Suicide and Part III in "Maud"', *Notes and Queries*, vol. 24 (Oct. 1977), 402–4.
16. Earlier readings have been inclined to seek a meaning for Maud's voice in I.iv that is substantive and referential, outside the function of the discourse itself. David Shaw's view, for instance, in *Tennyson's Style* (Ithaca: Cornell University Press, 1976), that the voice is 'a disembodied hieroglyph for something beyond her' (p. 176), tends to minimise its function *as* hieroglyph (sign), and while James Kincaid's reading, in *Tennyson's Major Poems: The Comic and Ironic Patterns* (London: Yale University Press, 1975), suggests that the song really emerges from deep within the speaker, Kincaid's conclusion that Maud 'announces the fully realized self and calls the narrator to participation in a world of unified contraries' (p. 120) suppresses the force of the speaker's utterance that Maud troubles the mind with a 'joy' and a 'glory' which he will '*not find*' (my italics).

In my reading, the poem proposes the impossibility of a world of 'unified contraries', replacing that impossible and Romantic dream with an unfixed world of Romantic irony, of dialectical continuities and process. Dorothy Mermin's argument that 'Maud as an object of love is a *literary* object' (272) acknowledges Maud's status as a sign within literary discourse in general, but that reading severely delimits Maud's function as a signifier within the subjectivity of this speaker's discourse. See also Tucker's point that Maud's 'worth' as a sign arises from her place within a social system (Tucker, p. 417).
17. This thou perceiv'st, which makes thy love more strong,/To love that well which thou must leave ere long.
18. I am assuming here that the 'enchanted moan' alludes to the sound of Maud's voice, whether in providing the answer that he desires in stanza seven or in sexual ecstasy (either imagined or remembered). If the sound is only that of the waves, then he confronts Maud's absence once again. Tucker relates the image to 'the delicious Keatsian phrasing of the preceding lines' (p. 424), which provides a further possibility for reference.

19. See Marilyn J. Kurata, '"A Juggle Born of the Brain": A New Reading of *Maud*', *Victorian Poetry*, vol. 21 (1983), 369–78, for the view that no sexual consummation occurs, and Jonathan Wordsworth for the view that Maud is deflowered (not necessarily in this scene).
20. Two recent studies have stressed the features of this lyric as providing the germ for the poem: see Tucker, pp. 407–8, and Marion Shaw, *Alfred Lord Tennyson* (London: Harvester Wheatsheaf, 1988), pp. 30–2. Shaw suggests that 'it is almost as though the rest of the poem were written to explain, to cover up, finally to have done with, the unassuageable anguish and yearning of this early lyric of romantic love', and she goes on to argue that the original lyric already contained the flaw of such love within its 'linkage of loss and eroticism, and in its very irresolution and incompletion' (p. 31).

    My argument is that the rest of *Maud* also represents the inevitable irresolution of yearning and that the poem does nothing finally to cover up its unassuageable anguish – that indeed the poem shows how any recovery of lost joy and wholeness is possible 'only in death, or in a dream, or in the fantasy of romantic love' (Shaw, p. 31).
21. Christopher Ricks, *Tennyson* (London: Macmillan, 1972), p. 246.
22. For a discussion which eschews the usual focus on the poem as realistic narrative, see Chris R. Vanden Bossche, 'Realism Versus Romance: The War of Cultural Codes in Tennyson's *Maud*', *Victorian Poetry*, vol. 24 (1986), 69–82; Vanden Bossche argues that the poem's contexts 'are not the lives of the narrator, Maud, and their families, but the metaphors, dichotomies, and contradictions that enabled the Victorians to imagine their world' (72).
23. See, e.g., Dorothy Mermin who maintains that the hero's love represents a movement 'into imagination' and 'away from the real present' (273).
24. See Tucker's point about the 'interfusion of private with public discourse' (p. 418).
25. Sinfield relates this issue to idealist claims about the distinction between poetic and ordinary experience: 'By connecting poetic strategies of presence to the mind of a disturbed person, Tennyson undermines the whole status of poetic vision' (p. 173).
26. As Lisa Berglund points out, in '"Faultily Faultless": The Structure of Tennyson's *Maud*', *Victorian Poetry*, 27 (1989), 45–59, there are sixteen 'unanswerable questions' in the first section alone and there is at least one question in all but six of the poem's twenty-eight sections. See also her valuable argument that the speaker's persistent questioning derives from his need to fill the empty pit, 'to make sense of his father's suicide by eliminating the void it has made in his life' (48).
27. See also Samuel Schulman: 'In the intensity of his invocation [in I.xxii] the hero buries his interest in genuine communication' (643–4).
28. Cf. David Goslee, in '"Fairer than aught in the world beside": The Speaker's Invocation of Maud', *Victorian Poetry*, 23 (1985), 391–402,

who acknowledges the speaker's position among varying interpretative versions and who argues that it is through the power of these versions that this speaker, alone of Tennyson's characters, 'can fulfill the Romantic goal of recreating himself, his world and his beloved' (392). The speaker is thus Tennyson's 'consummate love poet' (392), with his madness a means 'of giving ultimate importance to what an "objective" observer would dismiss as a "simple girl"' (401).

I think Goslee takes too lightly, however, the shifting and uneasy ambiguities that are built into the poem's ecstasies. If Tennyson *was* 'systematically preparing the only epistemological ground upon which he as a Victorian poet could celebrate love with an Elizabethan breadth and grandeur' (Goslee, 393), then he discovered at the same time that this epistemology was no 'ground' at all. In my view it is precisely the paradox of a foregrounded epistemological groundlessness that makes *Maud* such a disturbing cultural document. As a poem of romance, it writes a critique of romantic poetry. In this poem, the Romantic and culturally approved desire to re-create the self through language can be fulfilled only as a fiction of expectation, as in I.xxii.

29. Robert E. Lougy, 'The Sounds and Silence of Madness: Language as Theme in Tennyson's *Maud*', *Victorian Poetry*, vol. 22 (1984), 407–26, emphasises Maud's personal silence, apart from her songs, throughout: 'Maud exists in silence, defined by a world in which she is variously seen as daughter, sister, and potential wife, submerged wholly within those primarily male-oriented sexual and social structures around her' (414).

30. Cf. Ian H. C. Kennedy who equates loss of reference with incoherence, in 'The Crisis of Language in Tennyson's *Maud*', *Texas Studies in Language and Literature*, vol. 19 (1977), 161–78.

31. It is important to keep in mind that I am distinguishing between the discourse *as* discourse and the referential reality that is the produced fiction of that discourse; otherwise I would be merely reiterating a truism about any fictional context. My point, then, is that the 'garden' in II.v refers not to Maud's 'actual' garden that was part of the fictionally produced context of Part I, but to the garden of the speaker's discourse, its presence as sign, and the network of traces which that presence invokes. The complicating factor in this poem is that the 'actual' garden always was already produced as a symbolic moment within the speaker's expression.

32. Luke 12.3: 'Therefore whatsoever ye have spoken in darkness shall be heard in the light; and that which ye have spoken in the ear in closets shall be proclaimed upon the housetops' (King James Version).

33. There has of course been considerable discussion of Tennyson's intentions ever since the poem was first published, but his addition of the final stanza to a later edition (in 1856) may suggest some uncertainty on his part or at least the feeling that his views were misrepresented. Representative discussions of this issue are provided by E. F. Shannon, 'The Critical Reception of Tennyson's *Maud*', *PMLA*, vol. 68 (1953), 397–417, and James R. Bennett, 'The

Historical Abuse of Literature: Tennyson's *Maud: A Monodrama* and the Crimean War', *English Studies*, vol. 62 (1981), 34–45.

34. Readers who argue for the speaker's continuing insanity in Part III tend to focus on the speaker's personal psychology: see, e.g., Roy P. Baslar, 'Tennyson the Psychologist', *South Atlantic Quarterly*, vol. 43 (1944), 143–59; Ian Kennedy; Margaret E. Belcher, '"Sane but Shattered": The Ending of Tennyson's *Maud*', *AUMLA*, vol. 50 (1978), 224–34; Marilyn Kurata; Ann C. Colley, *Tennyson and Madness* (Athens, Ga.: University of Georgia Press, 1983); Robert Lougy.
35. See also James R. Bennett, '*Maud*, Part III: Maud's Battle-Song', *Victorian Poetry*, vol. 18 (1980), 35–49: 'Maud enjoins [the speaker] to be a *man* by embracing the epic-heroic code of combat' (44, my italics).
36. Stanza five of Part III was added in 1856.
37. See Belcher: 'It is shocking to realise that the new "deathful-grinning mouths" are but old dabbled lips and "red-ribbed ledges" writ insanely' (232).

CHAPTER 4: FACT AND FACTITIOUS IN *AMOURS DE VOYAGE*

1. Arthur Hugh Clough, *Amours de Voyage*, ed. Patrick Scott (University of Queensland Press, 1974), Canto V, letter v, ll. 95–7, p. 36. All quotations are taken from this comprehensively edited text (hereafter cited as Scott); future references will be given internally, citing canto, letter, and line number (the numbering is continuous within each canto). The poem was largely drafted in 1849, reworked during succeeding years and first published in the *Atlantic Monthly* in 1858. Clough also left a large number of cancelled passages and the textual notes in Scott's edition provide full selections from this unpublished material.
2. Other editions place a comma after line 101. An earlier variant of line 102, found in Bodleian MS.Eng.Poet.d.130 and 132, reads 'vague and unfixed' instead of 'changeable, vague' (cited in Scott, p. 70).
3. See, e.g., Thomas Carlyle, 'Characteristics', in *Critical and Miscellaneous Essays*, vol. III (London: Chapman Hall, 1899).
4. J. D. Jump, 'Clough's *Amours de Voyage*', *English*, vol. 9 (1953), 178.
5. Wendell V. Harris, *Arthur Hugh Clough* (New York: Twayne, 1970), p. 68; Masao Miyoshi, 'Clough's Poems of Self-Irony', *SEL*, vol. 5 (1965), 696.
6. See, for example, Walter E. Houghton, *The Poetry of Clough: An Essay in Revaluation* (Yale University Press, 1963), pp. 127–8; Eugene August, '*Amours de Voyage* and Matthew Arnold in Love: an Inquiry', *VNL*, vol. 60 (Fall 1981), 17; Katherine Chorley, *Arthur Hugh Clough: the Uncommitted Mind* (Oxford: Clarendon Press, 1962), p. 195; Michael Timko, *Innocent Victorian: the Satiric Poetry of Arthur Hugh Clough* (Ohio University Press, 1963), pp. 143–9, 151.
7. So far the only critic to suggest, albeit parenthetically, that the

contrasting opposites in the poem are themselves 'in continual flux', is Robert Micklus, in 'A Voyage of Juxtapositions: the Dynamic World of *Amours de Voyage*', *Victorian Poetry*, vol. 18 (1980), 408.

8. Robindra Kumar Biswas, *Arthur Hugh Clough: Towards a Reconsideration* (Oxford: Clarendon Press, 1972), p. 318.

9. John Goode, '*Amours de Voyage*: the Aqueous Poem', in *The Major Victorian Poets: Reconsiderations*, ed. Isobel Armstrong (London: Routledge & Kegan Paul, 1969), p. 277.

10. In about 1849, when considering questions of ethics, Clough toyed with belief in this idealist structure. His notebooks record the proposition that man's capacity for 'Spiritual Ethics' (the ability to withdraw and 'decline solicitations') 'depends on his consciousness of Time and Duration, the Transience of externa, The Perpetuity (permanence) of the Internum' (Scott, Appendix 3, p. 82).

11. See also John Goode, who uses the echo in this passage of the image of the stream and its association with the unruly mob to show how the rhetoric of chaos is built into the image of growth (p. 287).

12. This is a point made by Goode: 'The ... image ironises Genesis by making knowledge (which involved the fall) the high point of life, and ironises knowledge by making it a parasitic, fruitless and futile failure of growth to become anything other than process' (p. 295).

13. In III.iv.91 ('ye that extrude from the ocean your helpless faces'), 'the violently active verb taken with "helpless" implies an unresolved ambiguity in the relationship between freedom and necessity. In the anarchy of the sea, there is no defined and stable distinction between inner and outer' (Goode, p. 295).

14. Earlier MS versions of these lines had 'on the spot' instead of 'in a place' (see Scott, p. 53). My reading is reinforced by the effect of this change which is to make the link more vague, less specific in terms of a literal location.

15. Cf. Wendell Harris who finds each moment excessive: Claude's 'earlier description of Knowledge ... denied the possibilities of rational thought too strongly; the position to which he has now come errs in the other direction' (p. 75).

16. I am indebted to Professor Herbert Tucker for this point. As he succinctly suggested, 'Clough sentences his central consciousness not only to acting like a clause but also to being named after one' (private letter, 1 June 1988). The name also has origins in terms of *claudus* (lame, defective, wavering), which might relate to Claude's uncertainty and emotional timidity.

17. Biswas reads the elegiacs as acting in an ironic relationship with the hexameters of the letters: 'If these gracefully finished, traditionally accomplished elegiacs mock at the sprawling libertinage of the hexameters, the exceptional openness of the hexameters, their receptiveness to process, exposes, in turn, the illusory and unreal quality of this kind of loveliness. The two kinds of poetry, in fact, organize two radically different modes of experience' (p. 314).

My departure from this interpretation is at the point when it tends to place the elegiacs and hexameters in detached opposition:

in my reading, the two modes are differentiated, but not radically different; as two modes of experience, they exist in dialectical, not dualistic, relationship; neither mode is separable from the conditions of textuality which are common to each.
18. Wendell Harris, who as late as 1970 appears to be the first critic to consider the function of the elegiacs in any serious way, comments that 'the relationship of a number of these to the tale proper is not at all clear, principally because they are not consistently spoken by the same voice' (p. 76).
19. See Scott, note to III.15–16, p. 31.

CHAPTER 5: LANGUAGE AND TRUTH IN *THE RING AND THE BOOK*

1. Quotations from *The Ring and the Book* are from the final version in *The Poetical Works of Robert Browning*, vols viii, ix, x (London: Smith, Elder, 1889), and references are to book and line number within the poem itself; this version numbers the half-lines, similar to the issue of the first edition edited by Richard Altick (Penguin).
2. Richard D. Altick and James F. Loucks, II, for instance, in *Browning's Roman Murder Story: A Reading of "The Ring and the Book"* (University of Chicago Press, 1968), claim as a premise of the poem that 'while man's truth . . . is relative, God's truth is absolute' (p. 21), and through demonstrating Browning's discovery of 'a transcendental truth' in the case records, the poem enacts 'a parable of the ways of God to men' (p. 26); Gordon W. Thompson, in 'A Spirit Birth Conceived of Flesh: Browning's Concept of Art in *The Ring and the Book*', *Tennessee Studies in Literature*, vol. 14 (1969), 75–86, states that 'Browning conceives of Art and Love and Truth as . . . quite apart from the mere words of men' (75); in 'Multiple Narratives & Relative Truths: A Study of *The Ring and the Book, The Woman in White*, and *The Moonstone*', *Browning Institute Studies*, vol. 10 (1982), 143–61, Sue Lonoff suggests that 'Browning's truth' deals with the ways in which mankind may 'attain spiritual insight and approach The Word beyond mere words' (149); and in the most recent example of metaphysical reading, Paul Zietlow, in 'The Ascending Concerns of *The Ring and the Book*: Reality, Moral Vision, and Salvation', *SP*, vol. 84 (1987), 194–218, argues that 'Pompilia's tragedy offers luminous moments of reverberate truth whose impact cannot be formulated in words; it blossoms miraculously into reality in those infinite regions of the soul that lie beyond the boundaries of articulation' (209–10).

For non-transcendental readings, exceptions to the separation of language and truth, see Isobel Armstrong, 'The Ring and the Book: the Uses of Prolixity', in *The Major Victorian Poets: Reconsiderations*, ed. Isobel Armstrong (London: Routledge & Kegan Paul, 1969); Claudette Kemper Columbus, 'The Ring and the Book: A Masque for the Making of Meaning', *PQ*, vol. 53 (1974), 237–55; Susan Blalock, 'Browning's *The Ring and the Book*: "A Novel Country"',

Browning Institute Studies, vol. 11 (1983), 39–50; and Adam Potkay, 'The Problem of Identity and the Grounds for Judgment in *The Ring and the Book*', *Victorian Poetry*, vol. 25 (1987), 143–57. In 'The Dynamic Imagery of *The Ring and the Book*', *Studies in Browning and His Circle*, vol. 4 (1976), 7–29, Stephen C. Walker, despite his stress on Browning's restless and ambiguous imagery, nevertheless concludes that the dynamic symbolism of the poem 'transcends "mere imagery"', although what is incarnated is not so much God's truth as 'the restless irony of Browning's poetic insight' (29).

3. These contexts also extend to the reader, including you and me. In her use of the masque form as a model for the poem, Columbus demonstrates the reader's necessary involvement in the poem's production (see particularly her account of the carnival context, 244–5); Samuel L. Chell, in *The Dynamic Self: Browning's Poetry of Duration* (University of Victoria [B.C., Canada]: English Literary Studies, 1984), argues that it is the reader 'who ultimately holds the key to meaning' (p. 98); and Zietlow's claim that the poem represents the transcendent truth of Christian salvation depends on a repetition in the reader's mind of the Pope's 'witness' to spiritual power (see 195, 216). Zietlow does add that 'for the nineteenth- or twentieth-century reader to experience fully what Browning intends would in itself be a miracle' (218).

4. In Altick and Loucks, chap. 1, and in Mary Rose Sullivan, *Browning's Voices in 'The Ring and the Book': A Study of Method and Meaning* (University of Toronto Press, 1969), chap. 7.

5. Gordon Thompson provides a typical example: 'A poet is not a wordsmith, but a man of elevated vision who can make others share his sight, not through verbal dexterity, but with imagination' (78).

6. This powerful aesthetic has been subject to continual critical analysis in recent decades, notably by Paul de Man; see Christopher Norris, 'Paul de Man and the Critique of Aesthetic Ideology', *AUMLA*, vol. 69 (May 1988), 3–47; rpt. in *Paul de Man: Deconstruction and the Critique of Aesthetic Ideology* (London: Methuen, 1988), chap. 2.

7. See, for instance, Stopford A. Brooke, *The Poetry of Robert Browning* (London: Isbister, 1902), G. K. Chesterton, *Robert Browning* (1903; London: Macmillan, 1957), and Arthur Symons, *An Introduction to the Study of Browning* (London: Dent, 1906); for further discussion of this point, see Herbert F. Tucker, 'Dramatic Monologue and the Overhearing of Lyric', in *Lyric Poetry: Beyond New Criticism*, eds. Chaviva Hosek and Patricia Parker (Ithaca: Cornell University Press, 1985), pp. 226–43.

8. Most readings which emphasise metaphysical truth in the poem appear not to consider the comic and parodic qualities of this version. Hence Barton R. Friedman, in 'To Tell the Sun from the Druid Fire: Imagery of Good and Evil in *The Ring and the Book*', *SEL*, vol. 6 (1966), observes a 'struggle between good and evil, God and the devil' (706), and Kay Austen, in 'Browning Climbs the Beanstalk: the Alienated Poet in *The Ring and the Book*', *Studies in Browning and His Circle*, vol. 5 (1977), claims that 'In showing the truth of God

through the archetypal conflict between devil and saint, Browning attains the heaven for which he is striving in Book I – artistic and personal salvation' (37). In the poem, Tertium Quid and Pompilia acknowledge Guido's *human* condition, as a man whose mother, at least, loves him (IV.1593–6, VII.1715), and Guido himself mocks expectations about his horny-headed status (XI.554–7).

9. The performative function of the poem then allows the reader to repeat this process. See Altick and Loucks, who argue that while truth is not accessible to individual speakers, 'it is accessible to us, because Browning gives us the means of comparing all the discrepant versions and discounting palpable bias wherever it appears' (p. 270).

10. Henry James, 'The Novel in "The Ring and the Book"', *Notes on Novelists* (London: Dent, 1914), pp. 306–26; for the use of Bakhtin against James in relation to *The Ring and the Book*, see Blalock.

11. See, e.g., Altick and Loucks: Tertium Quid, Pompilia and the Pope, 'together ... embody Browning's opinions on the central moral themes of the poem' (p. 40). It is an amazing fact of criticism on the poem that despite the recognition of irony, duplicity and ambiguity in every other monologue, Pompilia's speech has been almost universally exempted from such linguistic corruptions. The exceptions have been Columbus, and William Walker, '*Pompilia* and Pompilia', *VP*, vol. 22 (1984), 47–63. See also Potkay: 'no one interpretation ... can claim absolute validity or transparent truth' (148).

12. The triadic structures suggested by Altick and Loucks, and later elaborated by Litzinger, work quite satisfactorily for books II–X (three groups of three monologuists related to popular thought, the protagonists' action and institutional responses), but they struggle to accommodate the remaining fourth of the poem, the other three books which fail to form a coherent unit of their own. See Altick and Loucks, pp. 39–40, 76–81, and Boyd Litzinger, 'The Structural Logic of *The Ring and the Book*', in *Nineteenth-Century Perspectives: Essays in Honor of Lionel Stevenson*, ed. Clyde de L. Ryals (Durham, N.C.: Duke University Press, 1974), pp. 105–14.

13. See Robert Langbaum, *The Poetry of Experience* (1957; New York, Norton, 1963), chap. 3, who also finds that the relativism is marred by books I and XII, which make 'our judgment ... forced from the beginning' (p. 135); and L. J. Swingle, 'Truth and *The Ring and the Book*: A Negative View', *VP*, vol. 6 (1968), 259–69, who argues that the poem is not about 'the search for and discovery of truth, but the loss of it' (267). Lee Erickson repeats Swingle's emphasis on an ontological theme, in *Robert Browning: His Poetry and His Audiences* (Ithaca: Cornell University Press, 1984), chap. 7.

14. John M. Menaghan, 'Embodied Truth: *The Ring and the Book* Reconsidered', *UTQ*, vol. 52 (1983), 263–76, argues that Browning represents a truth which is 'embodied, yet elusive' (275); in his view, Browning's intention is 'to bring us through an experience of the inaccessibility of, and at the same time fuel our hunger for, the truth' (266); this

15. reading closely approximates aspects of Romantic irony, notably Schlegel's sense of antagonism between 'the impossibility and the necessity of complete communication' (see Chapter 2).
15. The function of Celestino's text as a Zeno-like paradox has been noticed by William Walker and Potkay; Potkay proposes that no reader can 'get beyond the paradoxical structure of Fra Celestino's enunciation' (157); I agree with Potkay's suggestion that Celestino's paradox acts as an 'emblem' for the poem, but in terms of Derrida's 'vigilant practice', not in terms of the 'negative capability' which Potkay evokes – the Keatsian concept too readily restores a structure of idealist consciousness. See also Blalock, 49.
16. To this challenge that there is no divine referent, only changing verbal fictions, the Pope replies not by establishing a truth outside language, but by arguing the need for a religious model in order to promote right moral action.
17. In noting that 'truth' or 'true' occur some 317 times in the poem, Altick and Loucks appear not to distinguish between meaning as a signifier/signified relationship and meaning as a sign/referent relationship: for them the words 'truth' and 'true' struggle to survive 'as tokens of clear meaning' (p. 121).
18. When referring to the poet or to Browning in this discussion, I refer to the poet/speaker who is the produced subject of the language and content of book I and, later, book XII, and who, in the poem, takes responsibility for its production; I do not refer to the biological referent named Robert Browning.
19. The standard refinements of the ring image as an analogy for poetic creativity are Paul A. Cundiff, 'The Clarity of Browning's Ring-Metaphor', *PMLA*, vol. 63 (1948), 1276–82; George R. Wasserman, 'The Meaning of Browning's Ring-Figure', *MLN*, vol. 76 (1961), 420–26; and Mary Sullivan's extension of both these arguments (pp. 19–20).
20. As Walter M. Kendrick suggests, in 'The Vanishing Word', an unpublished Ph.D. thesis (Yale University, 1975), to make the ring 'the sign of more signs is to extend the figure to include figuration, to make the Ring a figure of a figure' (p. 228). I am indebted to this thesis for several suggestions about the ring metaphor: that it signifies the whole series of rings (p. 231), and that 'each ring is the sign of what precedes and follows it' (p. 233). Kendrick also argues that 'As an active sign, the Ring reconciles time and space, change and continuity. It is always different, yet always the same' (p. 233).
21. See Potkay: 'The Old Yellow Book does not . . . present "facts" in an empirical sense, but the inscriptions of interpretive testimonies, which are already at a remove from the inscrutable historical phenomena of the case' (156).
22. See also Kendrick: 'Rings, books, and men are only the signs of life, not life itself, unless they are being forged, being read, breathing and speaking' (p. 245).
23. The process by which all Browning's poetry enacts beginnings that

defer closure has been brilliantly described by Herbert Tucker in *Browning's Beginnings*.
24. Harvey Feinberg, 'The Four-Cornered Circle: Truth and Illusion in Browning's *The Ring and the Book*', *Studies in Browning and His Circle*, vol. 13 (1985), 76, 93.
25. Celestino's emblematic text about God's truth is in fact an example of this process. Itself a quotation, it is a variant of the text from Romans 3:4 that has already been cited (by Bottini) in book XII (453–4). The form of the first citation, 'Let God be true, and every man/A liar', with its grammar of command or wish rather than indicative statement, avoids the paradoxical force of Celestino's version, and such difference is part of the enactment of recontextualising. Celestino provides this text with a context in his sermon which assigns it meaning within the further context of the Franceschini case. The sermon (or its extract) is then recontextualised within Bottini's letter, where the paradox of the 'text' is noted and used against Celestino, accusing him of flattering the Pope (XII.650–3). Bottini's letter is in turn contextualised in book XII by Archangeli's letter and by the poet-speaker's disclosure that the further trial about Pompilia's wanton condition found in her favour.
26. See Altick and Loucks, pp. 199–201, Armstrong, 'The Uses of Prolixity', pp. 187–8.
27. See J. Hillis Miller, *The Disappearance of God* (1963; New York: Schocken, 1965): 'The philosophical and aesthetic moral of the poem is: "By multiplying points of view on the same event, you may transcend point of view, and reach at last God's own infinite perspective"' (p. 149).
28. For recognition that the form of the poem is open-ended, see Blalock, 43; Erickson, p. 234; and Potkay, 152–3.
29. I take the concept of serial texts from Douglas Standring, 'The Ring and the Book: Texts, and the Texture of Experience', unpublished M.A. thesis (Massey University, New Zealand, 1984).
30. See, e.g., Jacques Derrida, 'Living On: Border Lines', trans. James Hulbert, in *Deconstruction and Criticism*, eds. Harold Bloom, *et al.* (New York: Seabury Press, 1979): 'no meaning can be determined out of context, but no context permits saturation' (p. 81); for further discussion, see E. W. Slinn, 'Deconstruction and Meaning: The Textuality Game', *Philosophy and Literature*, vol. 12 (1988), 80–7. It is not my purpose here to represent the views of Robert Browning in his letters, but there is a remarkable passage in one letter to Elizabeth Barrett (11 January 1846) which could readily act as a gloss on *différance*: 'How I never say what I sit down to say! How saying the little makes me want to say the more! How the least of little things, once taken up as a thing to be imparted to you, seems to need explanations and commentaries', in *The Letters of Robert Browning and Elizabeth Barrett Barrett, 1845–1846*, ed. Elvan Kintner, I (Cambridge, Mass.: Belknap Press, 1969), p. 381.

See also the Wedgwood correspondence, which relates directly to *The Ring and the Book*, where Julia Wedgwood uses the metaphor of a postscript to suggest a related point about supplementarity ('It is as if all utterance were the postscript to some letter that contained all that one really cared to say') and deferral ('I doubt if even my postscript is intelligible, or would be to another. I have a wonderful sense that you can drop some grain into these muddy thoughts, that will make them clear'), in *Robert Browning and Julia Wedgwood: A Broken Friendship as Revealed by Their Letters*, ed. Richard Curle (New York: Stokes, 1937), p. 160.

31. See Blalock: 'The reader is forced to reformulate his judgments with every repetition and absorb an increasing amount of uncertainty instead of arriving at a firmer grasp on "true events"' (45).

32. Jacques Derrida, in *Of Grammatology*, trans. Gayatri Chakravorty Spivak (Baltimore: The Johns Hopkins University Press, 1976), locates the first break in the 'entrenched Western tradition' of the Logos, the authority of speech and grammar, with Nietzsche and with the 'graphic poetics' of the Fenellosa-Pound combination; in order to achieve this break it was necessary to disrupt the 'transcendental authority and dominant category of ... being' (p. 92). *The Ring and the Book* does not display a graphic poetics, but its disruption of verbal continuity and conceptual wholeness and its critique of transcendent truth would suggest that it can be linked to this break with logocentric tradition. It is also possible in the context of this study to suggest that Victorian poetry generally, insofar as it enacts a critique of the category of being established by the Cartesian *cogito*, anticipates such a break. See also Christine Froula, 'Browning's *Sordello* and the Parables of Modernist Poetics', *ELH*, vol. 52 (1985), 965–92, who makes a case for *Sordello* as 'a kind of "missing link" between Romantic humanism and modernist poetics' (966).

33. See Simon Petch, 'Browning's Roman Lawyers', in *Browning Centenary Essays: Special Edition of AUMLA*, eds. Simon Petch and Warwick Slinn, *AUMLA*, vol. 71 (May 1989), pp. 109–38. Petch's article is the first major study to stress the role of the lawyers in relation to the poem's concern with language: 'the law becomes the focus for the poem's central, social interest in language and discourse, institutions and authority' (p. 115). Cf. Zietlow who focuses only on religious language in the poem.

34. W. David Shaw emphasises the Pope's pragmatism in *The Dialectical Temper* (Ithaca: Cornell University Press, 1968), pp. 298–9.

35. Cf. Myron Tuman, in 'Browning's Historical Intention in *The Ring and the Book*', *Studies in Browning and His Circle*, vol. 3 (1975), 76–95, who, by placing the poem within the historicist tradition, reads 'Art' as a reference to history: 'Browning is saying that "Art" has a meaning that transcends the interest of any one group of readers' (94).

CHAPTER 6: THE POLITICS OF SELF IN *THE RING AND THE BOOK*

1. Approaches to the poem which argue that Browning intends readers to 'experience' for themselves the speeches and arguments in order to 'know' experientially, not just abstractly, the events of the murder case (see Armstrong, 'The Uses of Prolixity', and Zietlow), risk failing to consider the interdependence of experience and the representation (discourse) of experience; they may also, thereby, sustain a Romantic epistemology which privileges and internalises the self as centre. The post-structuralist point about experience is that it only achieves expression and meaning within the semiotic realm.
2. See the Conclusion to Walter Pater's *The Renaissance*.
3. See Paul Ricoeur, 'History as Narrative and Practice', *Philosophy Today*, vol. 29 (1985), 213–22: 'It is in telling our own stories that we give ourselves an identity. We recognize ourselves in the stories we tell about ourselves' (214). The role of narrative has become a central theme in recent discussions of psychoanalysis and literature, but for further discussion of the self as a narrative construct, see Anthony Paul Kerby, 'The Language of the Self', *Philosophy Today*, vol. 30 (1986), 210–23, and 'The Adequacy of Self-Narration: A Hermeneutical Approach', *Philosophy and Literature*, vol. 12 (1988), 232–43.
4. See also Samuel Chell: 'The temporal, incomplete nature of meaning and the inclusion of the past within the evolving, onward movement of the present are essential to the experience of self which it is the poet's task through language to represent' (p. 97). This formulation, however, still allows the existence of a separate self or separate experience (separate, that is, from discourse or semiosis) which is represented 'through language'; I am arguing that *The Ring and the Book* ultimately generates the more Hegelian and post-structuralist proposition of a subject who is tied to mediation, to semiotic structures.
5. This feature of earlier dramatic structures is parodied by Tertium Quid when he refers to the mob's desire for the Law to clear things up by producing a divine Truth in 'the play's fifth act' (IV.15–17).
6. Tertium Quid's anecdote about the Punch and Judy puppets (IV.1280–99) illustrates the way roles may be altered, judgements reversed, the genre transformed (tragedy becomes farce), and how there is time for 'one last worst fight more'. In the drama of writing there is no fixed character or formulation, only incompletion and reversal.
7. It is worth noting that Nietzsche does not deny that the subject exists; he redefines the nature of its existence. Consider the following extract from *The Will to Power*, trans. W. Kaufmann and R. J. Hollingdale, ed. W. Kaufmann (New York, 1968): '"The subject" is the fiction that many similar states in us are the effect of one substratum: but it is we who first created the "similarity" of these states; our adjusting them and making them similar is the fact, not their similarity (– which

ought rather to be denied –)' (p. 269). In this formulation, the self does indeed exist as fact, but as the fact of action-within-process, of the 'adjusting' and the 'making'. The constructed vision, the unitary self which can only exist as a conception, is a fiction, but the self as agent, located within its continuing and temporal action, nowhere fixed, is a fact.

8. Cf. Kris Davis, 'Browning's Caponsacchi: Stuck in the Gap', *Victorian Poetry*, vol. 25 (1987), 57–66, who refers to the court situation as the 'frame narrative' and to Caponsacchi's narrative as the 'kernel story' (57–8, 63). It is through the interactive nature of the narrative process that the double action of self may be observed – that double action whereby the self at once writes and is thereby written. Note that there is also another sense in which the subject of the enunciation, the producer of the speech, is the reader, since it is in the act of reading, always an act in the present, that the monologue is given life and meaning.

9. For Caponsacchi's passivity, see Constance W. Hassett, 'Browning's Caponsacchi: Convert and Apocalyptist', *PQ*, vol. 60 (1981), 487–500; Slinn, *Browning and the Fictions of Identity*, pp. 118–19; Davis, 57–66.

10. Kris Davis' reading of the analogy of the two martyrs as an image of security which 'returns Caponsacchi to the tomb-womb' (Davis, 61) complements very well my suggestions about sexual sublimation.

11. For most readers Pompilia has seemed the epitome of idealised womanhood; see, for example, a particularly effusive comment by William E. Harrold, in *The Variance and the Unity: A Study of the Complementary Poems of Robert Browning* (Athens: Ohio University Press, 1973): Pompilia is rendered 'symbolic of the essential feminine principles of intuition, emotion, love, subjectivity, existential epistemology, and organic development through inspired harmonious interaction of the parts' (p. 135). As noted earlier (see Chapter 5, n. 11), almost all readers, with the exceptions of Claudette Kemper Columbus and William Walker, have exempted Pompilia's monologue from the corruptions of ambiguity and irony.

12. The most obvious example of Pompilia's conscious sense of irony is when she addresses her auditors directly:

> And now you are not tired? How patient then
> All of you, – Oh yes, patient this long while
> Listening, and understanding, I am sure!
> Four days ago, when I was sound and well
> And like to live, no one would understand.
> (VII.905–9)

See also William Walker's discussion and documentation of Pompilia's irony and awareness of discrepancies (50–1).

13. There is also the odd interesting discrepancy about facts: for instance, Pompilia says first that she enjoyed 'thirteen' happy years before her marriage (373), but then later claims that she was 'barely twelve years old' when married (734). Is this a simple slip or a bending of

Notes to pp. 167–87

details in order to enlist sympathy? Consider also the discrepancy, noted by William Walker (60), between Pompilia's early declaration that she thought it was Gaetano's nurse at the Villa-door (59–60) and her later claim that it was Caponsacchi she expected to see (1808).

14. A similar shift occurs when Pompilia acclaims Caponsacchi's success: 'I say, the angel saved me: I am safe!' (1643). The next lines stress her *own* sense of purified completion, as she stands 'Traced round about with white to front the world' (1646).

15. Her tolerant and wondering tone is accompanied by moments of explicit condemnation (270–1, 312, 654–5, 1585–96) or of bitterness and anger (517–20, 1347).

16. See also the later passage when he too claims the mark of God: 'Me, the immeasurably marked, by God,/Master of the whole world of such as you' (XI.1505–6).

17. There is an interesting textual revision with respect to this need, or will, to changelessness. Guido responds to the offered crucifix late in the monologue by saying, 'Vainly you try to change what should not change,/And shall not' (2223–4). The first edition reads: "T in vain you try to change, what should not change,/And cannot' (*The Ring and the Book*, vol. IV [Smith, Elder, 1869], p. 186, XI.2221–2). The first version claims there is no possibility of change; the later version (it remained unaltered in the second edition) allows the possibility of change, but stresses Guido's resistance to it, which is consistent with the *need* to believe in a fixed self despite the forces against it. It could be argued that this revision is at odds with Guido's moral strategy which claims a self for which he is not responsible (a self that cannot be changed is a self that cannot make moral choices), but the tussle between potential change and willed resistance is more in keeping with the contradictions and fluidity of discourse (and so of consciousness) in the monologue.

18. Guido himself is desperately afraid of cuckoldry – see XI.897–919.

19. See Lisa O'Connor, 'The Construction of a Self: Guido and Metaphor in Book XI of *The Ring and the Book*', in *Browning Centenary Essays: Special Edition of AUMLA*, eds. Simon Petch and Warwick Slinn, *AUMLA*, vol. 71 (May 1989), pp. 139–58.

20. See also O'Connor's discussion of Pompilia as 'pungent plague', 'taenia', 'pale poison' and 'wreath' (pp. 146–9); O'Connor points out that these images give Pompilia power of life and death over Guido (p. 156).

AFTERWORD: ON POETRY AS A SIGNIFICANT DISCOURSE

1. M. Sachs, 'Space Time and Elementary Interactions in Relativity', *Physics Today*, vol. 22 (Feb. 1969), 53; cited in Fritjof Capra, *The Tao of Physics* (1975; London: Fontana, 1983), p. 183, my italics. For the notion that idealism has ironically become the 'truth' of materialism, see also Solomon, *In the Spirit of Hegel*, pp. 186–7.

Index

Altick, Richard D. 59, 127, 141, 194 n.27, 201 n.2, 202 n.4, 203 n.9, 203 nn.11–12, 204 n.17, 205 n.26
Armstrong, Isobel 6, 11–12, 13, 185 n.4, 189 n.4, 190 n.13, 193 n.21, 201 n.2, 205 n.26, 207 n.1
Arnold, Matthew 32, 49, 98, 117, 193 n.16
   Empedocles on Etna 46–9, 60, 98
August, Eugene 199 n.6
Austen, Kay 202 n.8

Baslar, Roy P. 199 n.34
Belcher, Margaret E. 199 n.34, 199 n.37
Bennett, James R. 198 n.33, 199 n.35
Bentham, Jeremy 11
Berglund, Lisa 197 n.26
Biswas, Robindra 91, 200 n.8, 200 n.17
Blalock, Susan 201 n.2, 203 n.10, 204 n.15, 205 n.28, 206 n.31
Bloom, Harold 193 n.21
Brooke, Stopford A. 202 n.7
Browning, Robert 8, 14, 19, 20, 28, 33–5, 38, 49, 64, 65, 120–48 *passim*, 149, 151, 152, 187, 203 n.9, 204 n.18, 207 n.1
   'Andrea del Sarto' 37, 44, 61
   Archangelis (*The Ring and the Book*) 144–5, 182
   'Bishop Blougram's Apology' 33, 37
   'Bishop Orders his Tomb at Saint Praxed's Church, The' 37, 61
   Bottini (*The Ring and the Book*) 141, 143, 182
   'Caliban Upon Setebos' 27, 61–2
   Caponsacchi (*The Ring and the Book*) 127, 137, 153, 155–63, 166, 167–71, 181, 182, 208 n.9
   'Childe Roland to the Dark Tower Came' 61
   'Cristina' 20
   'Epilogue' to *Dramatis Personae* 33–6, 61, 187
   'Evelyn Hope' 37, 61
   Fifine at the Fair 28, 37
   Fra Celestino (*The Ring and the Book*) 123–4, 125, 139, 143, 146, 166, 204 n.15, 205 n.25
   'Fra Lippo Lippi' 20
   Guido Franceschini (*The Ring and the Book*) 124–5, 127, 130, 137, 141, 143, 145, 151, 153–5, 156–8, 163, 167, 170–83, 203 n.8, 209 nn.17–18, 209 n.20
   'Johannes Agricola in Meditation' 20, 37
   'Last Ride Together, The' 61
   'Mr Sludge, "the Medium"' 37, 61
   'My Last Duchess' (Duke of Ferrara) 20, 27, 37
   'Pictor Ignotus' 44, 61
   Pompilia (*The Ring and the Book*) 123, 137, 146, 153–4, 155–63, 163–72, 176–8, 182–3, 203 n.8, 203 n.11, 208 nn.11–13, 209 nn.14–15, 209 n.20
   Pope (*The Ring and the Book*) 122–6, 128, 137, 141, 143–6, 172, 174, 179, 182–3, 204 n.16, 206 n.34
   'Porphyria's Lover' 14, 20
   'Rabbi Ben Ezra' 61
   Ring and the Book, The 2, 3, 8, 19, 119–48, 149–84
   'Saul' 20
   Tertium Quid (*The Ring and the*

Index

Book) 137, 176, 178–81, 203 n.8, 207 n.5
'Too Late' 37, 61
'Two in the Campagna' 38, 53–60, 61, 64, 65
'Worst of It, The' 45

Carlyle, Thomas 91, 199 n.3
Carr, Arthur J. 194 n.1
Cartesian, see Descartes
Chell, Samuel L. 139, 202 n.3, 207 n.4
Chesterton, G.K. 202 n.7
Chorley, Katherine 199 n.6
Clough, Arthur Hugh 8, 20, 92, 200 n.10
   Amours de Voyage 3, 8, 20, 90–118, 199 n.1
Colley, Anne C. 194 n.29, 199 n.34
Columbus, Claudette Kemper 201 n.2, 202 n.3, 203 n.11, 208 n.11
Connor, Steven 195 n.2
Cundiff, Paul A. 204 n.19

Davis, Kris 158, 190 n.22, 208 n.8, 208 n.10
de Man, Paul 202 n.6
Derrida, Jacques 1, 3, 5, 8, 10, 16, 22, 25, 34, 38, 41–4, 48, 50–3, 58, 62, 63, 65, 93, 190 n.14, 191 n.26, 192 n.14, 193 n.19, 193 n.22, 195 n.6, 204 n.15, 205 n.30, 206 n.32
   'Freud and the Scene of Writing' 50–3
Descartes, René 9, 14, 28, 40, 86, 93, 97, 104, 116, 119, 122, 142, 151, 173, 183, 187, 188 n.5, 189 n.6
Descombes, Vincent 188 n.2
différance (Derridean) 8, 34, 43, 135, 184, 205 n.30
difference (Hegelian) 2, 8, 23, 26–8, 31–2, 34, 43, 45, 76, 184
dialectic
   as interconnectedness 5–6, 183
   as opposition 13, 39–40, 192 n.13
   as process, transformation 8, 13–14, 16, 74, 76, 91, 113, 117, 123, 142, 150, 182, 196 n.16
   Hegelian 4, 8, 16, 22–5, 28, 31–2, 36, 39, 41–2, 46, 61, 93, 103–4, 115–16, 139, 141, 185–7
   of self 25–37, 44–5
Dickens, Charles 7

Eliot, George 18
Erickson, Lee 203 n.13, 205 n.28

Feinberg, Harvey 205 n.24
Fichte, Johann Gottlieb 12, 14, 21, 24, 39
Findlay, J.N. 30, 190 n.18
Freud, Sigmund 50, 195 n.6, 195 n.8
Friedman, Barton R. 202 n.8
Froula, Christine 206 n.32
Fulweiler, Howard W. 189 n.3
Furst, Lilian 40, 192 nn.11–12

Gadamer, Hans-Georg 5, 31, 188 n.3, 190 n.20
Gaskell, Elizabeth 18
Giordano, Frank R., Jr. 196 n.15
Goethe, Johann W. 115
Goode, John 92, 102, 104, 200 n.9, 200 nn.11–13
Goslee, David 197 n.28

Hamlet 105, 112
Hamilton, Paul 192 n.10
Handwerk, Gary 40, 192 n.9
Haney, Janice L. 192 n.10
Harland, Richard 13, 42, 189 n.6
Harris, Wendell V. 199 n.5, 200 n.15, 201 n.18
Harrold, William E. 208 n.11
Hartman, Geoffrey 194 nn.29–30
Hassett, Constance W. 208 n.9
Hegel, Georg Wilhelm Friedrich 1, 3–4, 5, 8, 12–37, 38, 39, 41–5, 49, 63, 93, 109, 127, 128, 131, 135, 141, 185–7, 189 n.6, 189 n.8, 190 n.15, 191 nn.1–2, 192n n.12–14, 195 n.6
   Phenomenology of Mind, The 3, 13, 16, 21, 32, 13–32 *passim*, 41, 42, 43, 189 n.5, 189 n.11

Philosophy of Mind, The 30–1, 190 nn.18–19
see also idealism; language
Heidegger, Martin 10, 16
Hopkins, Gerard Manley 12
Houghton, Walter E. 199 n.6
Hume, David 92, 93

idealism
  objective (Hegelian) 13–18, 29–30, 32, 38, 41, 91, 109, 113, 185–7, 192 n.15, 209 n.1
  subjective (Romantic) 1–2, 6–8, 10–13, 16, 24, 26, 29, 31, 40, 44, 96–7, 104, 108, 111, 113, 116–17, 119, 170–3, 207 n.1
Inwood, M.J. 189 n.8

James, Henry 123, 203 n.10
Joseph, Gerhard 194 n.29
Jump, J.D. 199 n.4

Kant, Immanuel 12, 14, 15, 30, 39, 42, 111, 122, 187, 189 n.6, 191 n.26
Keats, John 59, 196 n.18, 204 n.15
Kendrick, Walter M. 204 n.20, 204 n.22
Kennedy, Ian H.C. 198 n.30, 199 n.34
Kerby, Anthony Paul 194 n.25, 207 n.3
Kermode, Frank 189 n.10
King Lear 68, 196 n.11
Kincaid, James 196 n.16
Kurata, Marilyn J. 197 n.19, 199 n.34

Lacan, Jacques 65, 194 n.2, 195n n.3–6, 195 n.8
Laing, R. D. 190 n.17
Langbaum, Robert 203 n.13
language
  and consciousness 7, 11, 44, 46–50, 50–53, 149–52, 183–4
  see also self as text; textualism
Litzinger, Boyd 203 n.12
Lonoff, Sue 201 n.2
Loucks, James F. 127, 141, 201 n.2, 202 n.4, 203 n.9, 203 nn.11–12, 204 n.17, 205 n.26

Lougy, Robert E. 8, 188 n.8, 198 n.29, 199 n.34

Martin, Loy D. 151, 188 n.5
Marx, Karl 12–13, 16, 27, 28
McGowan, John P. 188 n.1
Mehlman, Jeffrey 52, 193 n.24
Mellor, Anne K. 191 n.6
Menaghan, John M. 203 n.14
Mermin, Dorothy 7–8, 188 n.6, 194 n.1, 196 n.16, 197 n.23
Michaels, Walter Benn 52, 193 n.25
Micklus, Robert 200 n.7
Miller, J. Hillis 205 n.27
Milton, John 120
mirror, mind as 7, 9–11, 15, 25, 40
Miyoshi, Masao 199 n.5

Nietzsche, Friedrich 10, 16, 44, 48–9, 57, 151, 189 n.3, 193n n.17–18, 193 n.20, 206 n.32, 207 n.7
Norris, Christopher 16, 42, 189 n.3, 202 n.6

O'Connor, Lisa 178, 181, 191 n.25, 209 nn.19–20

Paradise Lost 120, 122
Pater, Walter 207 n.2
Peacock, Thomas Love 11
Peirce, Charles Sanders 52, 60
Peltason, Timothy 193 n.21
Petch, Simon S. 142, 144, 194 n.1, 206 n.33
Plato 5, 14, 189 n.6, 191 n.1
Potkay, Adam 145, 202 n.2, 203 n.11, 204 n.15, 204 n.21, 205 n.28

Rajan, Tilottama 7, 188 n.7
Ricoeur, Paul 150, 207 n.3
Ricks, Christopher 197 n.21
Romantic irony 38–41, 139, 191 n.6, 192 n.12, 196 n.16, 204 n.14
Rorty, Richard 9, 10, 188 n.1
Ryals, Clyde de L. 191 n.6, 193 n.21

Sachs, Mendel 187, 209 n.1
Sartre, Jean-Paul 28

Index

Saussure, Ferdinand de 43
Schelling, Friedrich Wilhelm 39
Schlegel, Friedrich 38–40, 191 n.3, 192 nn.9–10, 204 n.14
Schulman, Samuel E. 86, 194 n.1, 197 n.27
Scott, Patrick 199 nn.1–2, 200 n.10, 200 n.14, 201 n.19
self
  and other 23, 27, 28–30, 31, 36, 45, 53, 108, 150–2, 162, 171, 188 n.5, 195 n.6
  and world 33, 37, 76, 80, 86, 88, 98, 106, 108, 117, 142, 181, 187
  as absence, lack 64–6, 69, 73
  as difference, division 25, 65, 95, 98, 113, 117, 175
  as text, writing 1–2, 49, 53, 62, 98, 105–8, 110, 114, 149–52, 171–2, 174–5
  production of 2, 33–6, 44–5, 184, 207 n.7
  transcendent 1, 12, 26, 31, 32, 39, 47, 111, 113, 119, 138, 150
  see also dialectic; language
Shakespeare, William 74
Shannon, E. F. 198 n.33
Shatto, Susan 86, 195 n.7, 195 n.9, 196 n.13
Shaw, Marion 197 n.20
Shaw, W. David 21, 185–7, 189 n.2, 189 n.3, 196 n.16, 206 n.34
Shelley, Percy Bysshe 11
Silverman, Kaja 194 n.2, 195 nn.3–4
Sinfield, Alan 76, 81, 188 n.2, 190 n.21, 194 nn.1–2, 195 n.5, 197 n.25
Slinn, E. Warwick 193 n.21, 205 n.30, 208 n.9
Solomon, Robert 15, 16, 19, 21, 28, 41, 185, 189 n.7, 189 n.9, 189 n.13, 190 nn.16–17, 191 n.2, 209 n.1
Spatz, Jonas 196 n.15
Spinoza, Benedict 40, 189 n.6
Standring, Douglas 141, 205 n.29
Starzyk, Lawrence J. 188 n.2

Stevenson, Lionel 188 n.2
subjectivism, *see* idealism (subjective)
Sullivan, Mary Rose 120–2, 202 n.4, 204 n.19
Swingle, L.J. 203 n.13
Symons, Arthur 202 n.7

Tennyson, Alfred 8, 14, 20, 49, 63–6, 69, 71, 75–7, 84, 87, 186, 190 n.21, 195 n.5, 198 n.28, 198 n.33
  In Memoriam 7, 19, 33, 61, 184, 186
  'Lady of Shalott, The' 62–3, 194 n.29
  Maud 3, 7, 8, 19, 61, 66–89, 184, 195 nn.6–7
  'St Simeon Stylites' 14, 20
  'Tithonus' 37, 44, 61, 64
  'Ulysses' 20, 37, 45, 64
textualism 1–2, 25, 38, 42, 46, 105–8, 114, 117, 119, 126–8, 132–4, 140, 146–8, 183–4, 187
  see also Derrida; language; self as text
Thompson, Gordon W. 201 n.2, 202 n.5
Thorslev, Peter 192 n.13
Timko, Michael 199 n.6
Tucker, Herbert F. 34, 35, 69, 77, 85, 86, 88, 191 n.24, 193 n.21, 194 n.30, 195 n.6, 196 n.14, 196 n.16, 196 n.18, 197 n.20, 197 n.24, 200 n.16, 202 n.7, 205 n.23
Tuman, Myron 206 n.35

Vanden Bossche, Chris R. 197 n.22

Walker, Stephen C. 202 n.2
Walker, William 203 n.11, 204 n.15, 208 nn.11–13
Warren, Alba H. 188 n.2
Wasserman, George R. 204 n.19
Wedgwood, Julia 205 n.30
Wordsworth, Ann 49–50, 193 n.21
Wordsworth, Jonathan 195 n.10, 196 n.19

Zietlow, Paul 201 n.2, 202 n.3, 206 n.33, 207 n.1

OHIO UNIVERSITY LIBRARY

Please return this book as soon as you have finished with it. In order to avoid a fine it must be returned by the latest date stamped below.

QUARTER LOAN

JUN 1 4 1992

APR 0 5 1996
MAR 2 2 1996
MAY 0 5 1992

JAN 4 1993

Quarter Loan

NOV 1 2 1992
RETURN BY
SEP 0 3 1993

NOV 1 6 1993
QUARTER LOAN

JAN 1 0 1996

FEB 1 2 1992